IMAGES
of America

SAN YSIDRO AND THE TIJUANA RIVER VALLEY

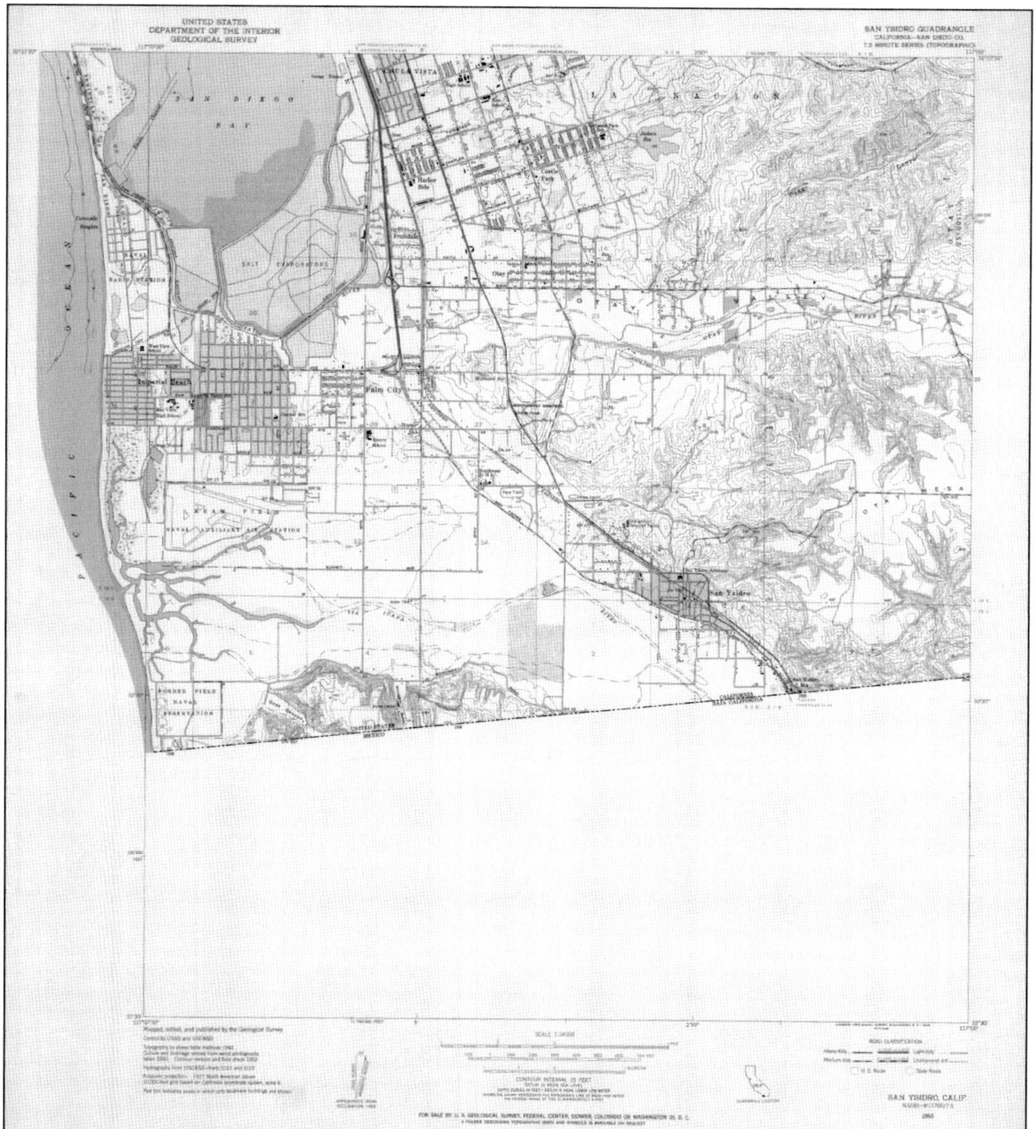

This map from 1953 depicts San Ysidro and the Tijuana River Valley, which, at the time, mainly consisted of farms and ranches. Four boundary markers—numbered 255, 256, 257, and 258—stand along the border of the United States and Mexico. The Tijuana River spans five miles from the border through the valley until it spills into an estuary. (Courtesy of the US Geological Survey.)

On the Cover: In this 1940 photograph, a Fourth of July parade passes the Safeway Store and a hardware store as it travels down San Ysidro Boulevard. (Courtesy of Evelyn Sevel.)

IMAGES
of America

San Ysidro and the Tijuana River Valley

Barbara Zaragoza

ARCADIA
PUBLISHING

ISBN 978-1-4671-3188-9

Published by Arcadia Publishing
Charleston, South Carolina

Printed in the United States of America

Library of Congress Control Number: 2013955117

For all general information, please contact Arcadia Publishing:
Telephone 843-853-2070
Fax 843-853-0044
E-mail sales@arcadiapublishing.com
For customer service and orders:
Toll-Free 1-888-313-2665

Visit us on the Internet at www.arcadiapublishing.com

Dedicated to the residents, past and present, of San Ysidro, who cultivate a small-town feel in spite of the federally managed San Ysidro Land Port of Entry encroaching upon their community; to the farmers who still grow food in the Tijuana River Valley; and to Mike and Patricia McCoy, who have been pioneers in protecting our border ecology.

Contents

Acknowledgments

I would like to thank the many donors who generously shared their time, memories, photographs, and more for this project. Their names are listed in the captions.

My appreciation also extends to the Tijuana River National Estuarine Research Reserve, especially to Mike McCoy and staff members Jeff Crooks and Anne Marie Tipton. Thank you to Ellen Sweet, from the County of San Diego Department of Parks and Recreation (CSDDP) History Office, who provided me with a treasure trove of information on the early history. David Flores and Andrea Skorepa of Casa Familiar gave me a rundown of contemporary Hispanic history as well as the current issues facing San Ysidro. Thanks go to the San Ysidro Chamber of Commerce, in particular Luz Vega, for fielding my numerous calls. To Cindy Stankowski at the San Diego Archeological Center, in Escondido, and Karen Lacy at the Museum of Man for their help with Native American history. To Thomas Giaquinto at the San Diego Police Historical Association (SDPHA) for sharing pictures from their vast photographic collection. Thanks to Carol Myers and Christine Travers at the San Diego History Center (SDHC) and to Iris Nelson at the Chula Vista Public Library. Additional help in constructing the history came from Professor Emeritus Steve Schoenherr, Michael Freedman, Paloma Aguirre, Therese Muranaka, and the Los Amigos group that meets monthly as Friends of San Ysidro. Finally, thanks to David Egger and Mary Odermatt for gathering family photographs and providing me with a comprehensive oral history of farming in the Tijuana River Valley.

Several secondary historical sources were invaluable to my research. Historian Charles Hughes has written the best reports for the California Department of Parks and Recreation that include details of the military presence at Border Field, a comprehensive history of the border region in the late 1800s, and much more. Robert M. Hanft wrote the definitive railroad history entitled *San Diego & Arizona: The Impossible Railroad*. Herbert Hensley and Sally Johns wrote a detailed account of Little Landers and the 1911 revolution in *Chula Vista—The Early Years*, Volume Four. A great thanks to the San Ysidro Public Library for providing me with a history of San Ysidro promulgated by caring librarians for several decades. One student-written document, *The San Ysidro Community History Project*, edited by Dr. Richard Griswold from San Diego State University, was particularly helpful in gathering post-annexation information.

Introduction

For thousands of years, the Kumeyaay lived in the fertile region now known as San Ysidro and the Tijuana River Valley. Their seasonal cycles led them to live on top of mesas and harness the plentiful rainwater during a time when the climate was significantly cooler and wetter. They then walked trails leading to the Pacific Ocean, where they hunted for game, fished in boats, and collected shellfish.

The first encroachment upon Native American land began with Fr. Junipero Serra's trek through Goat Canyon during his Sacred Expedition in the 1760s. About 50 years later, Mexico gained independence from Spain and handed out land grants to foreigners who settled the region, forever altering the lives of Native Americans. However, the most lasting impact upon the San Ysidro area came when the Treaty of Guadalupe Hidalgo was signed at the end of the U.S.-Mexican War in 1848. The US and Mexican governments designated that the boundary line would cut through the Tijuana River, a decision that split land between the two countries, even if that land was privately owned.

Both ecology and culture were no longer contiguous due to an abstract boundary line decided upon by faraway capital cities. Initially, a simple marble obelisk designated the change from one country to another, and the marker drew tourists in droves. Real-estate developers saw the profit potential, and a land boom began with entrepreneurs flooding the region to offer stagecoach rides and lavish hotel accommodations. Towns cropped up throughout the Tijuana River Valley, where the mild weather was touted as a cure for illnesses. Soon, however, visions of wealth and an upscale tourist spot went bust, and many of the towns remained in existence on paper only at the county assessor's office.

The US Treasury Department still saw its coin, establishing the first customhouse in the 1870s. The Mexican government followed suit, and both countries levied taxes for crossing the border. Inevitably, criminals soon began smuggling goods and people. Customs officials also said that animals crossed from one country into the other, causing farmers to complain, so the governments then constructed a flimsy wire fence that remained for several decades.

With or without a fence, customs and immigration continued to strengthen its presence. When Prohibition laws went into effect in the United States, Tijuana became known as "Vice City," and the town of San Ysidro catered to tourists going back and forth between the line, including celebrities such as John Wayne and Rita Hayworth. San Ysidro Boulevard became an important thoroughfare packed with shops, a library, and a civic center. When crime in Tijuana or political events, such as World War I, shut down the border crossing for longer periods, San Ysidro's economy suffered.

Mexicans and Americans generally passed through the boundary unimpeded, with people working on one side and living on the other. Ranchers bred horses, including Seabiscuit, who was boarded on a ranch in the Tijuana River Valley. Dairy farmers—many of Japanese and Swiss descent—also lived next to the border. Robert Egger was a dairy farmer who also grew a variety of vegetables thanks to the year-round mild weather. The Navy leased property at the boundary, creating an auxiliary base to the many military establishments throughout San Diego.

In 1957, residents of San Ysidro voted for San Diego to annex their town. They hoped to receive better services such as funds for proper irrigation. After the annexation, people again discussed the idea of a tourist destination along the border. Proposals included a Skyride spanning from San Ysidro to Tijuana and an upscale marina located along the boundary line at the Pacific Ocean, but most of these ideas failed. However, the City of San Diego did construct two major freeways—which managed to displace hundreds of homes and businesses—leading to the border. The close-knit town fragmented, and San Ysidro's Land Port of Entry became the busiest in the world.

The Tijuana River Valley remained a farming and ranch community, but in 1964, the government ended the bracero program that brought Mexican nationals into the United States legally as guest workers. Those who crossed the boundary line in search of work now tended to stay, often settling in San Ysidro. The Spanish-speaking population reached 80 percent just as the United States fell into a recession, the peso experienced massive devaluations, and media attention increasingly turned to the "crisis" of illegal immigration. In response, the federal government began to construct more fencing along the boundary.

In response, the Chicano movement arrived at the border with Herman Baca launching protests in 1977 and again in 1979. Cesar Chavez also held many rallies at the Civic Center in San Ysidro. Their grassroots activism inspired many present-day organizations—such as Hearts & Hands, the San Ysidro Health Clinic, and Casa Familiar—that address concerns in the border community.

By 2008, the federal government received carte blanche to disregard all laws that would impede the rapid construction of a double border fence. They filled Smuggler's Gulch with dirt and placed the marble obelisk behind thick mesh. The International Water Commission, however, still made sure that four holes between the two countries would allow for sewage to flow freely into the Tijuana River and out to the Pacific Ocean. Further activism ensued, ranging from Border Angels to WildCoast cleanups.

Today, farmers keep tilling the fertile soil, and closer to the Pacific Ocean, a nature preserve protects the largest coastal wetland in Southern California. Every year, 47 million people pass through San Ysidro to cross the border, and as in the late 1800s, city officials still continue to create plans that may turn this area into an upscale tourist destination. However, residents already know that living at *la frontera* makes San Ysidro and the Tijuana River Valley unique in the world—a community that must manage what today remains a contiguous ecology and culture in spite of an artificial split created by a heavily guarded fence.

One

Ecology and the Ancients

The Tijuana River Valley ends at an estuary where the river meets the Pacific Ocean. There, the largest coastal wetland in Southern California provides a home to one of the most biologically productive ecosystems in the world, including 370 species of birds.

Around 11,000 years ago, the region resembled the Pacific Northwest but with a wetter, cooler climate. Seashells reveal that humans occupied the area between 7,000 and 9,000 years ago. By 3,000 years ago, the climate turned dry and warm—similar to the modern-day weather in the region. Excavated pottery shards indicate that pots were used to store food and water, and the ancient peoples also used sophisticated stone tools.

In 1769, during the Crespi-Rivera Expedition, Fr. Juan Crespi became the first European to come through the Tijuana River Valley. Several months later, Fr. Junipero Serra followed, walking with the Serra-Portola Expedition that included Spanish soldiers and Native Americans from Baja California through present-day Goat Canyon.

At that time, three Kumeyaay villages existed—Chiap (La Punta), near the southern end of San Diego bay; the Melijo (Melijo), on the southern bank of the Tijuana River; and another village in San Ysidro. As hunter-gatherers, they relied on seasonal cycles of movement from the coast to the mountains. With the founding of the mission of San Diego de Alcalá, Native Americans had to adjust those cycles. The Spanish cultivation of grains, the grazing of animals, and the felling of oak trees that provided acorns—a dietary staple for Native Americans—meant that the tribes' way of life was quickly coming to an end.

The Kumeyaay did not necessarily welcome the new intruders. Indian raids became common, including during the night and early morning of November 5, 1775, when Kumeyaay warriors from at least 15 villages attacked the San Diego mission, setting it aflame and attacking the Spaniards sleeping inside; Chiap and Melijo village members were among the warriors who participated.

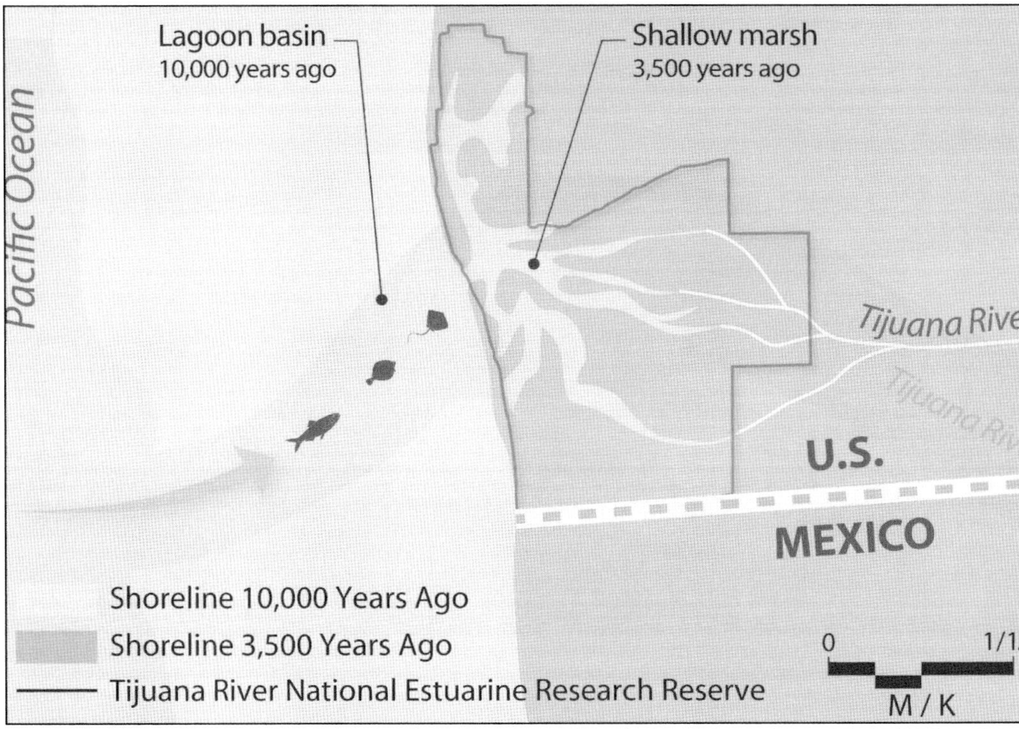

A deep-water lagoon existed here 10,000 years ago. The tide brought in fish and shellfish. About 3,500 years ago, the sea level rose, and the Tijuana River valley filled with sediment that created the present-day salt marsh ecosystem. Archeological evidence suggests that many groups of early Californians came by sea, traveling along the "kelp highway" from Asia to Alaska and down the Pacific Coast. (California State Parks.)

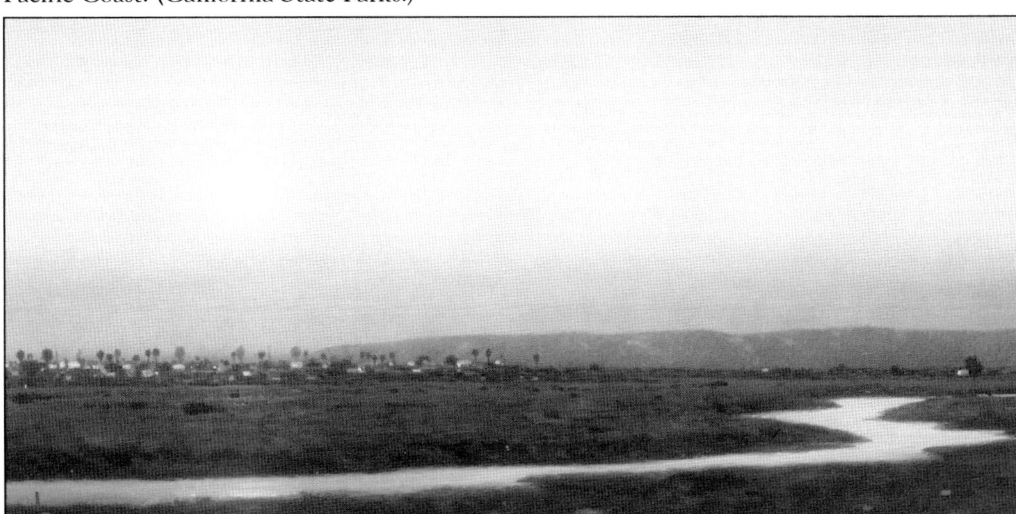

At the end of the valley, by the Pacific Ocean, the Tijuana Estuary forms part of the largest coastal wetland in Southern California. The estuary acts as a natural filter for pollutants thanks to plants and bacteria in the mud; it is also home to an abundance of species. This painting, created by local artist Glenn Crooks, shows the estuary and the salt marsh with its cord grass. (Glenn Crooks.)

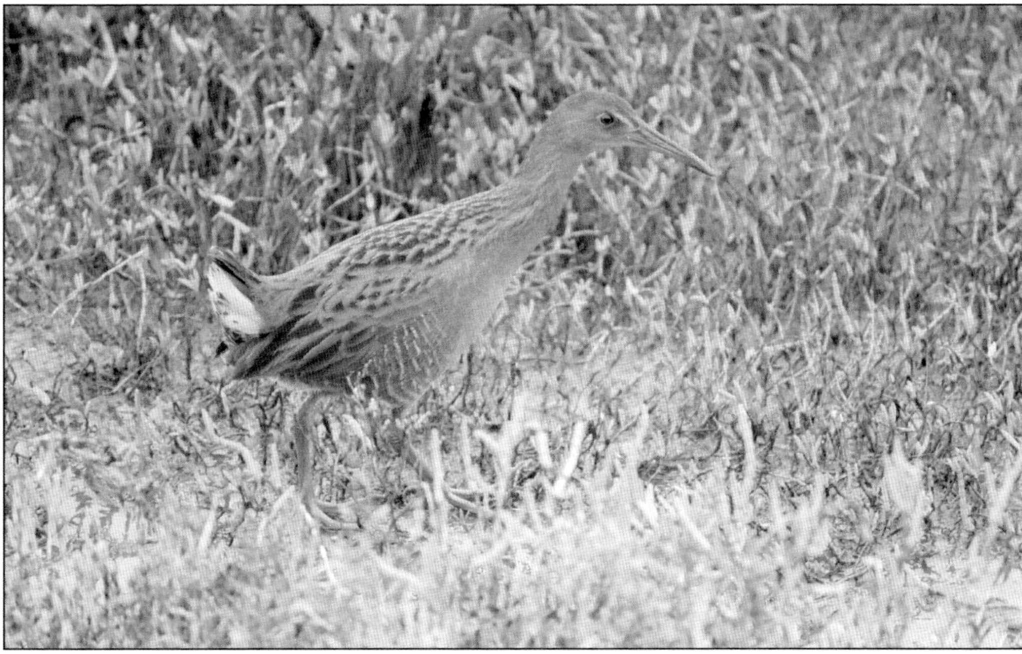

The Tijuana River Valley lies along the Pacific Flyway where more than 320 species of birds migrate and more than 50 permanently reside. The estuary is also home to 12 endangered species, including this light-footed clapper rail, a bird that builds nests made of buoyant cord grass stems in the marshes to protect its chicks from predators. (Winand Hess.)

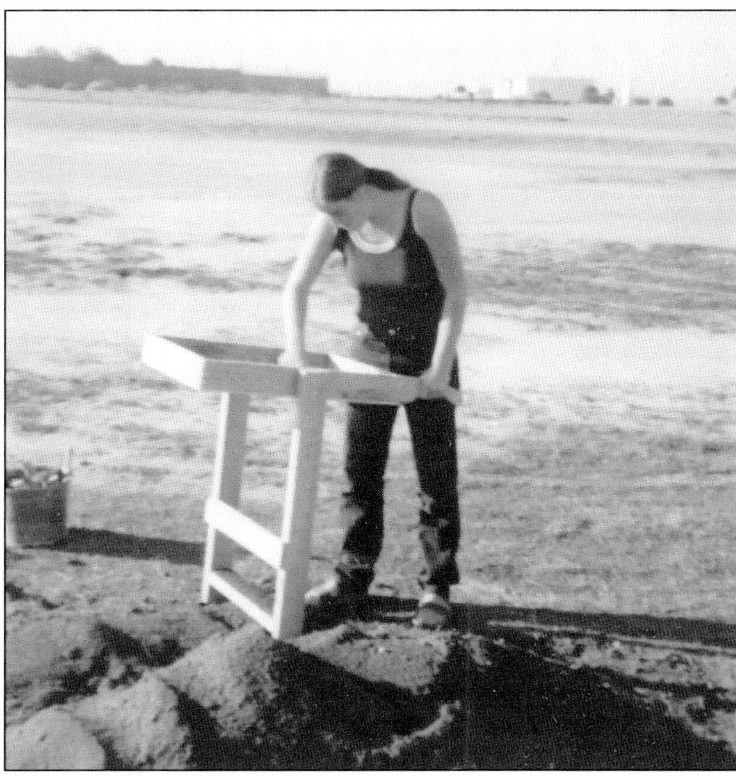

The earliest settlers of this region, known as the San Dieguito, date back approximately 8,000 years. They often resided on the mesas at least 200 feet above sea level. The La Jollans arrived about 2,000 years ago and established themselves near the Pacific Ocean. In 1976, an archeological dig on this region's mesa found artifacts from the La Jollans. (California State Parks.)

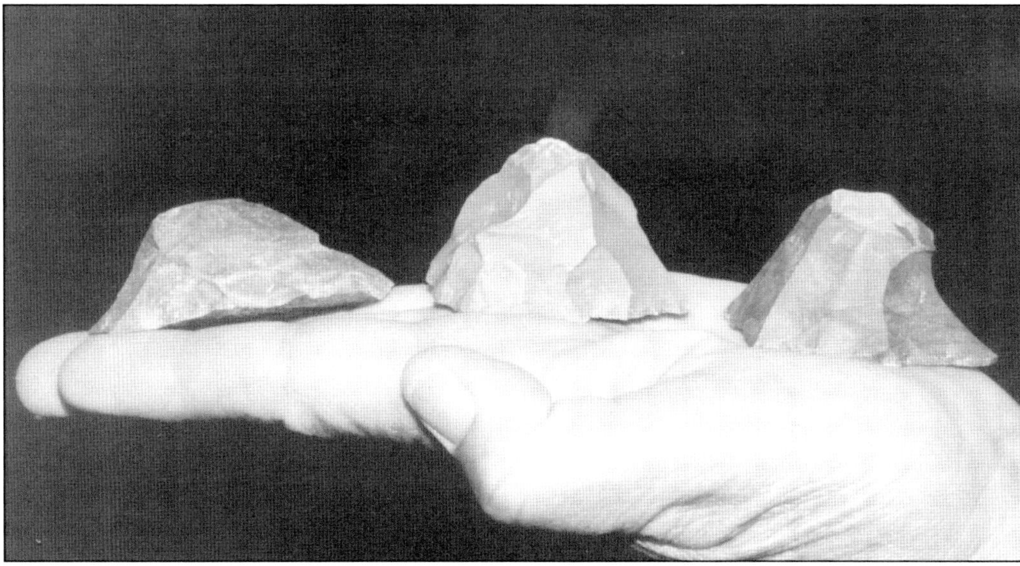

These hand scrapers are some of the stone tools used by Native Americans about 6,000 to 8,000 years ago. The natives made these tools through percussion flaking or by striking a hammer stone against an intended tool to shape it. These scrapers could have been used to clean animal skins or scrape wood and plant material, or they could have served as arrowheads. (San Diego Archeological Center.)

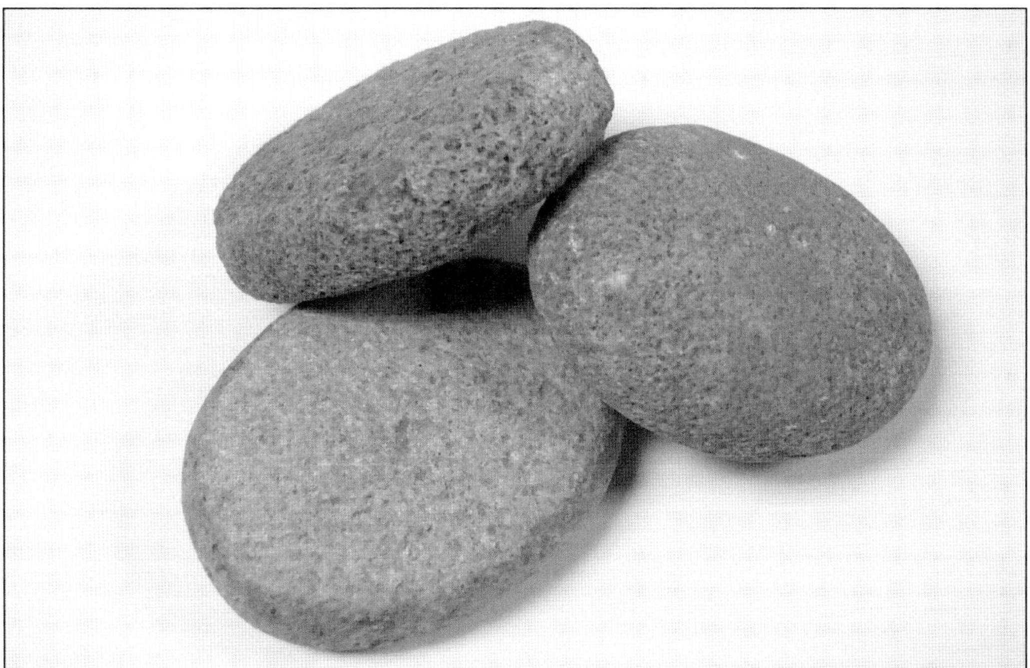

Manos, or grinding stones, were used to pound seeds and other plant foods but also to crush the bones of small animals. The marrow from animal bones provided a source of calcium, protein, and fat. Grinding stones were also used to pulverize clay prior to making pottery and to grind pigments for rock art. The manos are riverbed cobbles that probably required little modification. (San Diego Archeological Center.)

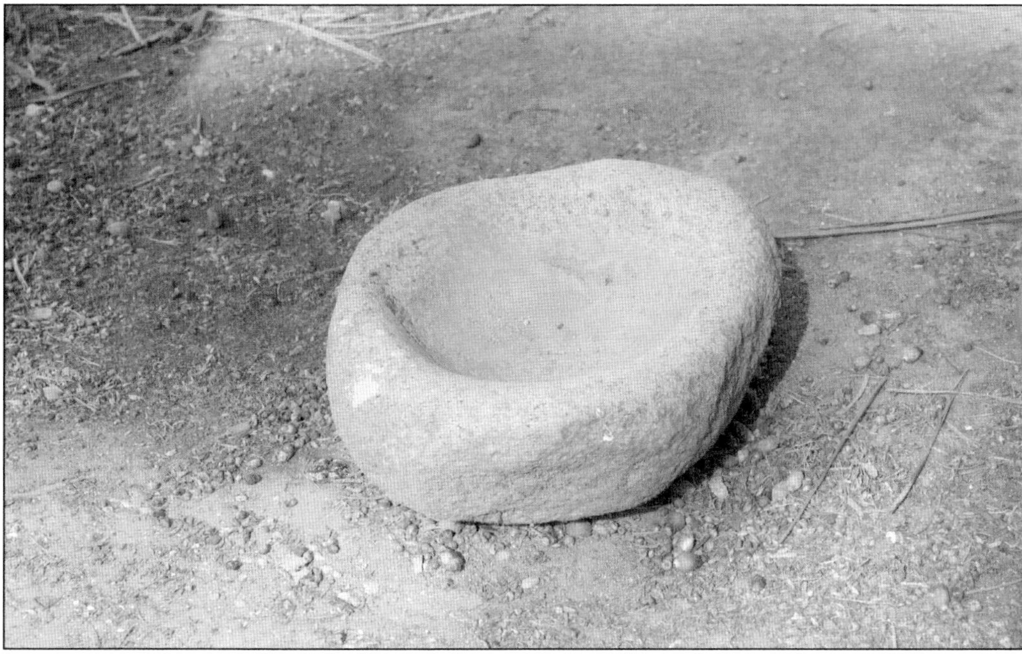

This metate, a borrowed Spanish word meaning "grinding platform," was found on the farmland of David Egger in the Tijuana River Valley. The San Dieguito peoples did not use the metate, so the La Jollan people probably introduced these stone tools into the area. Metates were usually made of sandstone and were used for grinding acorns, seeds, and bones. (Author.)

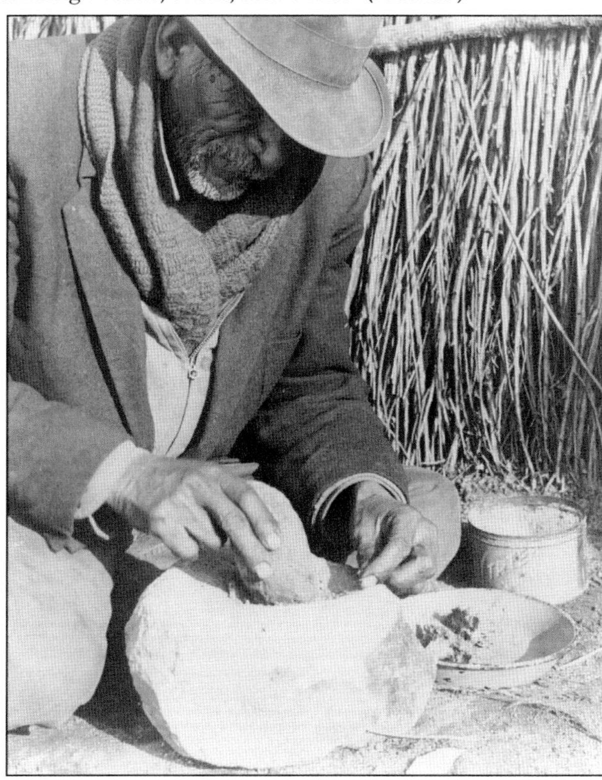

In this picture, Rufino Uchurte, a Kumeyaay, grinds rabbit bones using a metate and manos. According to archeologists, the Kumeyaay arrived in the Tijuana River Valley about 1,000 years ago. They used these stone tools for grinding acorns, their single most important food source. This photograph was taken in 1962 at Santa Caterina in Baja California, Mexico. (San Diego Museum of Man; photograph by Ralph C. Michelsen.)

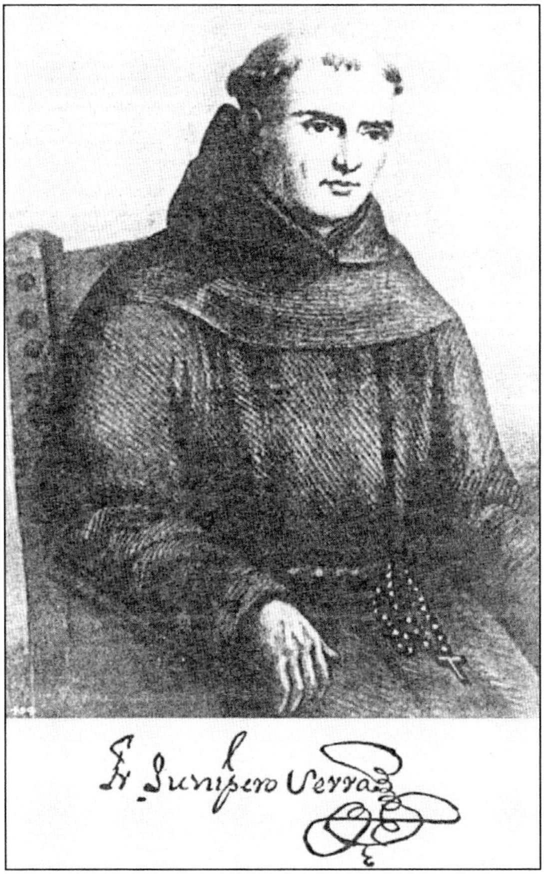

In 1769, Fr. Junipero Serra traveled over rugged, difficult terrain by foot with an expedition of soldiers and Native American guides from missions in Baja California. His overland trek, known as the "Sacred Expedition," was meant to expand the Spanish Empire. (San Diego Mission de Alcalá, Library Archives.)

Father Serra and his group camped overnight in a place he called San Pablo. He wrote that he found nice pastureland and a pleasant river of good water. Although scholars first believed that Father Serra walked through Smuggler's Gulch, they now maintain that his expedition traveled through Goat Canyon, where he briefly passed by on his way to establishing the San Diego Mission de Alcalá. This picture shows present-day Goat Canyon. (Author.)

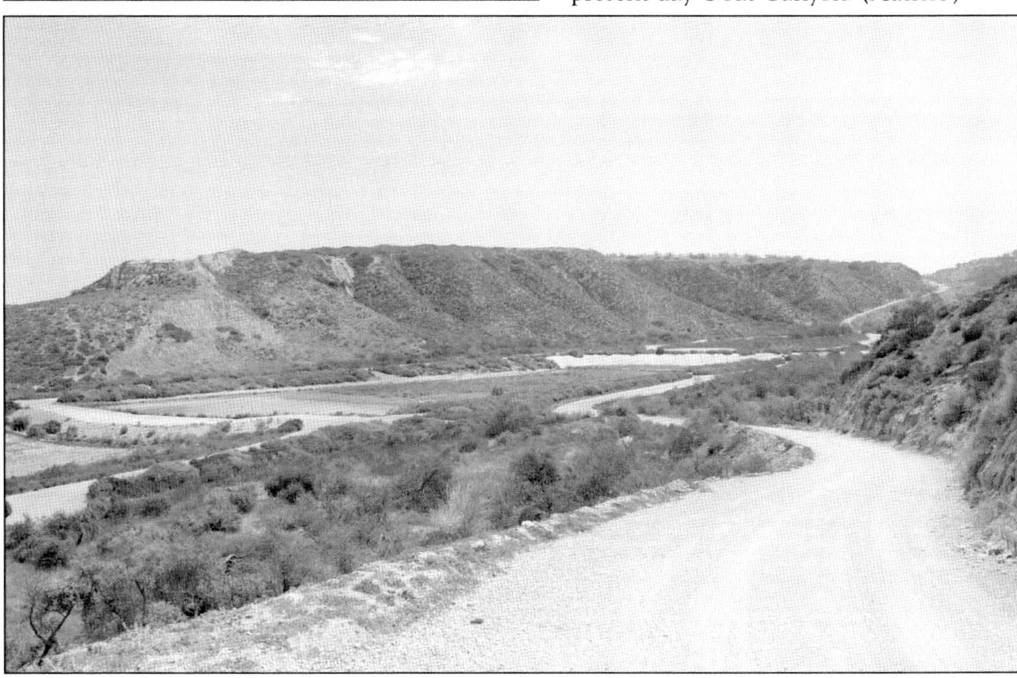

Two

THE MARBLE OBELISK

When Mexico gained independence from Spain in 1821, the new government wanted to promote settlement in its barren northern territory of California. Officials awarded approximately 600 land grants, often to soldiers, that spanned from Ensenada to Sacramento. Santiago Argüello Moraga, commandant of the Presidio of San Diego, received a grant for Rancho Tia Juana that encompassed approximately 10,000 acres. Although his grant stretched from the Pacific Ocean through the Tijuana River Valley, the actual boundaries were left ill-defined due to lack of need.

Two years later, Argüello's son, Emigdio, received a grant for the adjacent Rancho Melijo, where he built an adobe house known as La Punta. The property was considered the oldest home between Old Town and the international boundary. There, the Argüellos and their friends enjoyed summers at the beach, although the property had to be abandoned at least twice due to raids by Native Americans.

A decade after the Argüellos settled in the Tijuana River Valley, the U.S.-Mexican War ended in 1848 with the signing of the Treaty of Guadalupe Hidalgo. A Joint United States and Mexican Boundary Commission was created and surveyors descended upon the region from the American and Mexican sides to determine the exact location of the boundary. When they finished their work, the agreed upon international line cut through the Argüellos's property.

In 1851, the Boundary Commission placed a marble obelisk overlooking the Pacific Ocean at today's Border Field State Park to demarcate the line between the two countries. It designated this boundary monument as No. 1.

Thanks to the completion of the National City & Otay railroad in the 1880s that stretched down to the border, the obelisk became an immediate tourist attraction that purportedly brought more than 100,000 visitors each year. Real-estate speculators sought their wealth near the obelisk, and enthusiastic investors purchased tracts of land and tried to establish health resorts, tourist hotels, and residential lots. The land boom, however, went bust when real estate prices suddenly declined. A devastating flood in 1891 washed out the hopeful tourist town of Tia Juana (where San Ysidro exists today). Many other "paper towns" of the region never became realities, remaining towns that were filed "on paper" at the county assessor's office only.

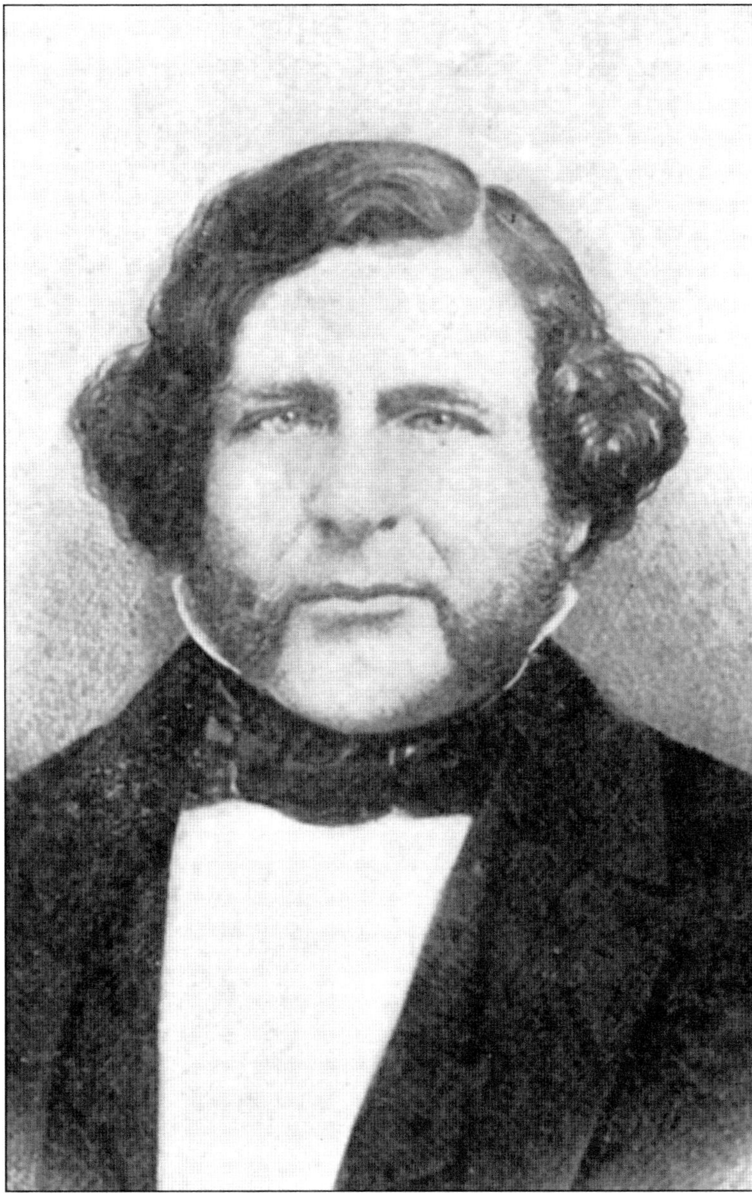

The earliest recorded reference to the name "Tia Juana" is on the baptismal certificate of Native American Jose Sanchez, who was baptized in 1809. In Kumeyaay, the name of the ranch may have meant "by the sea." Little else is known about property ownership in this region until Santiago Argüello Moraga (1792–1862) received a land grant for Rancho Tia Juana in 1829. A decorated soldier, Santiago Argüello was also commandant of the Presidio of San Diego and held a variety of political offices, including revenue officer and collector of the port. He received a land grant from Gov. Jose Maria Echeandia that totaled about 10,000 acres. Four years later, Argüello's son, Santiago Emigdio Argüello (1813–1857), received a grant for Rancho Melijo from Echeandia's successor, Gov. Jose Figueroa. Emigdio (pictured), like his father, distinguished himself as a soldier, aiding the United States during the U.S.-Mexican War and serving as a corporal during the Indian uprisings of 1851 and 1852. The Argüello ranchos extended from the Pacific Ocean through the Tijuana River Valley and beyond. (CSDDP.)

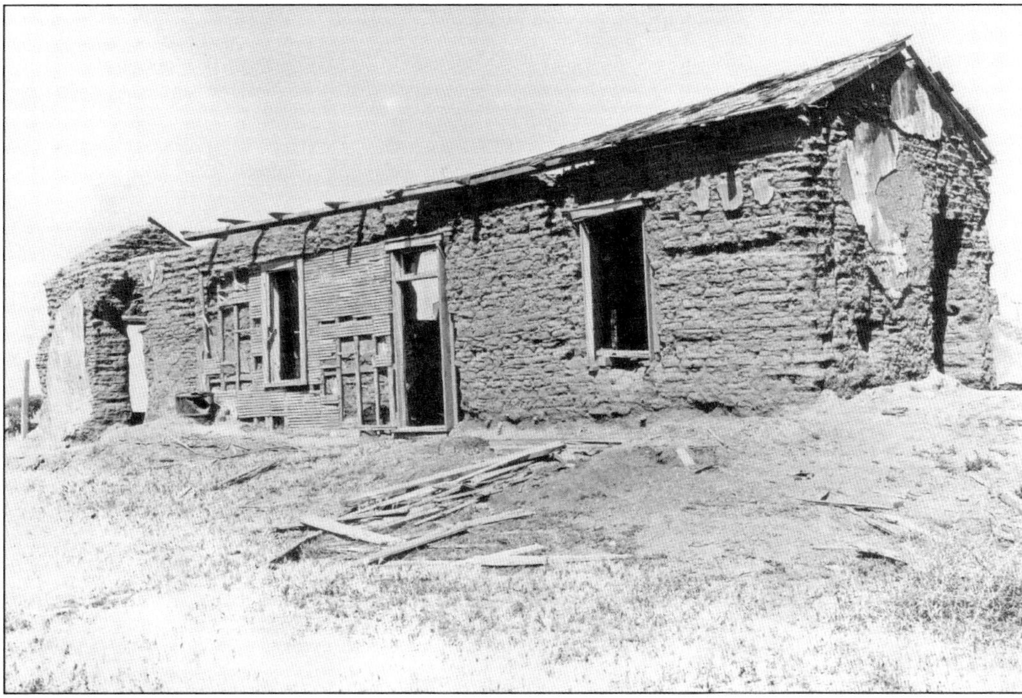

In 1834 or 1835, Emigdio Argüello built an adobe house, known as La Punta, overlooking the Pacific Ocean. The house was considered the oldest residence in the South Bay. Emigdio purportedly raised 22 children with his wife, Maria Guadalupe Jacoba Eugenia Estudillo. The home had nine rooms, and due to the mild weather, the family spent many summers entertaining visitors here and enjoying the nearby beach. (Chula Vista Public Library, Local History Collection.)

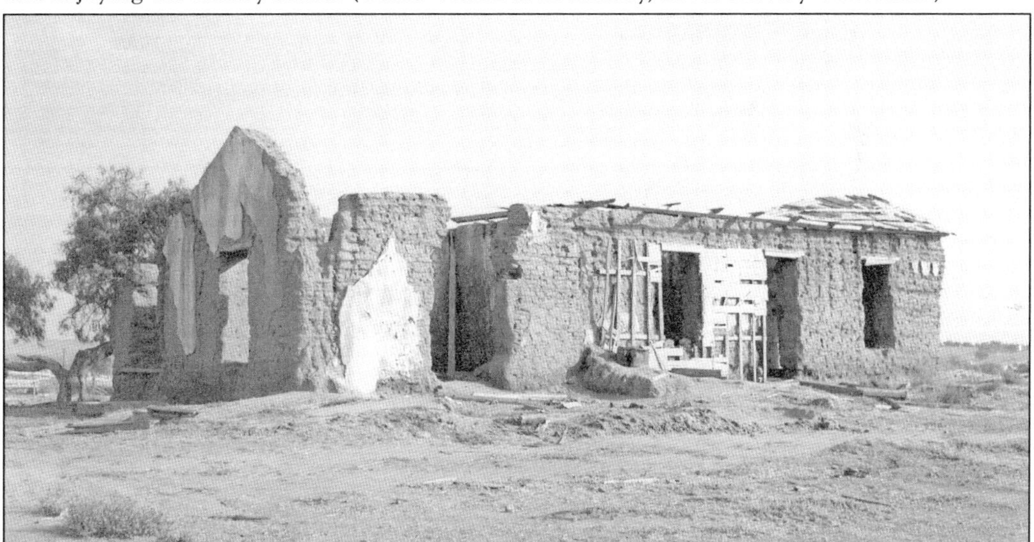

For thousands of years, the Kumeyaay tribes walked along the Tijuana River Valley trails to access the sea, where they gathered food. The Argüello ranch did away with this tradition and, as a consequence, Indians began raiding the property. The Argüellos had to temporarily abandon their rancho for fear of Indian raids in 1837 and again in 1851. (Chula Vista Public Library, Local History Collection.)

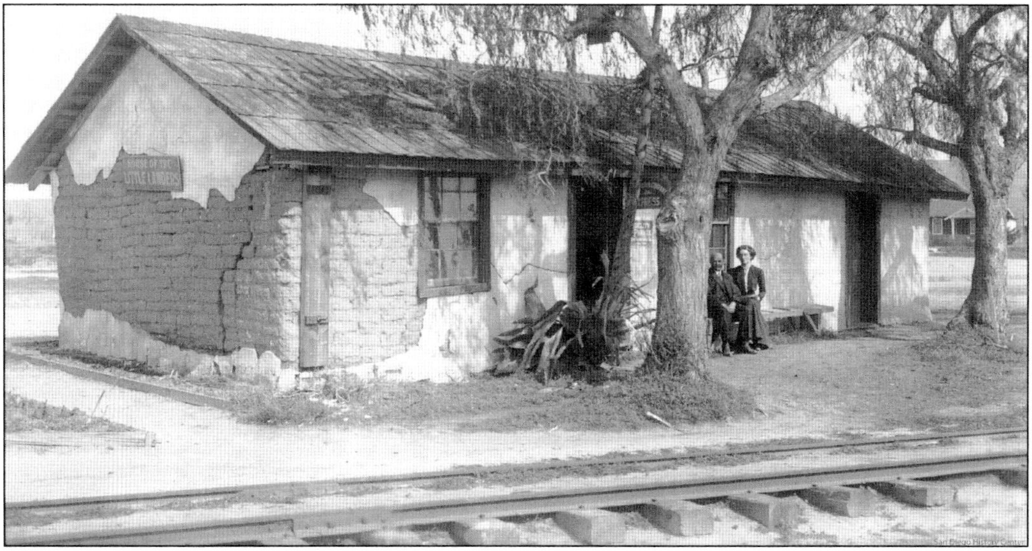

Juan Ybarra owned this ranch, located in present-day San Ysidro, in the 1880s. He had a faithful Indian servant who warned him of an upcoming raid. Despite taking precautions, Ybarra and two of his hired hands were murdered. His two grown daughters were then carried into the mountains as captives. His adobe house (pictured) was later used by the Little Landers colony. (SDHC.)

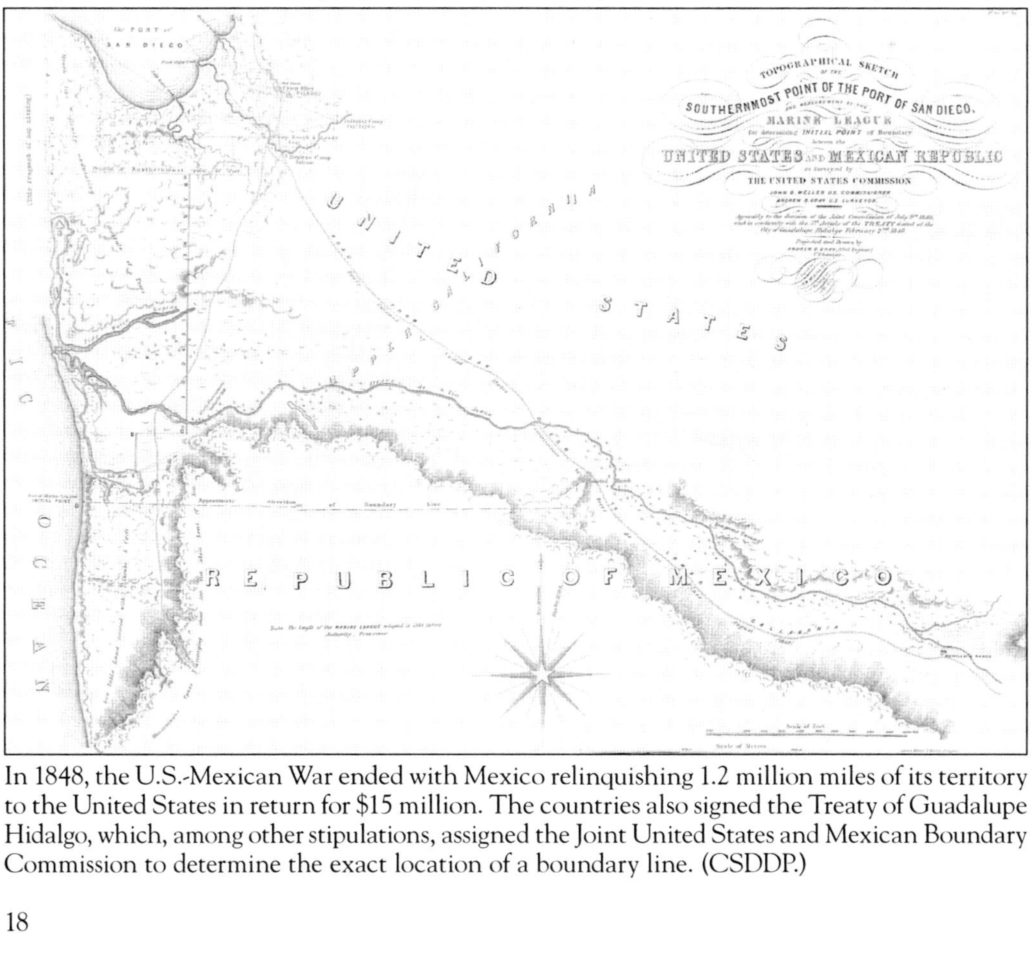

In 1848, the U.S.-Mexican War ended with Mexico relinquishing 1.2 million miles of its territory to the United States in return for $15 million. The countries also signed the Treaty of Guadalupe Hidalgo, which, among other stipulations, assigned the Joint United States and Mexican Boundary Commission to determine the exact location of a boundary line. (CSDDP.)

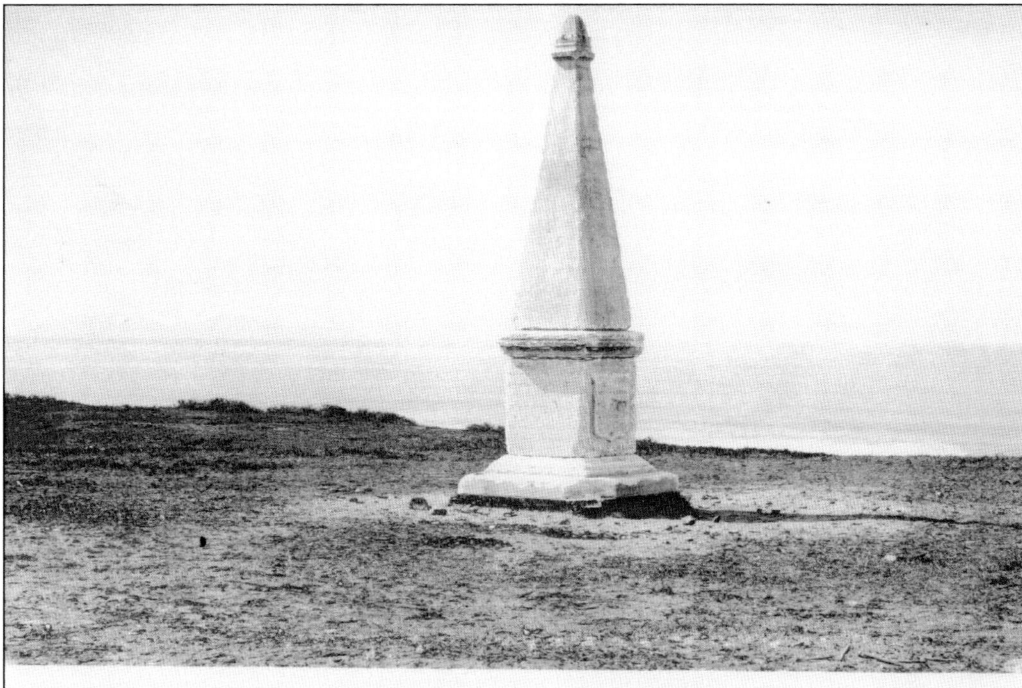
Initial Monument, marking Mexican Boundary.

Drawing the boundary line took two years to complete—from 1849 to 1851. Gen. Pedro García Conde served as the commissioner and Jose Salazar Ylarregui served as the surveyor for the Mexicans. John B. Weller was the commissioner and Andrew Gray was the surveyor for the Americans. Gray established one of the two camps near the anticipated boundary. The commission included 39 surveyors and 150 army men for military protection, as well as draftsmen and interpreters. The two countries agreed that the boundary should be approximately one league south of the San Diego Harbor—the area located in the middle of Argüello's property. The boundary commission then ordered a boundary marker from a New York firm called "At the Sign of the Quadrant." The marker was made of Italian marble and was 14 feet high. "Republica Mexicana" and, on the reverse side, "United States of America," were etched into the stone. (Above, CSDDP; right, Special Collections & University Archives, San Diego State University Library & Information Access.)

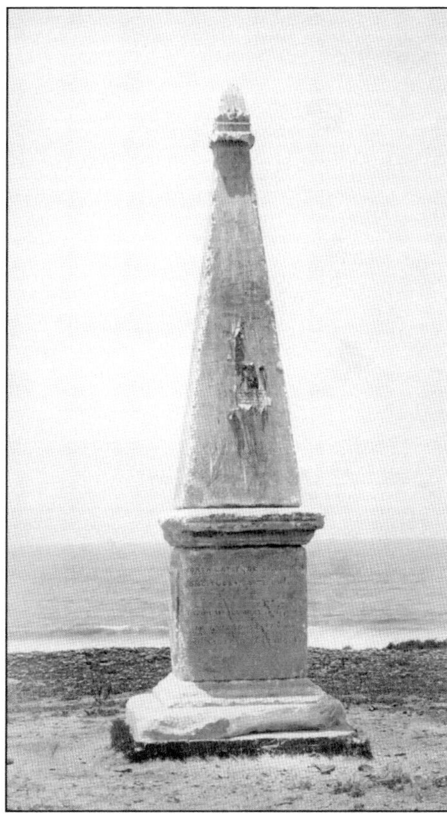

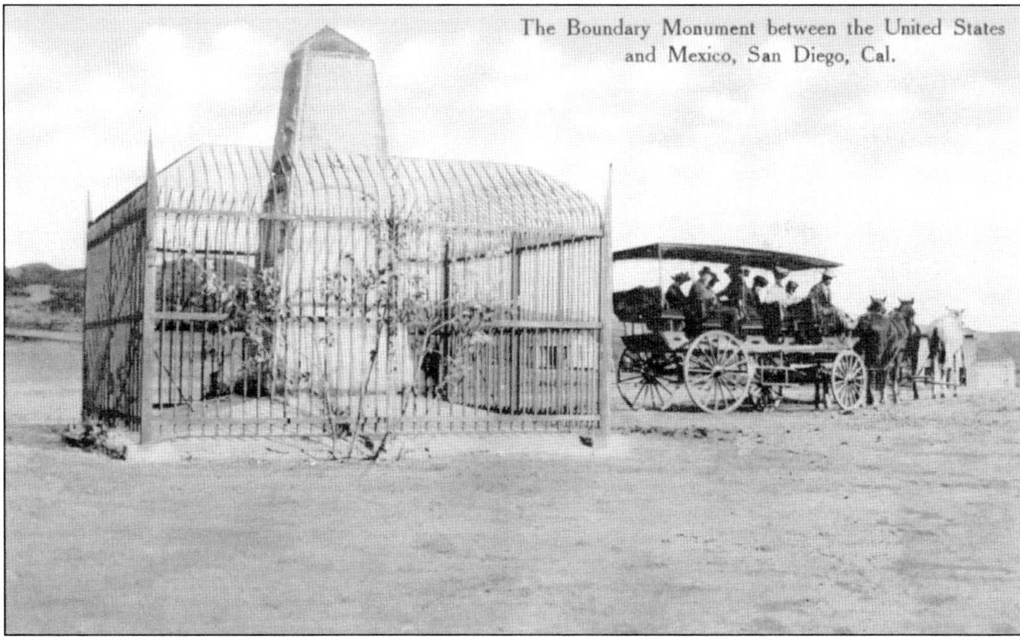

The border monument became a popular tourist attraction, and by some estimates, more than 100,000 visitors came each year by the end of the 19th century. The "Pioneer Omnibus and Stage Coach Line" ran services between Old Town and the monument. Visitors who came often broke off small chips of marble as souvenirs. Over time, this caused significant damage to the obelisk. (CSDDP.)

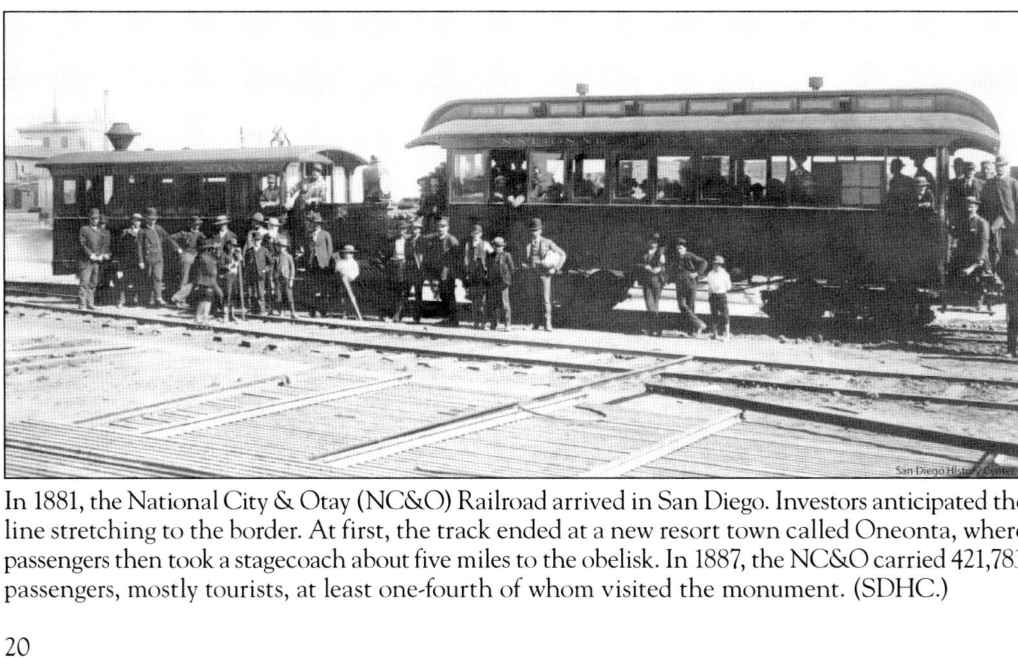

In 1881, the National City & Otay (NC&O) Railroad arrived in San Diego. Investors anticipated the line stretching to the border. At first, the track ended at a new resort town called Oneonta, where passengers then took a stagecoach about five miles to the obelisk. In 1887, the NC&O carried 421,783 passengers, mostly tourists, at least one-fourth of whom visited the monument. (SDHC.)

Designs boomed for new towns along the border. In 1888, Carlson & Higgins promoted the development of International City, a commercial border town at the obelisk. It filed a subdivision map with the county recorder's office. Other "paper towns" that cropped up included Palm City (1884), South San Diego (1887), Tia Juana (1887), and Oneonta (1888). I.N. Hart purchased a tract of land in Oneonta, built a home, and set up a daily stagecoach service to the monument. The Oneonta Land, Town and Water Company also built a first-class, two-story hotel. (County Records Office, San Diego.)

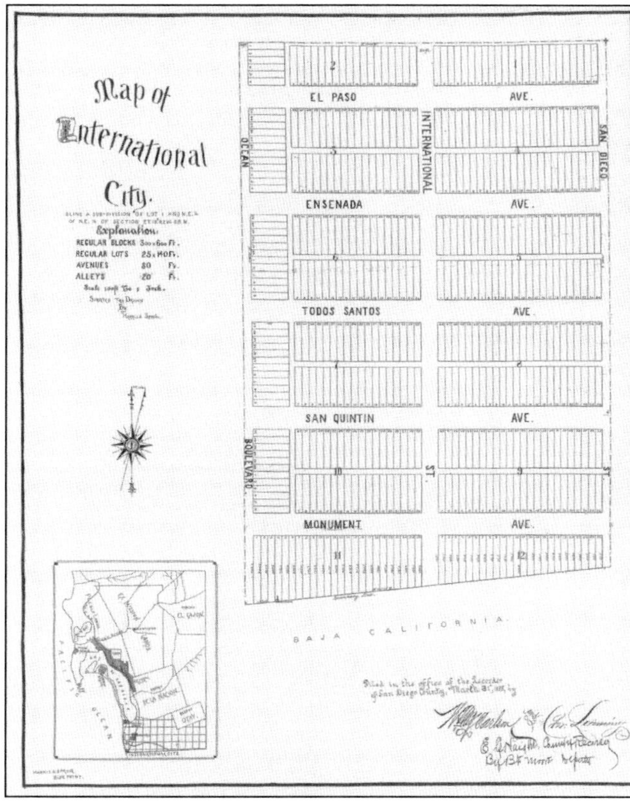

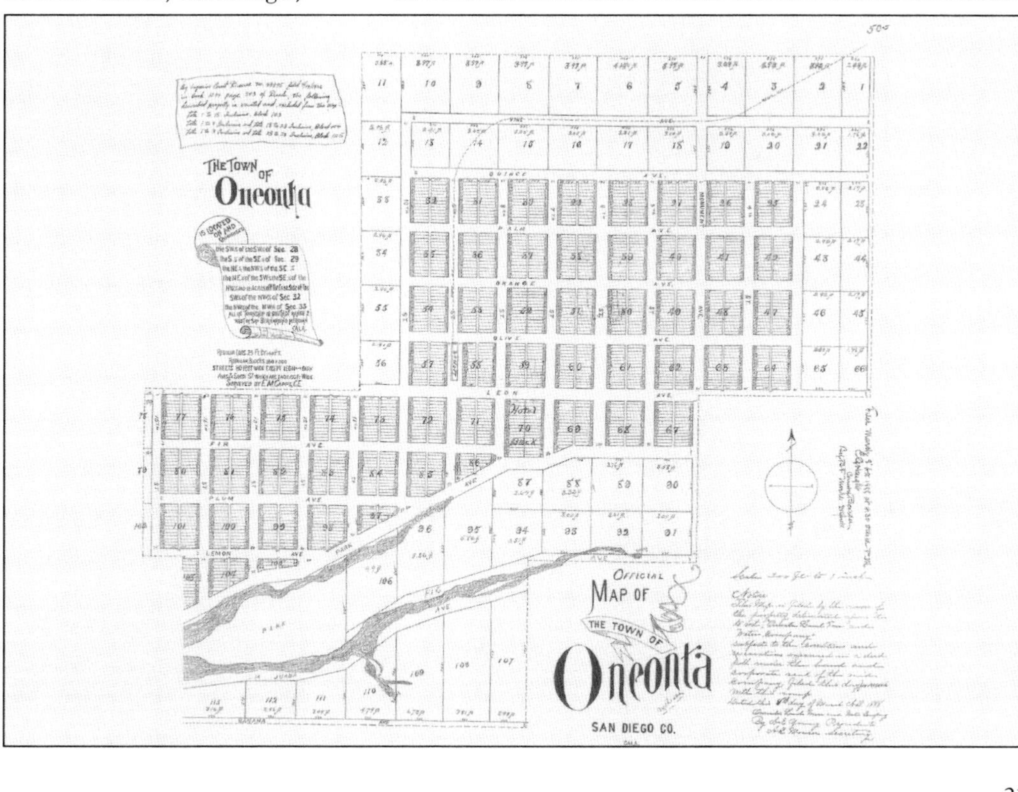

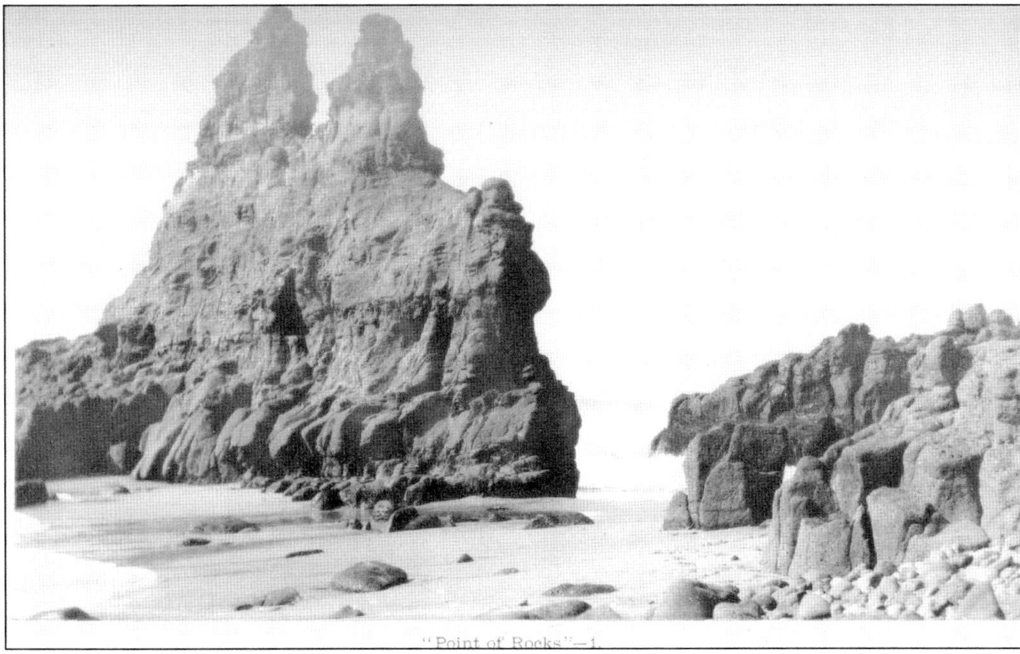

The entire Tijuana River Valley region became an attraction for tourists who, at first, arrived by stagecoach to enjoy the mild beach weather. Slightly beyond the monument was the Point of Rocks, considered one of the finest coastline attractions. The rocks could be seen from as far away as the Hotel Del Coronado on the other side of the Bay. (CSDDP.)

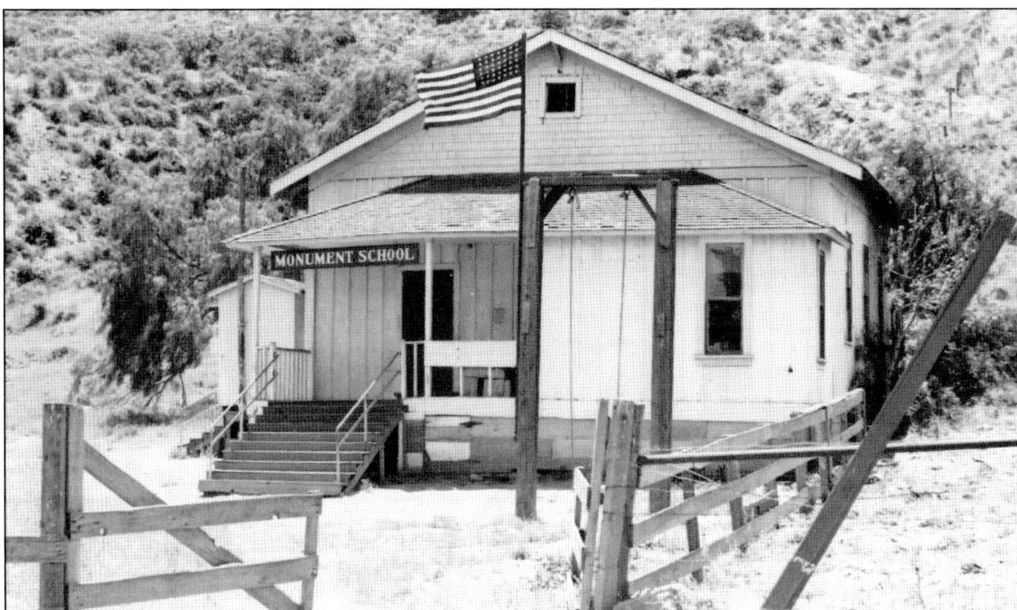

Near the boundary monument, a new town called Monument City was laid out in 1869. Surveyors began laying out roads, a voting precinct, and a post office. The Monument School pictured here also started accepting students. Promoters believed that the Pacific Ocean and the boundary monument provided the best location for future development. In the end, however, the projected new residents never arrived. (Evelyn Sevel.)

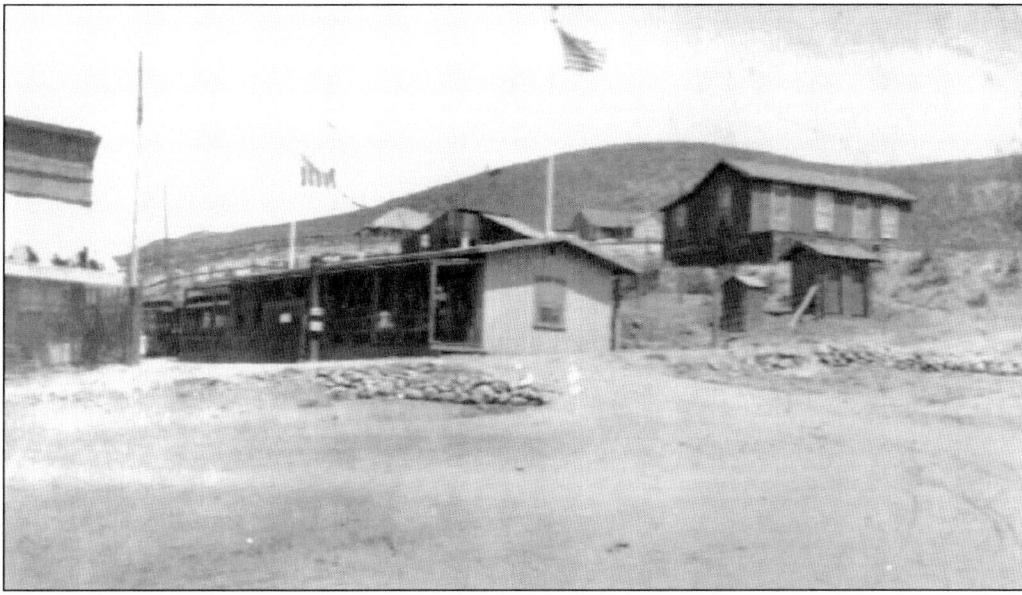

The governments of the United States and Mexico sought to capitalize on the boom as well. In 1873, the US Treasury Department began to collect tariffs on livestock and other goods crossing the border. In 1874, the Mexican government followed suit, establishing its customs building. This c. 1907 picture is the oldest in existence that depicts the US Customs House. (SDPHA.)

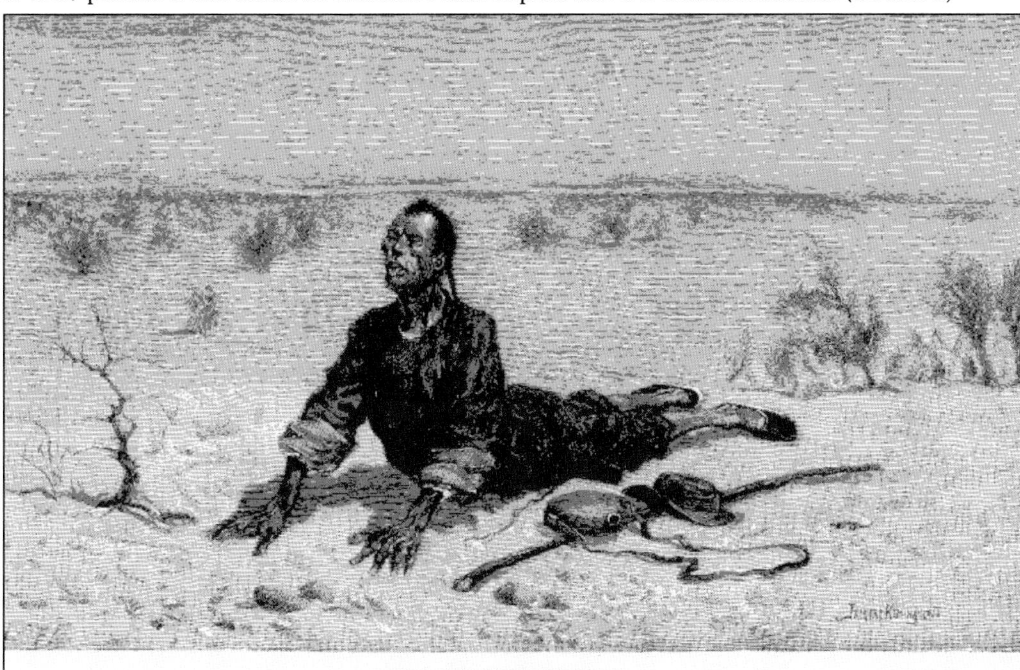

Customs and immigration at the border also meant the beginning of illegal smuggling. After the passage of the Chinese Exclusion Act in 1882, smuggling of Chinese immigrants across the border from Baja California became widespread. Special Chinese inspectors were even hired at the border. This image, from an 1891 issue of *Harper's New Monthly Magazine*, shows the harsh conditions that befell Chinese immigrants as they tried to cross the desert.

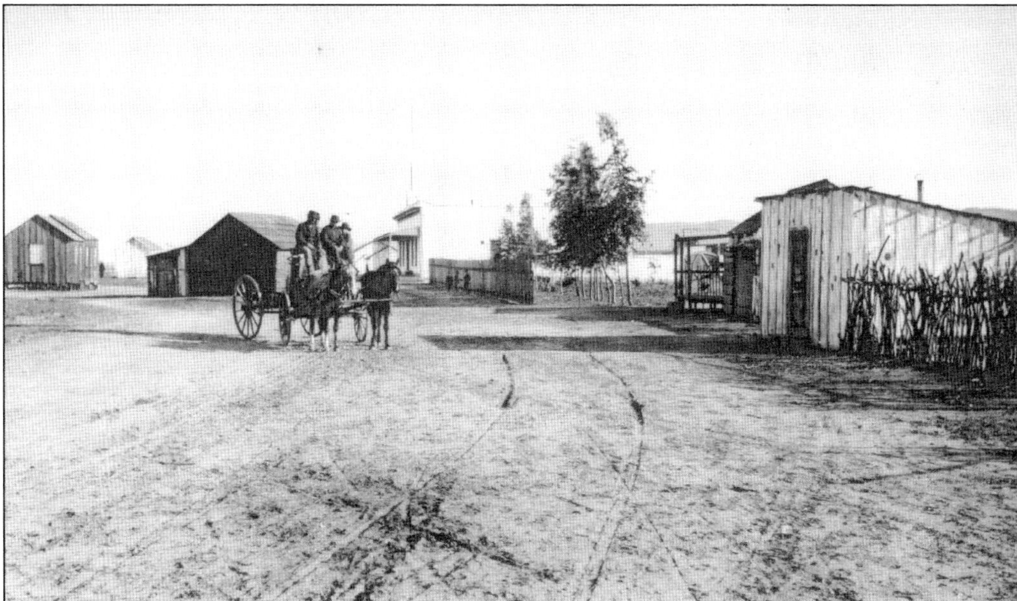

Tia Juana—Mexican Side.

By 1885, real estate firm Hart & Stern developed a subdivision called Tia Juana City in present-day San Ysidro. In "Tijuana," as it was called on the Mexican side, the population totaled about 200 people. The town consisted of a customhouse, a hotel, a restaurant, a butcher shop, a church, a school, and a few adobe structures. (CSDDP.)

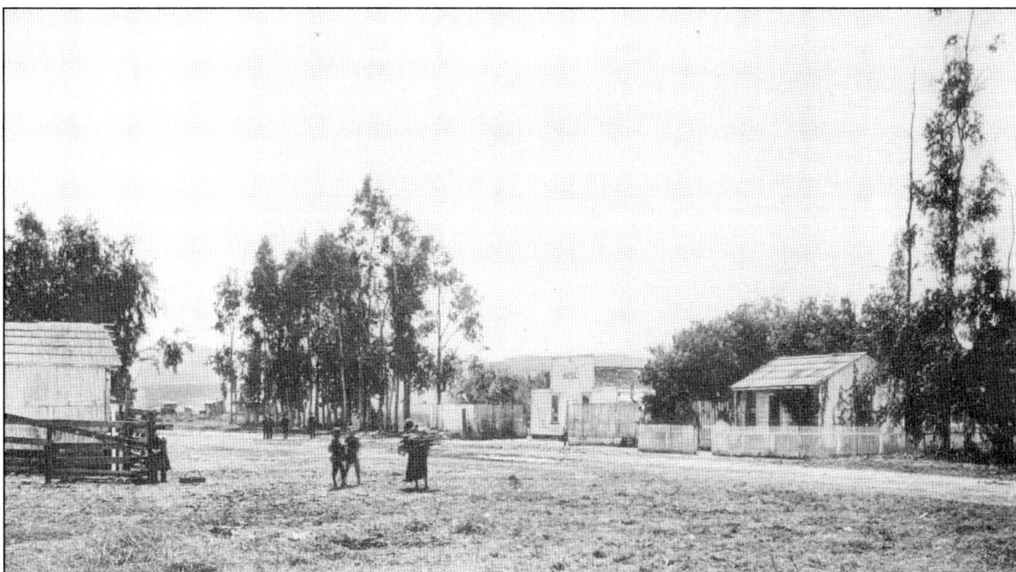

Tia Juana—American Side.

The American side of Tia Juana included a three-story, 56-room hotel. The Americans called the town Tia Juana, believing it to be a Mexican word for "Aunt Jane." George Washington Barber opened the first general store and restaurant in the town. Both American and Mexican real-estate speculators came here in search of profits, but their hopes were dashed when a flood destroyed the town in 1891. (CSDDP.)

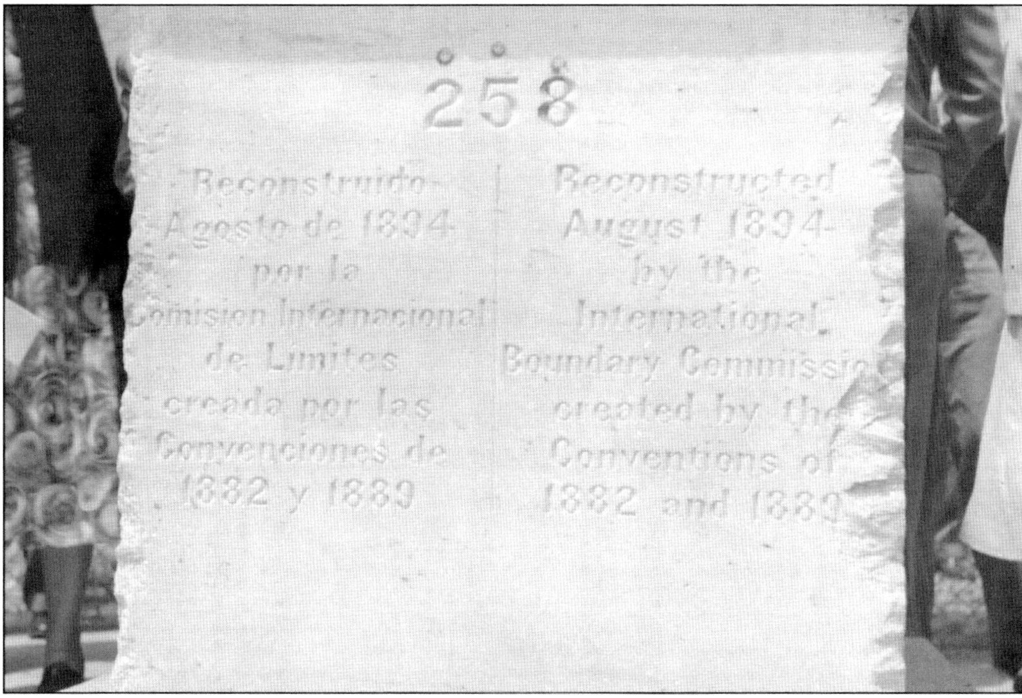

With more settlement along the border, disputes arose over the boundary's precise location and on which side residents lived. From 1894 to 1898, Mexico and the United States addressed the issue by resurveying the line. The Barlow-Blanco Commission placed 258 boundary monuments across 689 miles of the border. They labeled the El Paso marker No. 1. The last marker, once considered the initial point at the Pacific Ocean, was relabeled as No. 258. (CSDDP.)

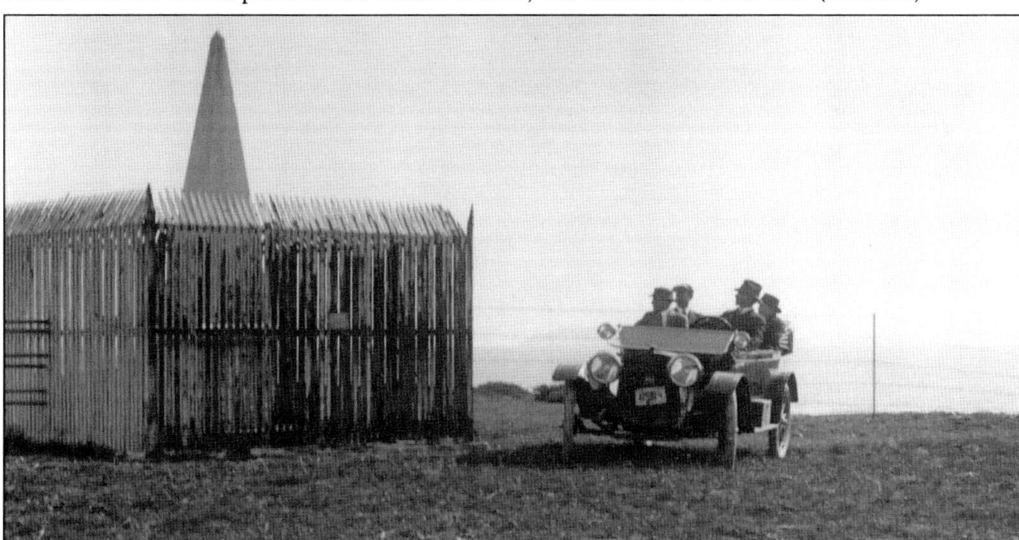

The Barlow-Blanco Commission agreed that marker No. 258 was in terrible shape. Visitors who chipped marble pieces off of the obelisk had almost destroyed it, so the boundary marker was sent to a San Diego marble yard and fixed. When the commission replaced it at the boundary along the Pacific in 1894, it protected the monument with an eight-foot-high steel picket fence. (Miguel Guerrero, Joyce Hettich Collection.)

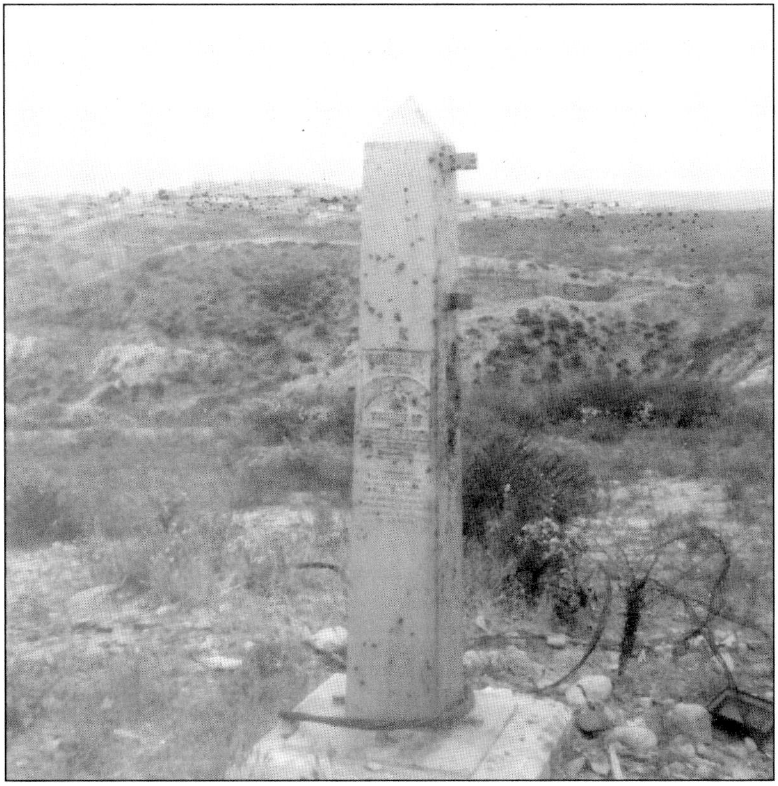

The entire Barlow-Blanco Commission survey was completed in 19 months by Mexican and American commissioners and engineers working together. The total employees numbered about 60, all of whom hauled along wagons and supplies. They placed two solid iron monuments, Nos. 256 and 257, east of the obelisk. This 1970s image shows No. 257. (California State Parks.)

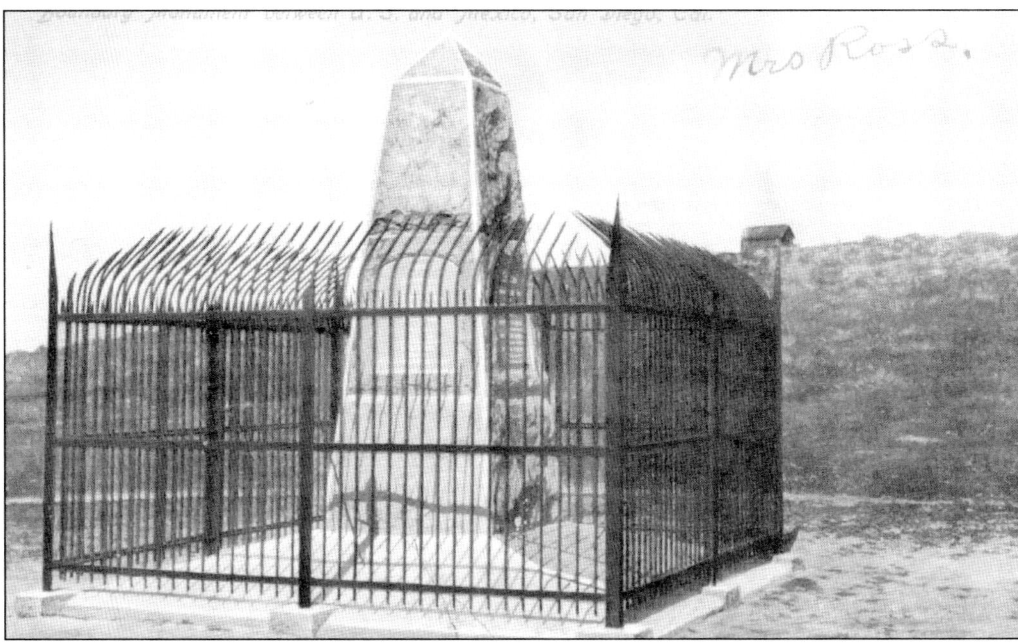

The Barlow-Blanco Commission placed monument No. 255 in what was then still referred to as Tia Juana (present-day San Ysidro). As this picture demonstrates, a steel picket fence also protected this monument that resided next to the National City & Otay railroad. Vandals, however, were still able to chip pieces off the monument. (CSDDP.)

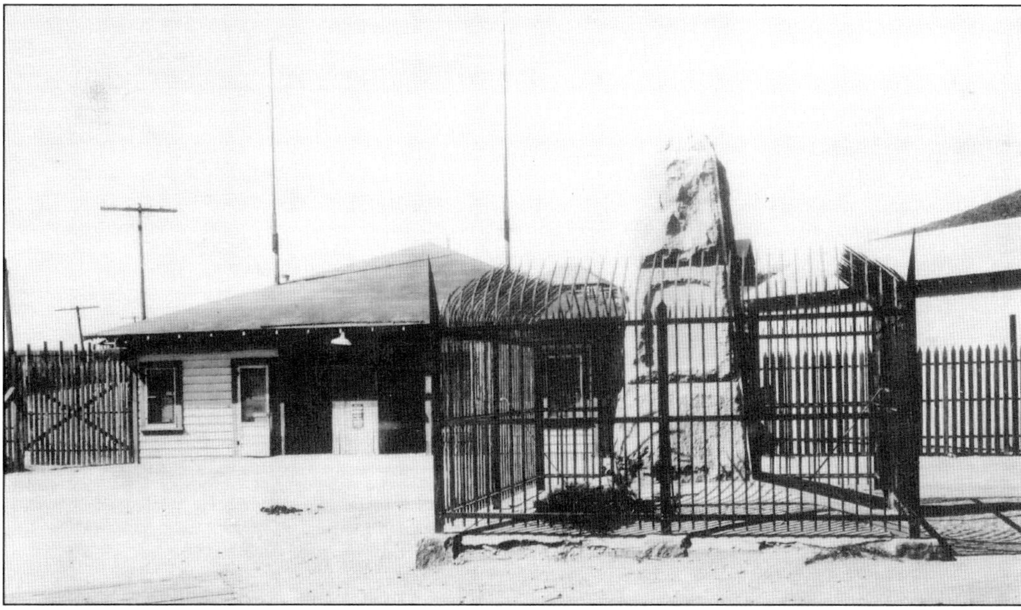

This photograph shows a view of monument No. 255 with the San Diego–Arizona Railroad Depot in the background. Around 1910, just four years after the town of Tia Juana had been destroyed by a flood in January 1895, the Tijuana River flooded again during heavy rains, and the monument washed away. (CSDDP.)

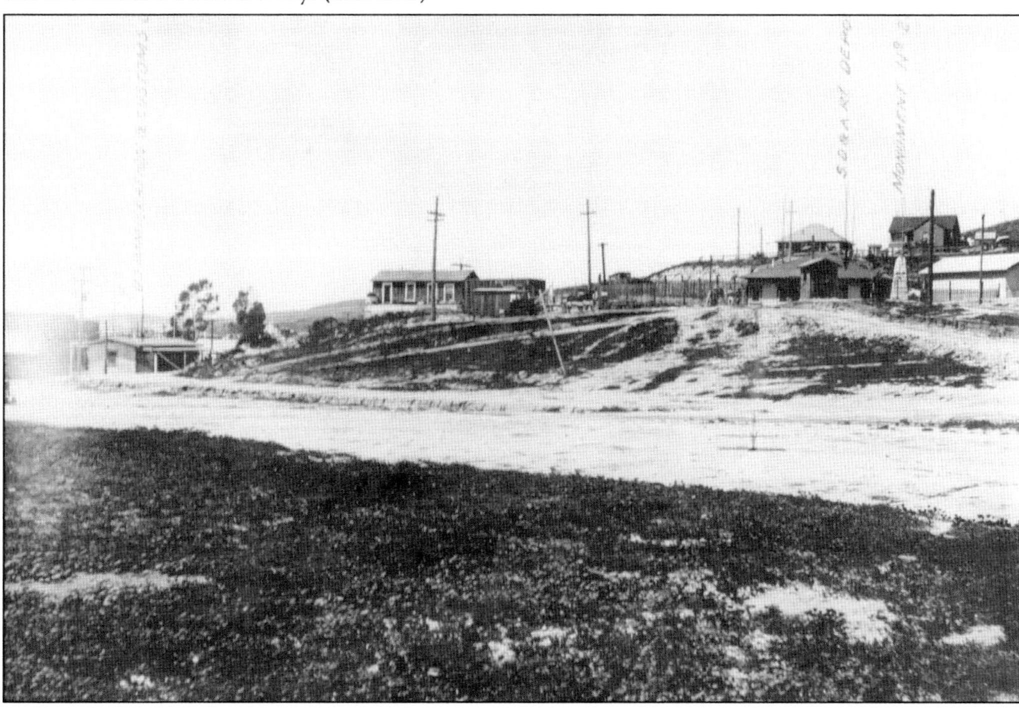

Rather than trying to recover monument No. 255, the Barlow-Blanco Commission created a new monument and moved it to higher ground. In this picture, monument No. 255 is in its new location. The US Immigration and Customs Office is at the bottom of the hill, and the San Diego–Arizona Railroad Depot is adjacent to the monument. (Miguel Guerrero, Joyce Hettich Collection.)

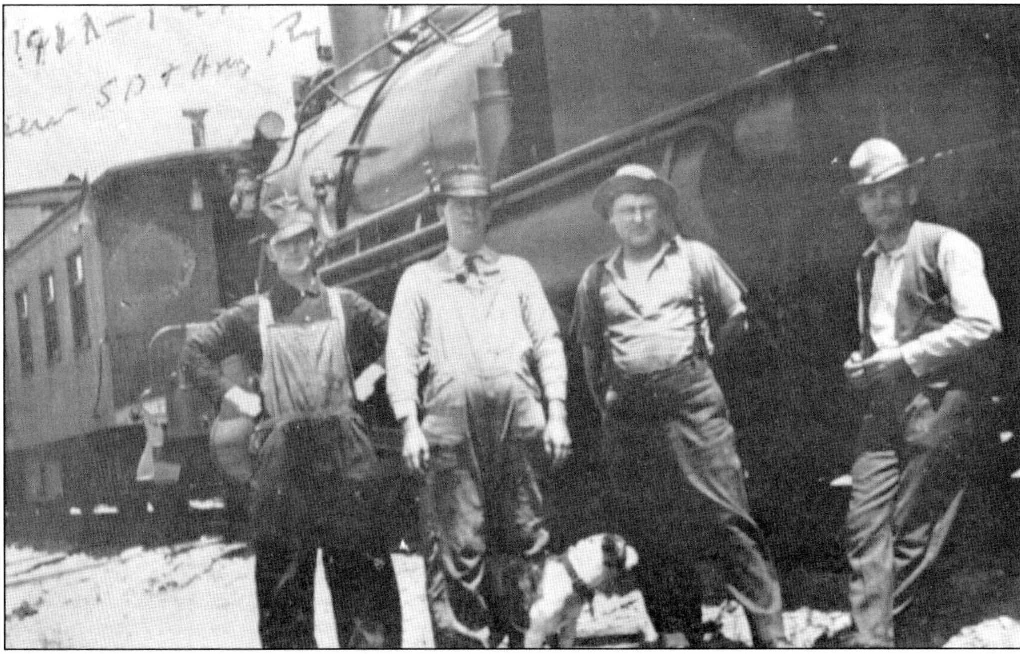

Although the National City & Otay (NC&O) Railroad train started running in 1886, it took another nine years before the tracks finally reached the Mexican border. The train proved to be popular for traffic to and from Mexico, and tourists flocked to the area by train. The railroad also carried freight, including several million pounds of produce annually for the South Bay communities. (Miguel Guerrero, Joyce Hettich Collection.)

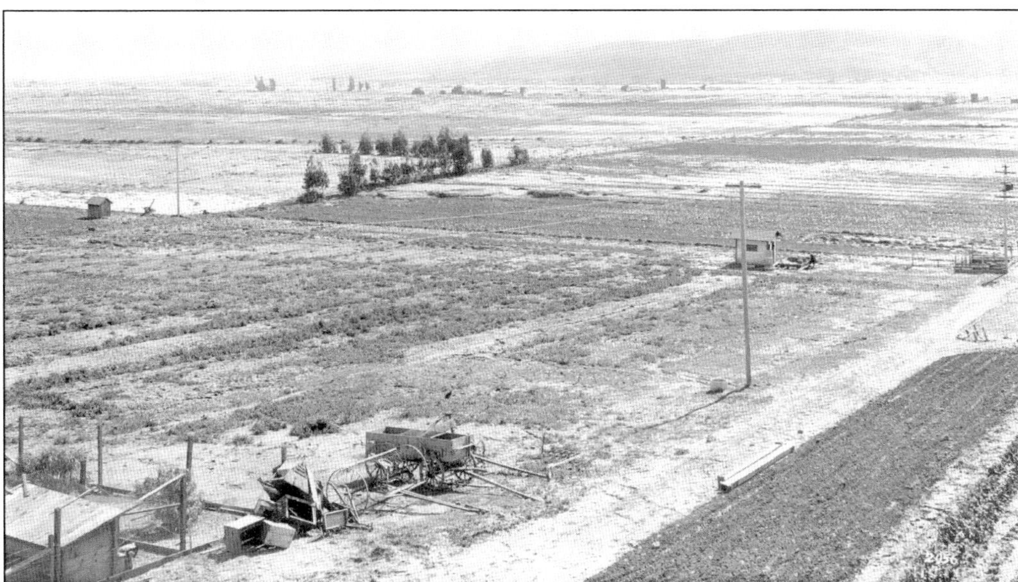

The Tijuana River Valley remained settled by farmers who began moving into the area in the 1860s to fill homestead claims. With good soil and water from the river, farmers also grew wheat, peaches, apricots, figs, and more. An Italian, Felipe Pazza, even cultured silk from mulberry leaves. This 1910 picture of the valley offers a glimpse at the fertile area during that time. (Chula Vista Public Library, Local History Collection.)

Three

Little Landers

By 1907, a new San Diego–Arizona railroad reached to the boundary and San Ysidro as well as the Tijuana River Valley became a location once again in the local and national public eye. With transportation readily available, as well as open fertile soil, a Massachusetts journalist named William E. Smythe saw the region's potential.

Smythe lived during a time when the vicissitudes of industrialization led to great disillusionment with modernization. Americans worked in factories that exploited their labor for very little in return. Smythe wanted to address these ills by fostering a "back to the soil" movement. Although Smythe himself was never a farmer, he believed that men could easily live well off an acre of land. He took his utopian vision out west, and together with George P. Hall—a former horticultural commissioner for San Diego County—he wanted to establish a colony in Old Town, but prices were too high. They eventually settled on a location that they named San Ysidro after St. Isidore, the patron saint of farmers.

In 1909, through his promotion company, Smythe bought three small undeveloped ranches for $15,000. He settled in San Ysidro and called his colony "Little Landers No. 1." His hope was to create more of these utopian colonies throughout the United States.

A master at publicity, Smythe wrote about Little Landers in San Diego newspapers. He also circulated a pamphlet called "Why Be A Little Lander?" At the height of Little Landers' existence, 300 families lived in the community. The colony gradually turned into a town reaching almost to the boundary fence, and, eventually, even the Customs Port of Entry used "San Ysidro" as the town name.

Smythe's utopian ideal was fraught with problems, however. At least half of the families needed a second income in order to survive on their acre. While they owned the land, they could not afford appropriate irrigation, which remained a constant problem due to the fact that they settled the region during the worst drought in San Diego history. By 1915, colonists, as well as newspapers, criticized Smythe for having created and fostered false hopes.

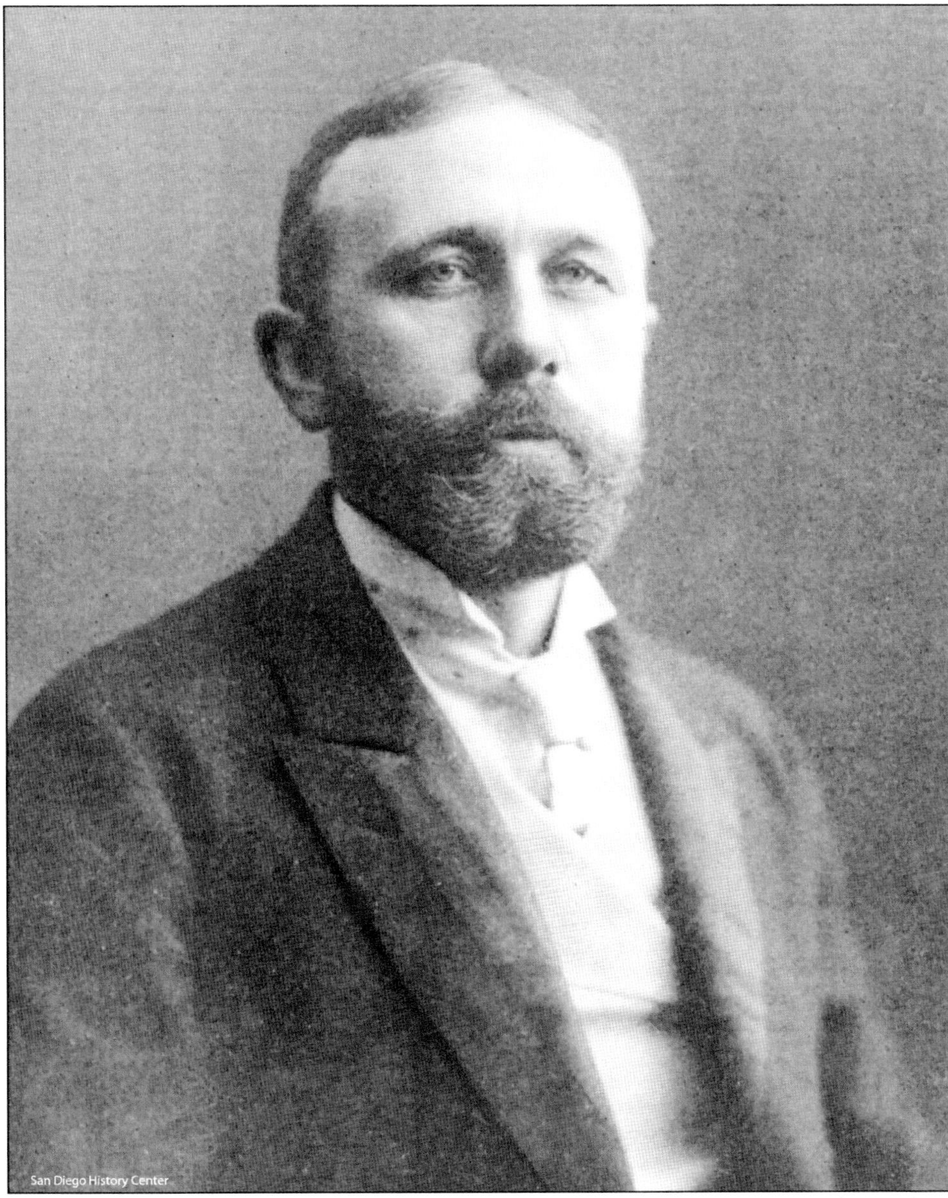

William Ellsworth Smythe (1861–1922) was born in Worcester, Massachusetts. In his early years, he became an editor for Nebraska newspapers. Struck by the Great Plains drought, he began to write about the history of irrigation and then helped irrigate the nearly abandoned western counties of Nebraska. The region flourished, becoming the best farming land in the state. He then went to Idaho and founded a cooperative land development called New Plymouth. After advising other developers near Sacramento and Lassen County, Smythe moved to San Diego in 1902, where he began to write the *History of San Diego,* among other books. Influenced by the "back-to-the-soil" movement, Smythe claimed that an average man could make a living on an acre of land. To prove his claim, he organized Little Landers in present-day San Ysidro. He lived in the colony from 1909 to 1914, serving as vice president and president, but he hoped to create Little Landers throughout the United States. To that end, he helped organize a community near Glendale (now Tujunga) and a poultry colony called Runnymede. (SDHC.)

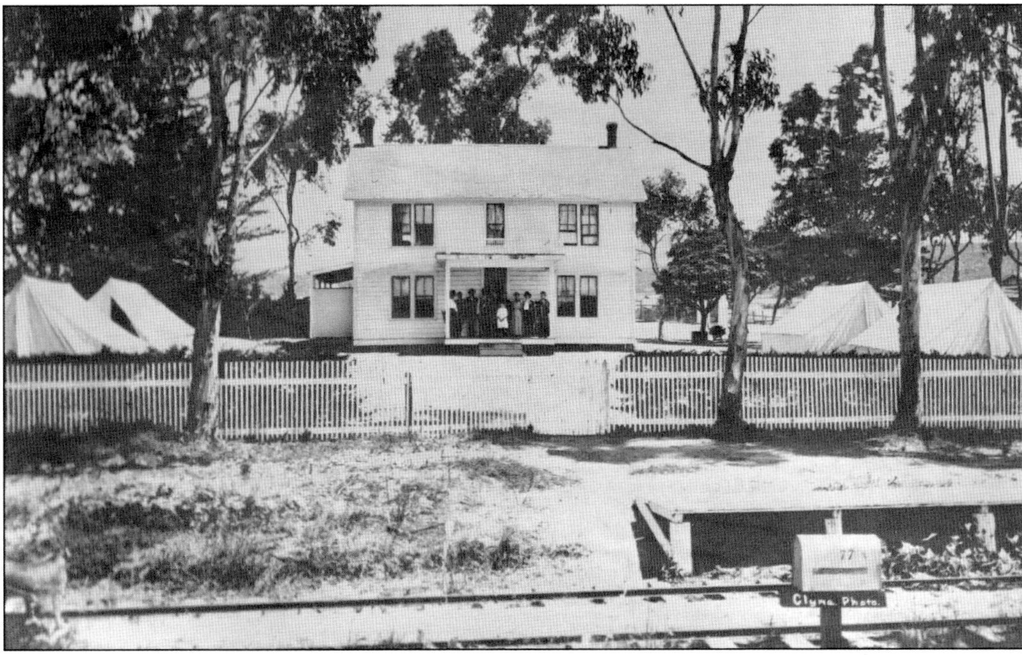

On January 11, 1909, William Smythe and George P. Hall welcomed potential colonists to the San Ysidro Hotel. People came in three carloads and drew numbers from a hat for the acre tracts, which were priced from $350 to $550 depending upon location and quality of soil. Twenty families began living in the colony. This picture displays colonists in front of the hotel. Tents are on either side that, at first, provided living quarters. (Evelyn Sevel.)

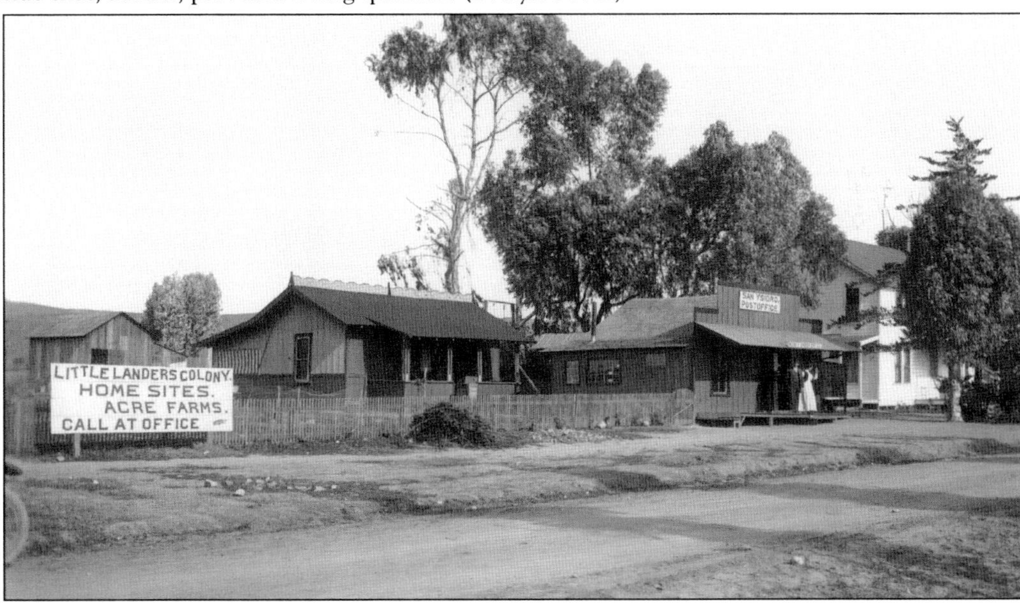

The motto "a little land and a living" expressed the working principle of the colony. Smythe explained that a family could gain a livelihood from cultivating an acre of land. Little Landers was formally incorporated on August 1, 1908. Through his promotion company, Smythe paid $15,000. The capital stock of the company was $100,000, and 10,000 shares of stock were authorized. (SDHC.)

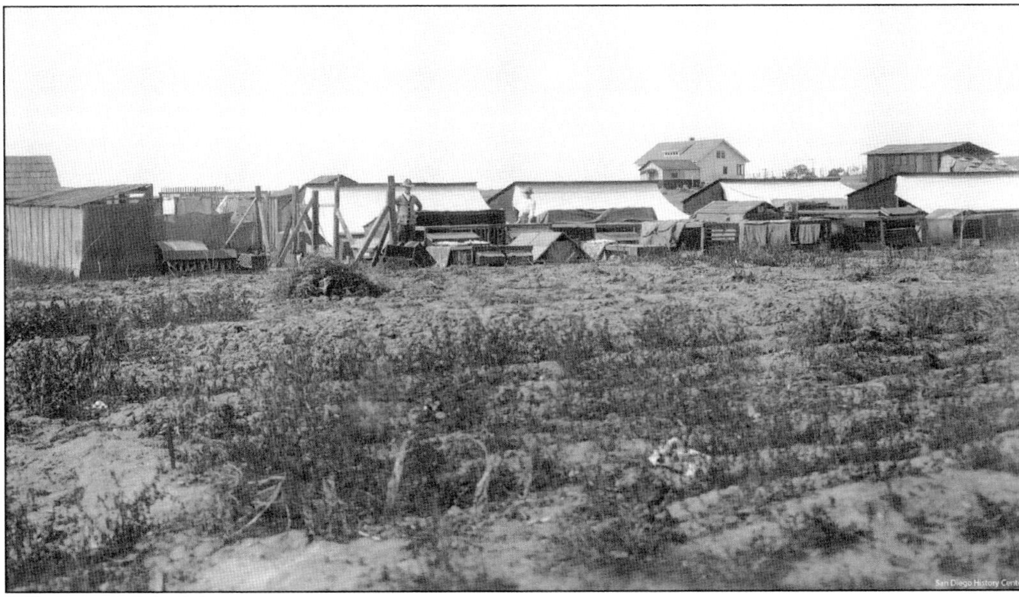

Within a few weeks of the August 1908 incorporation, 20 families were living in the colony. Residents erected domiciles above the ruined border village, which had flooded about two decades earlier. At first, many community members lived in tents next to the homes they were building. For irrigation, they pumped water from the Tijuana River into a small reservoir. (SDHC.)

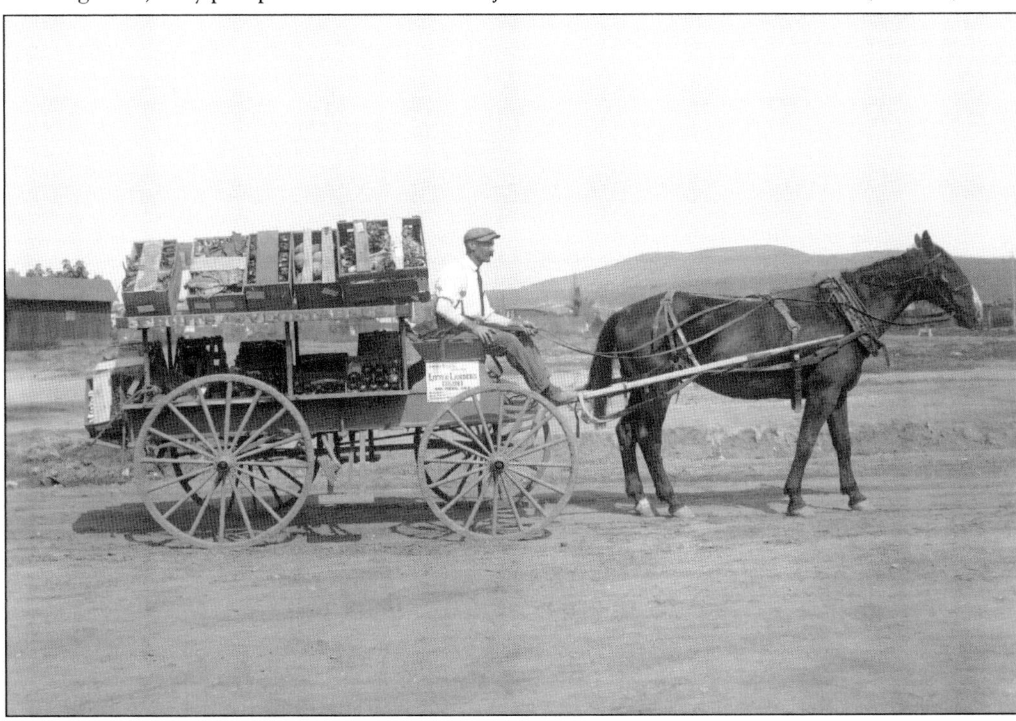

Little Landers residents wanted to cultivate their own land, but they also wanted to earn income by selling their surplus crops to San Diegans. In the beginning years, a wagon and cart (like the one pictured here) visited each colonist to pick up produce and take it to the city, where it could be sold house to house. (SDHC.)

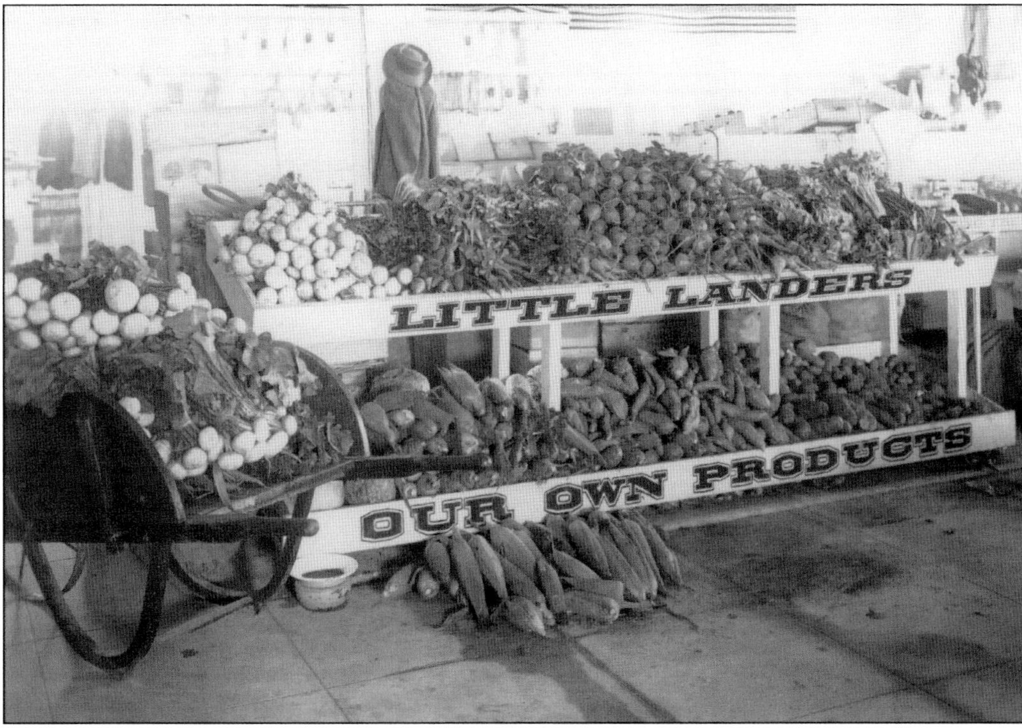

By October 21, 1913, the Little Landers Market was incorporated as a nonprofit cooperative. This general cooperative store was maintained at San Ysidro in the adobe house once owned by Juan Ybarra. Products for sale included food, farm tools, and household appliances. The colonists produced a wide variety of crops, including figs, oranges, lemons, apricots, peaches, cabbages, spinach, celery, asparagus, radishes, and lettuce. (SDHC.)

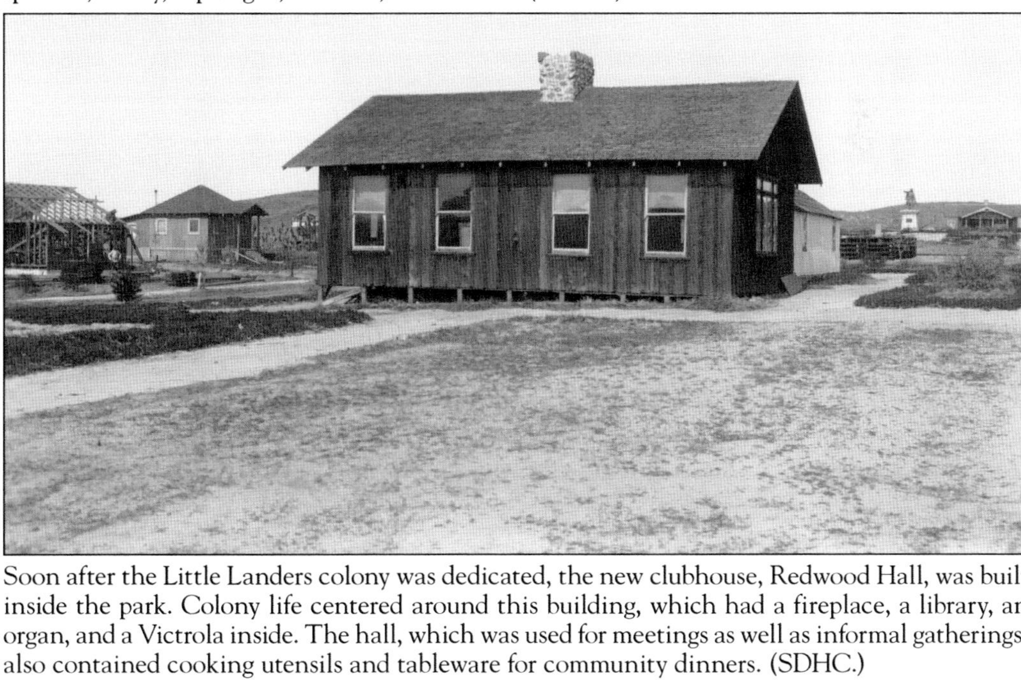

Soon after the Little Landers colony was dedicated, the new clubhouse, Redwood Hall, was built inside the park. Colony life centered around this building, which had a fireplace, a library, an organ, and a Victrola inside. The hall, which was used for meetings as well as informal gatherings, also contained cooking utensils and tableware for community dinners. (SDHC.)

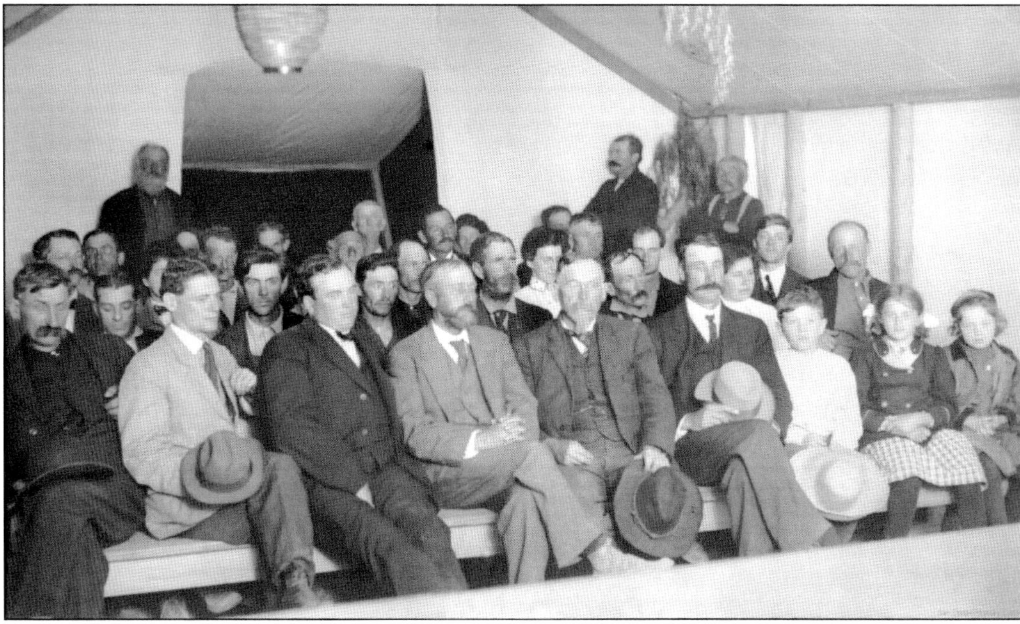

The Little Landers held business meetings weekly, quarterly, and annually on Monday evenings inside the clubhouse, which also hosted purely social meetings. The colonists elected officers to serve for one year, including a president, a vice president, and a secretary-treasurer. In this image, William Smythe is fourth from the left and George Hall is fifth from the left in the first row. (SDHC.)

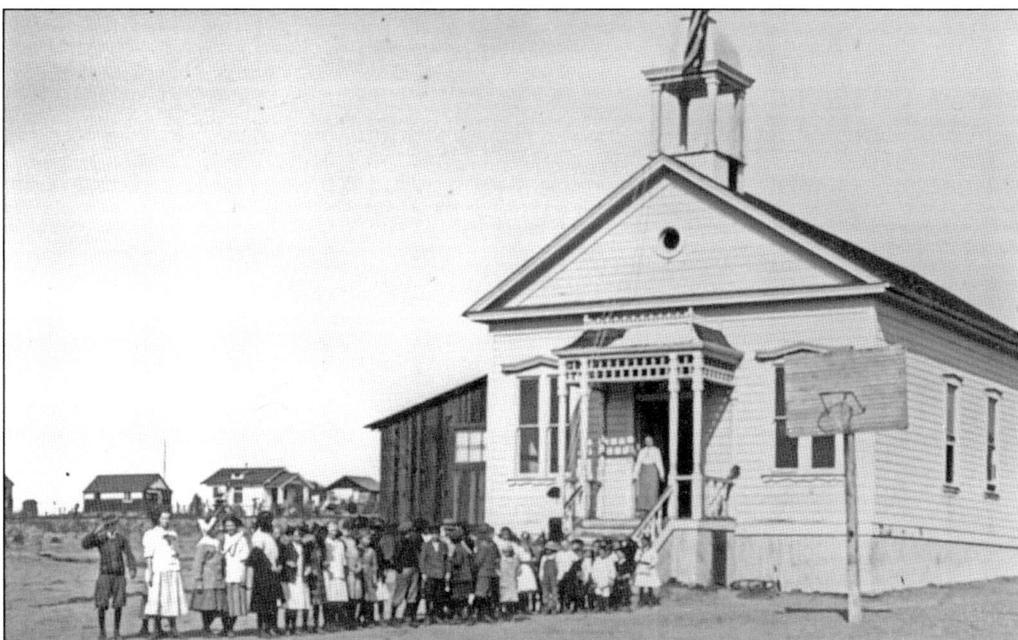

The founders intended for Little Landers to become a model town. Streets, lots, and a park were marked out, and J.W. Lewis was appointed both contractor and general manager of the settlement. An elementary school was built a few blocks away from the clubhouse. The school included grades from elementary through the first year of high school. (Chula Vista Public Library, Local History Collection.)

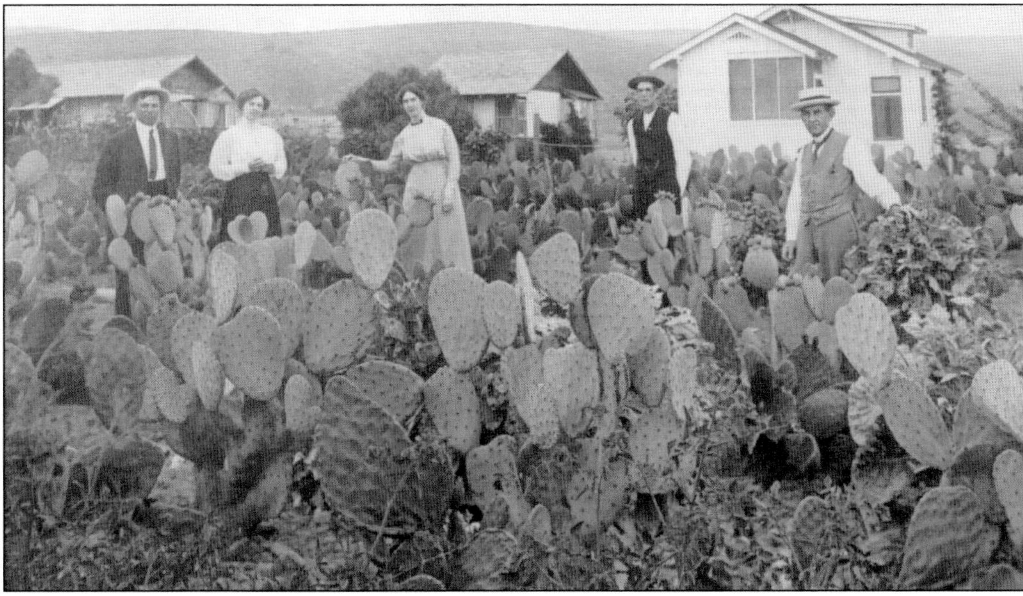

By the fall of 1910, only 38 families lived in Little Landers. William Smythe's corporation faced bankruptcy in November and the company's liabilities were assessed at $14,000. Colonists did not have the money to install wells and pumps, so they were unable to irrigate their crops. Many blamed Smythe for luring people to the area without providing a proper water-pumping system. These were also years of drought. In this picture, colonists pose with cactus plants, displaying the dry conditions of the land. (SDHC.)

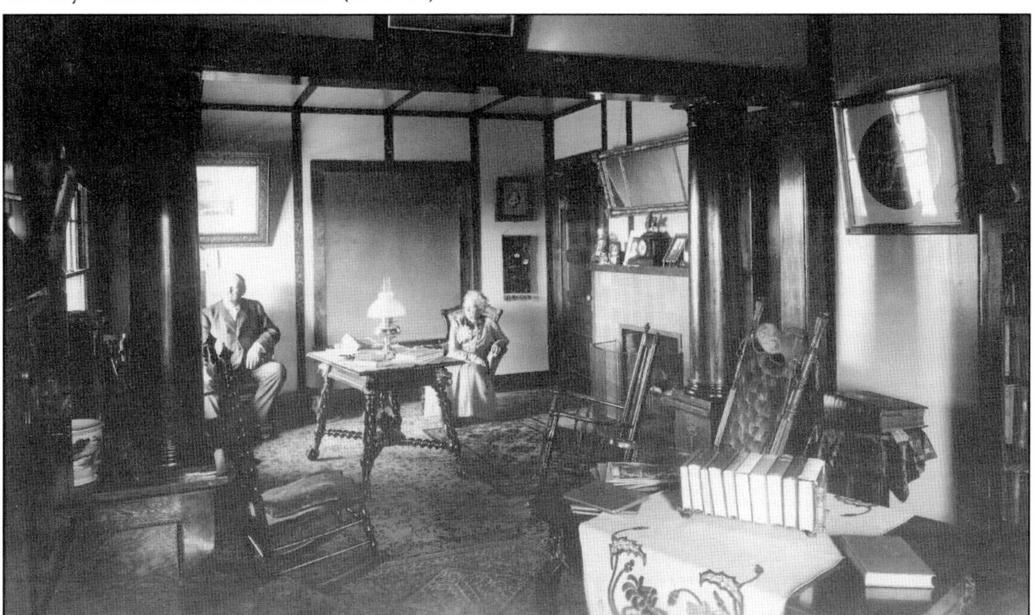

In 1910, the bylaws in the Little Landers colony excluded "Negroes, Orientals and Mexicans" from settling and owning property in the colony. New laws allowed white settlers to purchase only a town lot, rather than a farm, moving the colony away from its original agricultural ideals. The elderly also became overrepresented. In this picture, an elderly couple sits in their Little Landers home. (SDHC.)

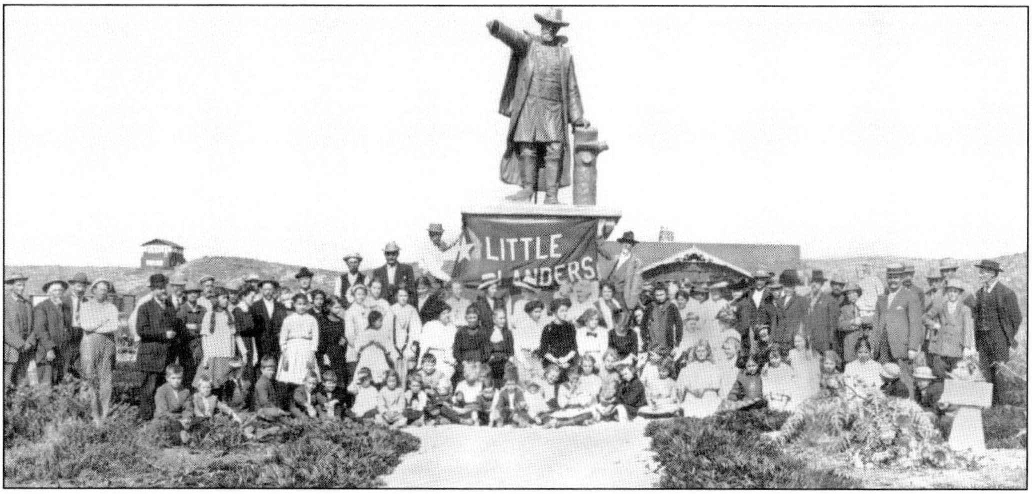

In 1913, after finally incorporating an irrigation district, the community of 69 families held a grand celebration that was also intended to honor what would have been the 89th birthday of the late Pres. Ulysses S. Grant. During the celebration, a statue of Grant (purchased by 70-year-old George Hall) was unveiled in San Ysidro Park on a concrete pedestal. (SDHC.)

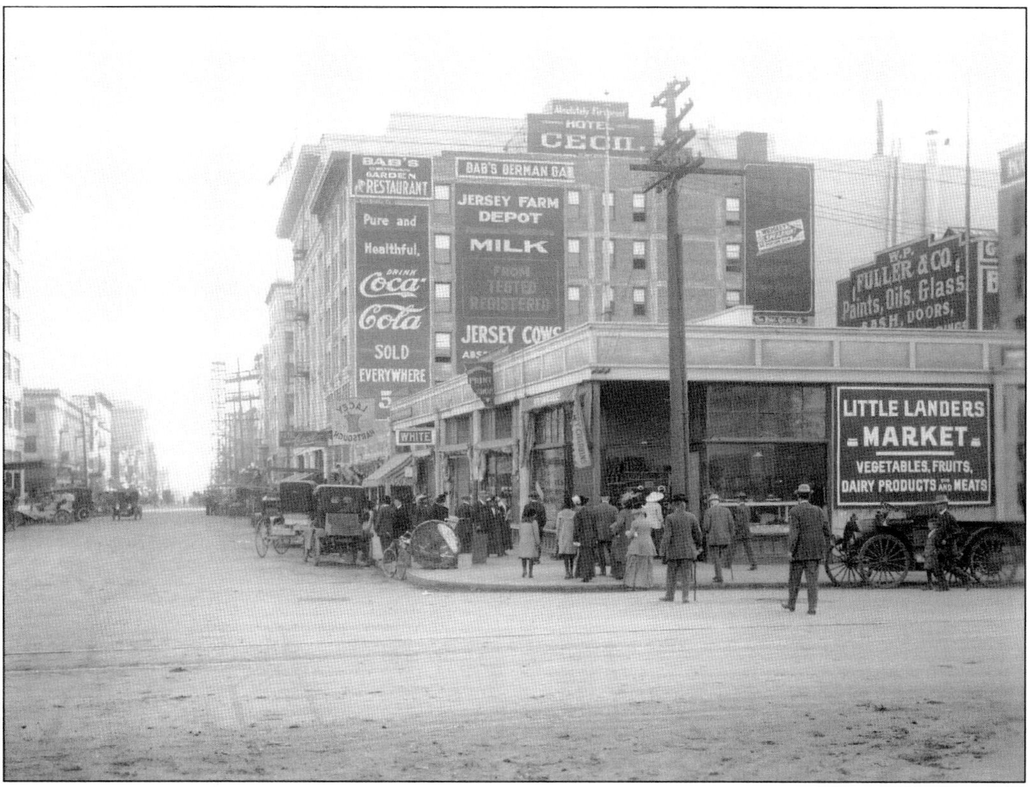

In 1912, about 67 colonists participated in the establishment of a cooperative store called the Little Landers Market at Sixth and B Streets in downtown San Diego. However, many felt they were not being adequately paid and withdrew from the cooperative. Under continuous fire, William Smythe left San Ysidro in 1914 to establish another Little Landers elsewhere. The Little Landers Market was suspended one year later, in 1915. (SDHC.)

Four

REVOLUTION AND FLOOD

While the utopian dream of Little Landers slowly withered, the boundary line separating the United States and Mexico had a deep impact upon the area's ecology and culture. Customs officers pleaded with the government for more patrols and boundary fences running through the territory.

In 1911, the Mexican Revolution broke out in Tijuana. In Mexico, dictator Porfirio Diaz was overthrown, and instability spread throughout Baja California. Revolutionists organized under an anarchist labor movement called the Industrial Workers of the World (IWW). From Los Angeles, leader Ricardo Flores Magon gathered an army of American, European, and Mexican insurgents who dispersed along the border to fight in small groups.

On January 29, 1911, a 12-man force captured Mexicali. For three months, other IWW insurgents fought around Mexicali, Tecate, and El Alamo. By May 8, an IWW faction led by Carl Rhys Pryce reached Tijuana. While most residents fled, up to 150 Mexican soldiers and citizen volunteers defended the town, and a 16-hour fight raged through May 9.

Surprisingly, IWW rebels were victorious. They took over Tijuana and lawlessness reigned—for one month. On June 22, Federal Mexican Troops launched a Second Battle of Tijuana and overthrew the IWW rebels, who were apprehended at the border and taken to a prisoner camp.

After peace returned to the border, the Panama-California Exposition in Balboa Park sparked the attention of business owners and the mayor in Tijuana. It created a "Tijuana Fair" in the same year to attract San Diego tourists, replete with entertainments that were illegal in California, including gambling, bullfighting, and horse racing. Hundreds of thousands of tourists passed through San Ysidro and the Tijuana River Valley during this time.

Tragedy struck in January 1916, when heavy rains made the Tijuana River overflow its banks during what became known as the worst flood in the recorded history of San Diego County. The raging waters destroyed farms, cattle, railroad tracks, bridges, and homes. Little Landers vanished, and residents of the area were forced to leave or rebuild. However, floods would continue to plague the region.

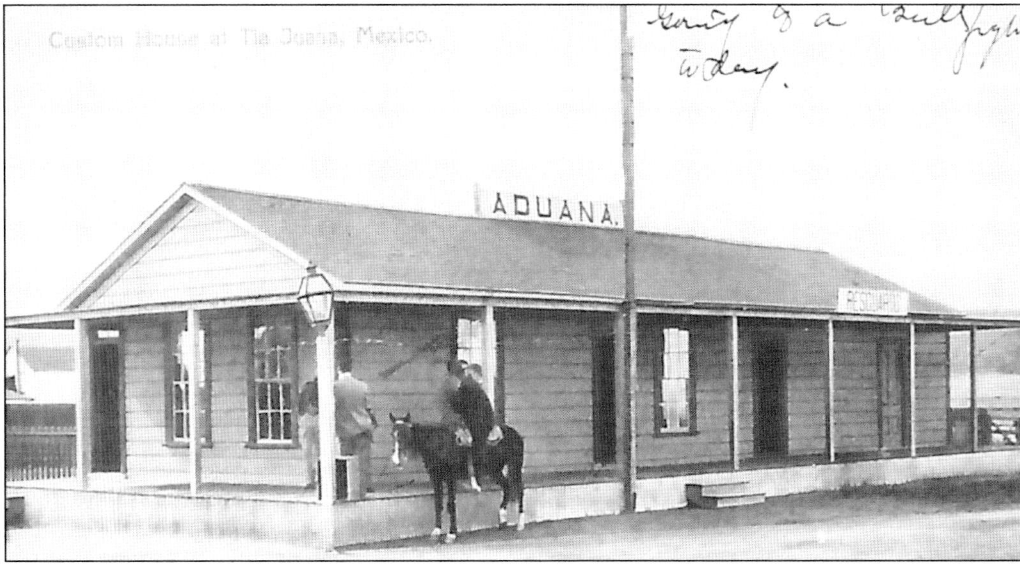

On May 8, 1911, a group of about 100 members of the Industrial Workers of the World (IWW), led by Welsh-born Gen. Carl Rhys Pryce, marched into Tijuana. Mexican soldiers in the federal garrison at Tijuana and citizen volunteers, totaling only between 50 and 150, fought for the city. The customhouse (pictured) had Mexican federals stranded inside. A group of 25 IWW insurgents killed them. (SDPHA.)

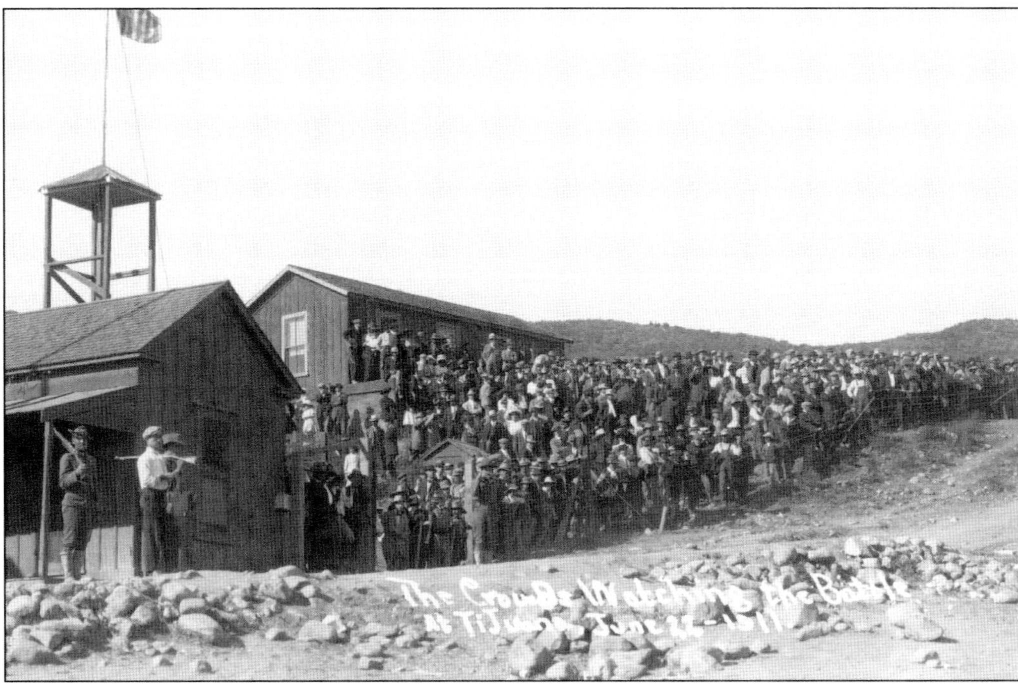

When San Diegans heard about insurgents marching into Tijuana, they rushed to the border by the thousands and lined the hills around San Ysidro to watch a live battle. Trains from San Diego brought carloads of spectators, but they were prohibited from crossing the border. The 16-hour battle left 32 dead and 24 wounded. The IWW insurgents captured Tijuana, victorious under General Pryce. (SDHC.)

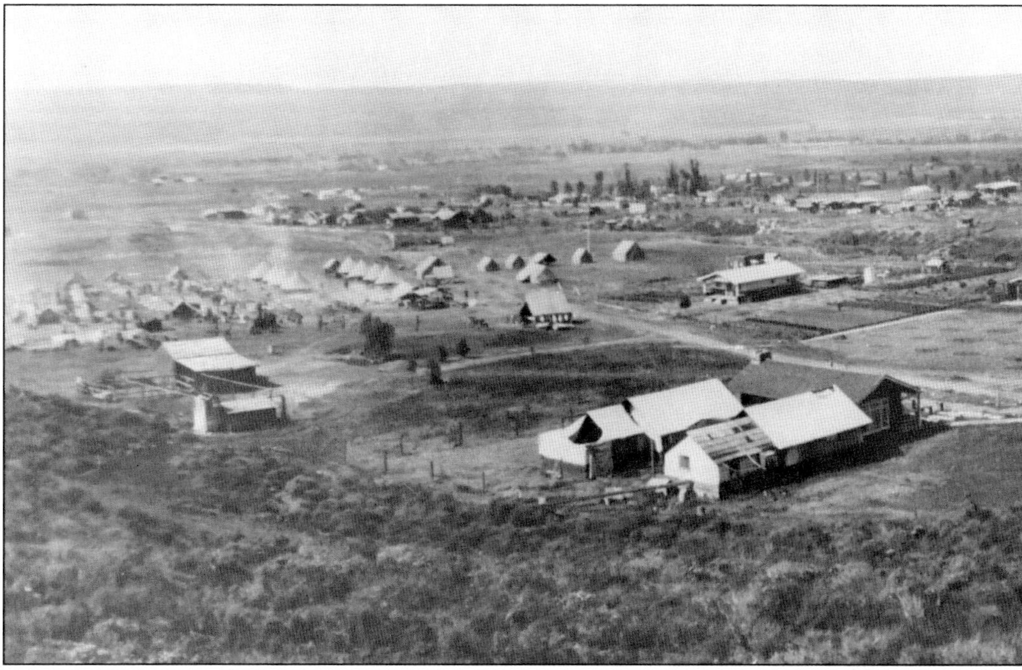

After the fighting ended, refugees were put up in a tent camp at San Ysidro. Numbering about 125 people, they were mostly American and Mexican merchants. Ironically, Industrial Workers of the World (IWW) insurgents told visitors coming to Mexico that they could carry off whatever they wished. Tourism boomed for Tijuana as American souvenir-hunters flocked across the border to ransack shops. (Evelyn Sevel.)

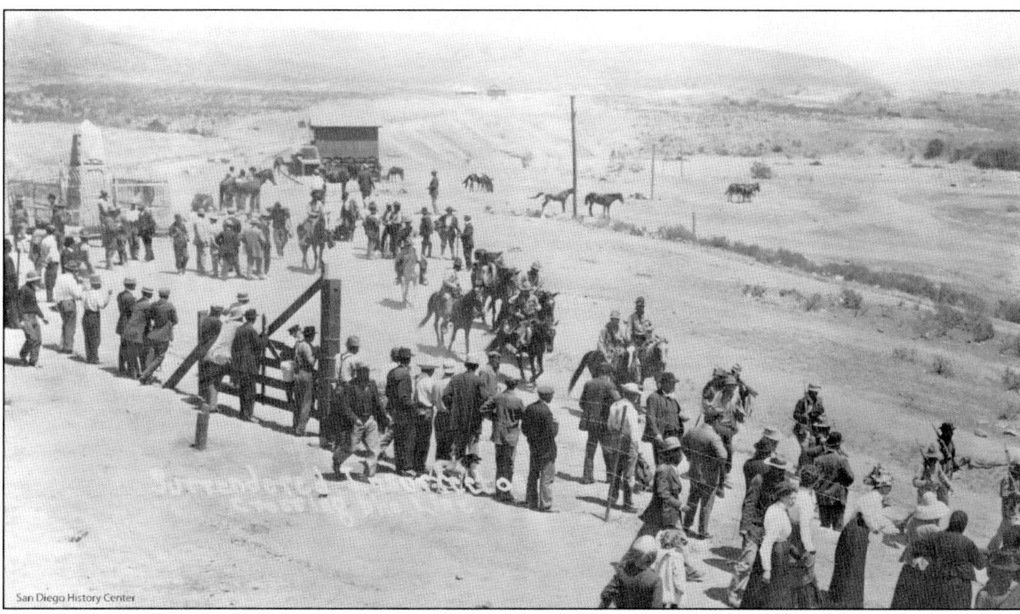

On June 22, 1911, Gov. Celso Vega marched with federal troops to launch a Second Battle of Tijuana. This time, they were victorious. After three hours of battle, they overthrew the 155 IWW members and 75 Mexicans who had gone over to the IWW side. The rebels then surrendered to Capt. Alfred H. Wilcox at the US border. (SDHC.)

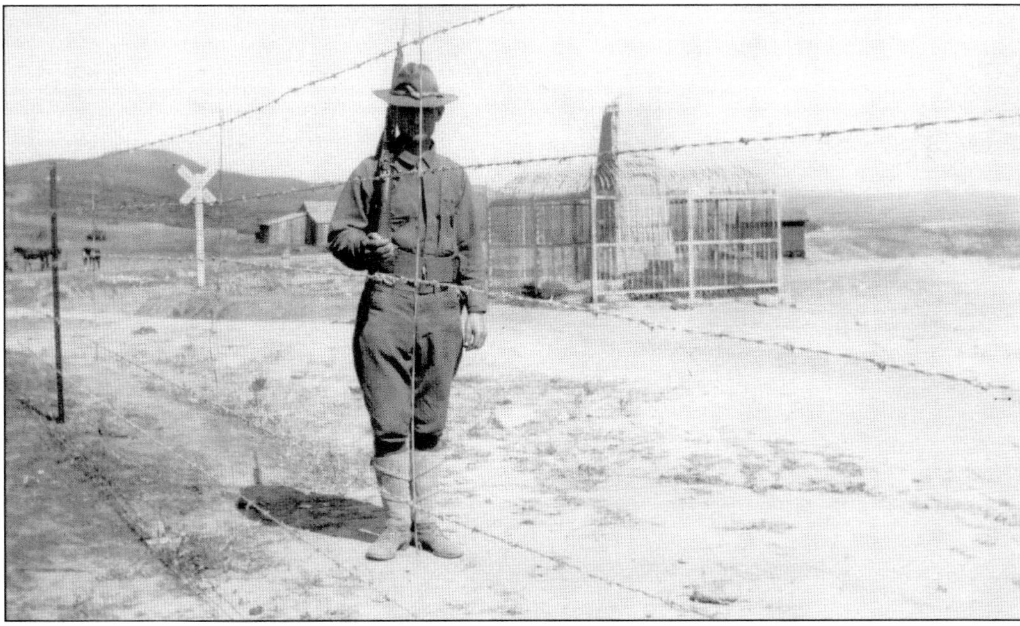

The Battle of Tijuana had a 20 percent casualty rate, higher than that of the U.S.-Mexican War. Although peace returned to the border region, the revolution showed how events in Mexico heavily impacted San Ysidro residents, including the Little Landers colony, which asked for further military reinforcements. In this picture, a US Army soldier poses with a border monument in the background. (SDHC.)

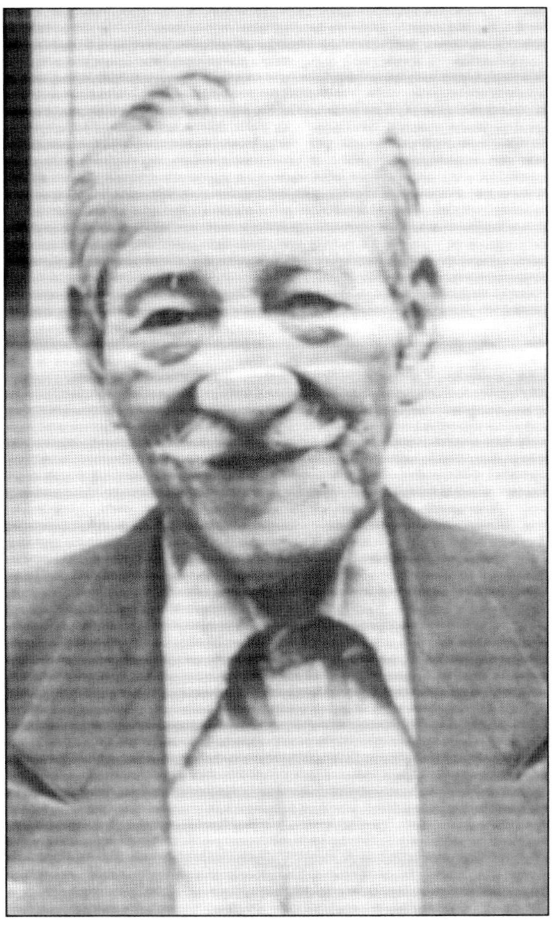

Political instability in Mexico meant families often immigrated to the United States. Guadalupe Gonzalez was said to be the first Mexican man to settle in San Ysidro with his family. His son Guadalupe L. Gonzalez (pictured) was born in 1884 and emigrated with his father at the age of nine. Guadalupe L. lived in San Ysidro for 60 years, the longest-time resident, and fought in the 1911 battle. (Conchita Lopez.)

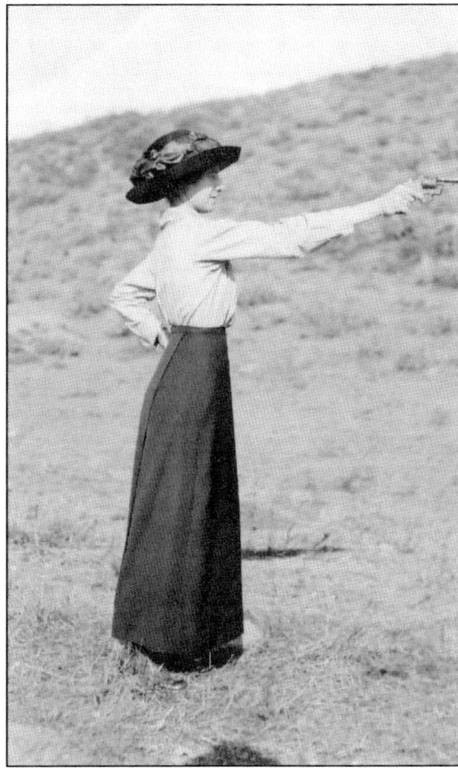

By the turn of the century, there were only three US customs officers, while the Mexican government had 14 customs officials. Mattie Larson (pictured at right and center below) initially came to the area in 1907. Six San Ysidro families invited her to teach their children. According to Larson, 30 children from Tijuana walked across the border each day to attend classes because the six families did not have enough children to support a schoolteacher by themselves. She then became a border inspector in 1911. In 1913, Larson married a young engineer who worked on the railroad. As a consequence, she left her position as a border inspector, which was a positive development; Larson was reportedly severely bored at the job because for days on end, only one person other than the mailman would make the border crossing. (Both, Yolanda Gaudet.)

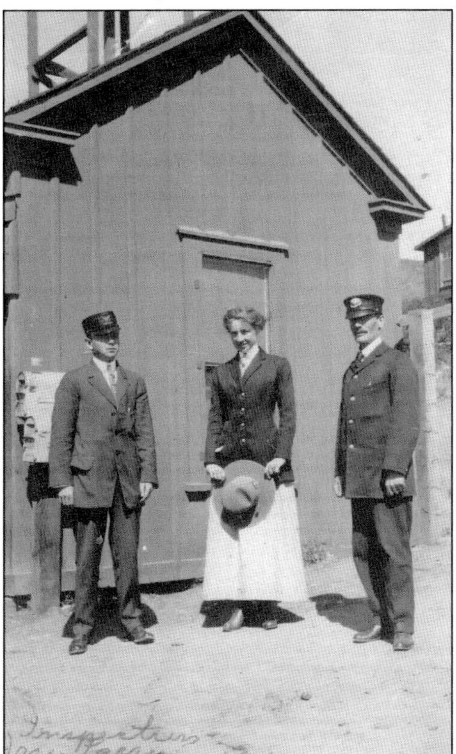

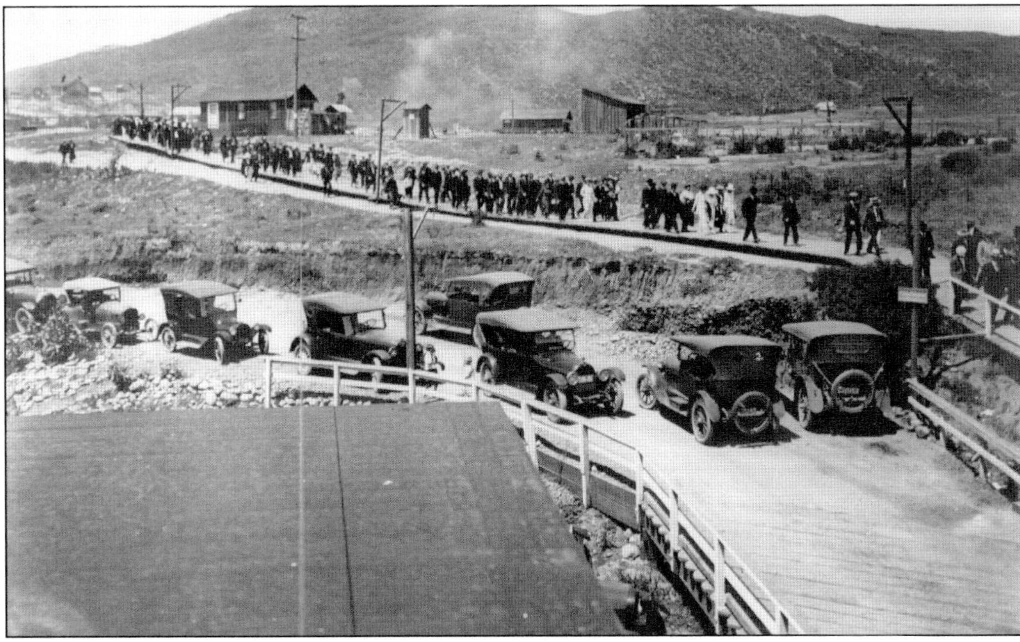

The Panama-California Exposition, which was held from March 1915 through January 1, 1917, brought many tourists to San Diego. Tijuana entrepreneurs saw the potential profits of this tourism and created a "Tijuana Fair" that included attractions outlawed in California like horse racing, bullfighting, cockfighting, and gambling. An estimated 8,000 tourists crossed the border in one day to take advantage of these entertainments. To accommodate the crowds, Mexican authorities built this 1,800-foot-long boardwalk from the border into Tijuana. (Evelyn Sevel.)

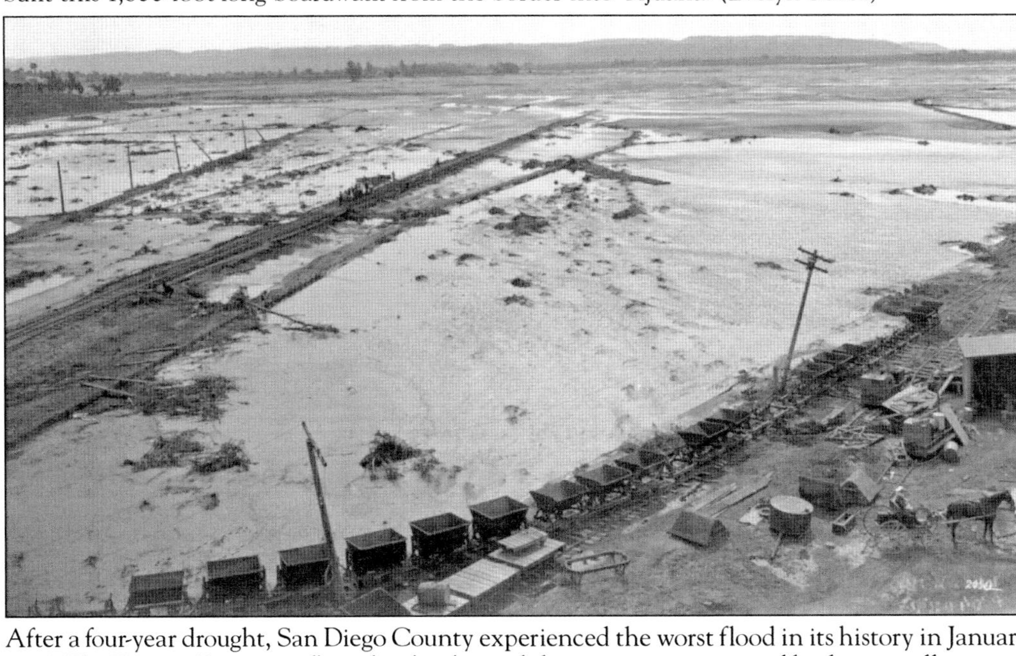

After a four-year drought, San Diego County experienced the worst flood in its history in January 1916. The Tijuana River overflowed its banks, and the raging waters caused bridges to collapse and railroad tracks to be destroyed. This picture shows the impact of the flood on the Tijuana River Valley looking toward San Ysidro. (Chula Vista Public Library, Local History Collection.)

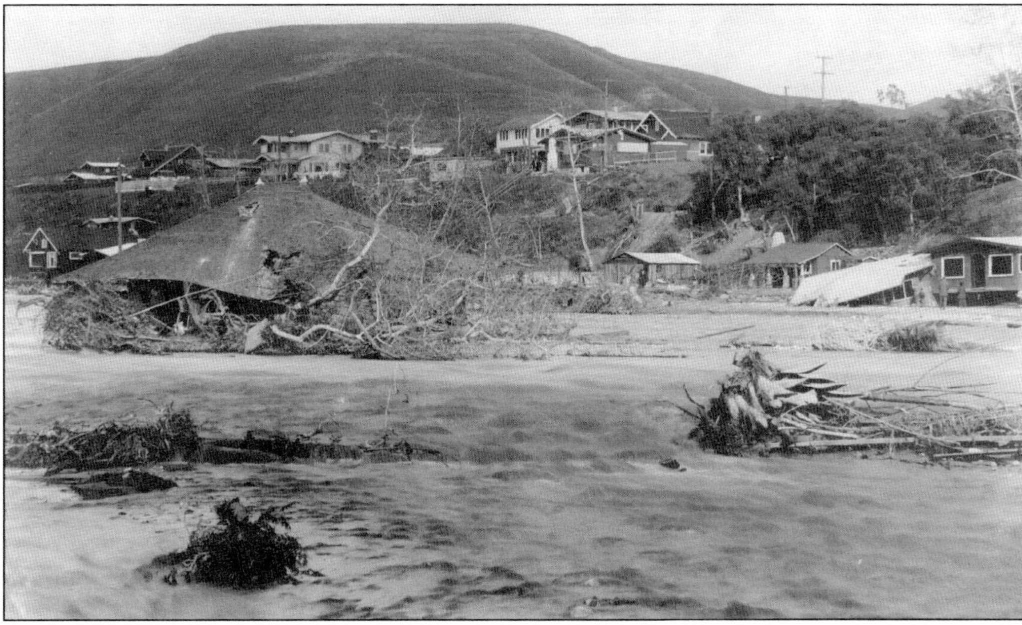

During the January 1916 flood, several torrential storms tore the Lower Otay Dam open, spilling 4.5 billion gallons of water into the entire South Bay. The Little Landers colony disappeared, leaving 135 settlers homeless. Two women drowned. Although Little Landers founder William Smythe returned to help with relief efforts, he became ill and left. Little Landers vanished. (Special Collections & University Archives, San Diego State University Library & Information Access.)

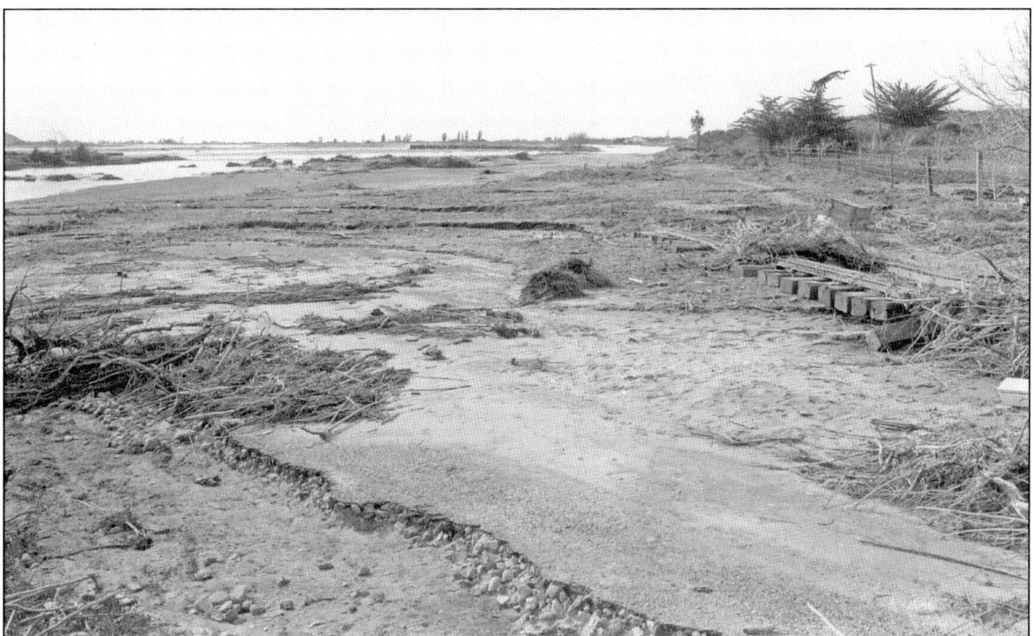

Flooding in the Tijuana River Valley region occurred again and again, causing problems for the community—especially for farmers. This picture shows how August Schnell's dairy farm was wiped out in 1916 and the Tijuana River swung far to the right of its usual course. (Chula Vista Public Library, Local History Collection.)

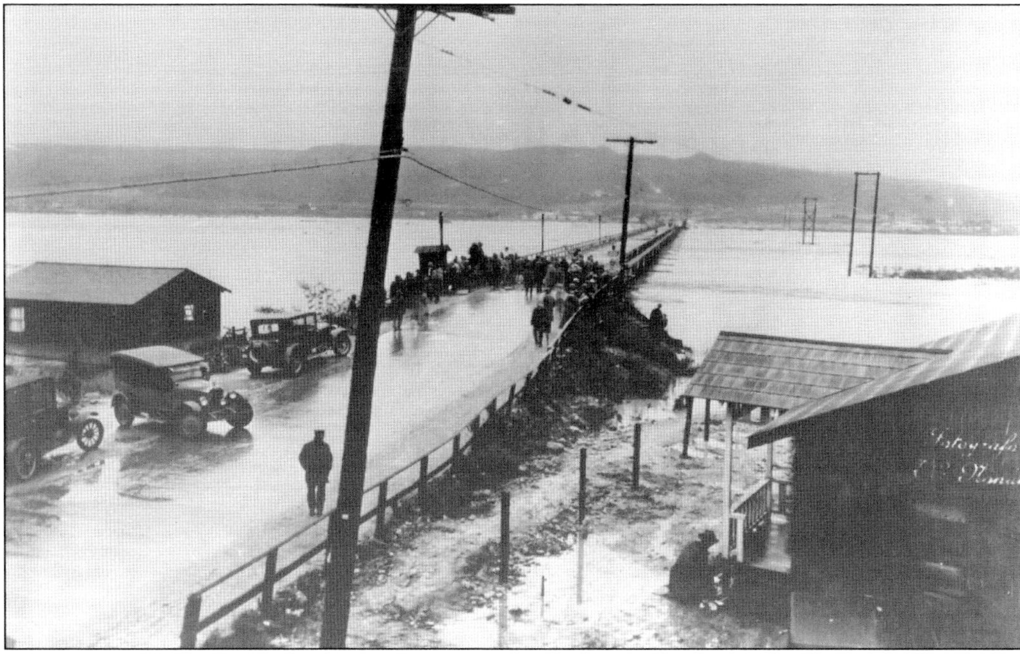

The 1916 flood caused the shutdown of the South Bay transportation system and all communications. Houses floated away. Because the Tijuana River Valley and San Ysidro were located in a flood plain, the region was subject to many more flood disasters. This 1925 picture shows the San Ysidro border crossing with its boardwalk flooded once again. (Evelyn Sevel.)

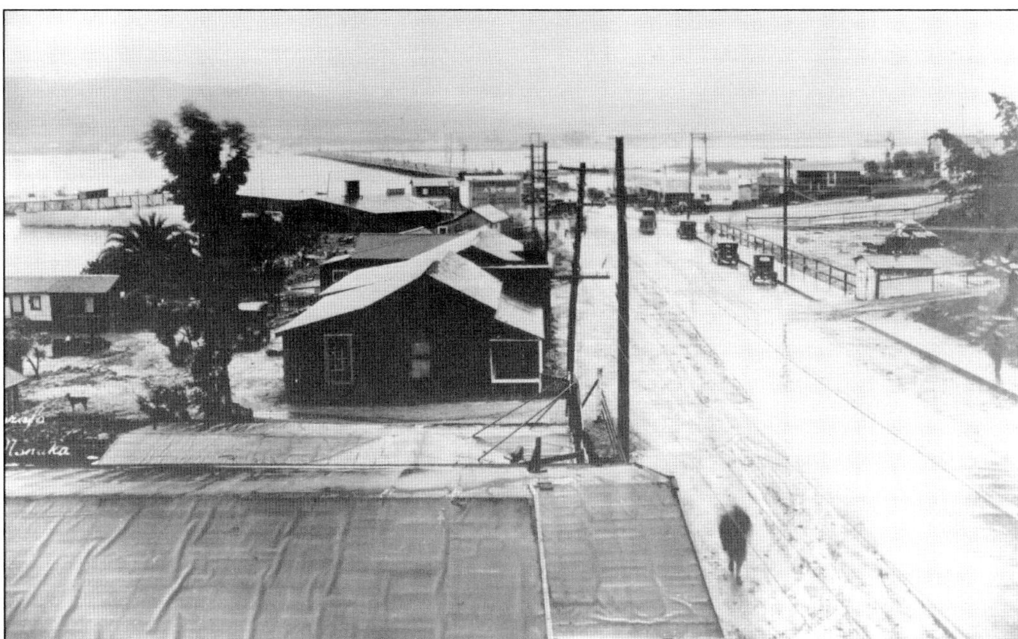

This is another view of the 1925 flood at the border. The Tijuana River flooded in 1891, 1895, 1916, 1921, 1925, 1937, and again in the 1980s and 1990s. Each time, the destruction cost lives, damaged property, and sent residents either fleeing to higher ground or determined to rebuild. (Evelyn Sevel.)

Five

A Small Town

After the 1917 Tijuana Fair, San Ysidro began to undergo dramatic change largely due to one man: Frank "Booze" Beyer. Capitalizing on entertainments that became illegal in California, American entrepreneurs saw fortunes in Tijuana's "vice" tourism. When the United States instituted Prohibition in 1919, fortunes catapulted across the border. Tourists swarmed to "Vice City" to enjoy entertainment that was illegal in the state of California. Beyer owned many establishments that catered to these tourists, but he chose to settle in the quieter town of San Ysidro, where he donated a library and a civic center and gave money to two churches.

As smuggling and debauchery marked life across the border, racetrack and saloon employees estimated at more than 300, sought quieter living in San Ysidro. The employees bought residential homes from former Little Landers colonists, and the laws prohibiting minorities from owning property were dropped.

To meet the needs of all residents, as well as to serve the tourists passing through—including movie stars like Rita Hayworth and John Wayne, San Ysidro Boulevard became a main thoroughfare with a movie theater, many stores, and a pharmacy. As the town became less tied to farming, its economy depended upon the politics between the United States and Mexico. Border closures often adversely affected the town's economy.

Around the time of the Great Depression, families of Mexican heritage who worked in the mines of Arizona came to San Ysidro, where they found work at Rohr industries or other large aircraft and military-related companies. Meanwhile, the Tijuana River Valley remained agricultural, and San Ysidro stores continued to provide goods to the predominantly Swiss, Japanese, Italian, and Mexican farmers of the area.

Residents who lived in San Ysidro and the Tijuana River Valley from the 1930s onward recall that everyone knew everyone. Even today, old-timers refer to San Ysidro as their "Mayberry."

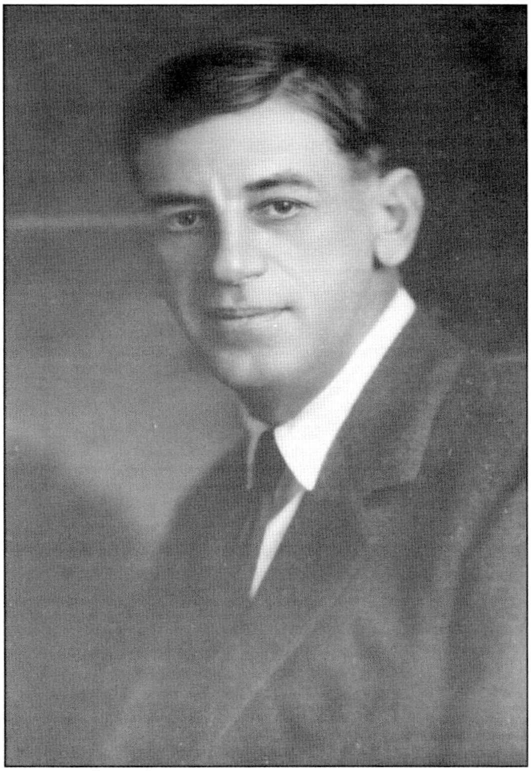

Frank "Booze" Beyer (1875–1931) was born in 1875 in Norristown, Pennsylvania. He became a mining engineer and followed the mining booms in Alaska, Colorado, and Arizona. In the early 1900s, he switched occupations to "roulette dealer" while in Tonopah, Nevada. Soon thereafter, he owned saloons and brothels in Bakersfield, California. Setting his sights on higher profits, he partnered with two Americans—Marvin Allen and Carl Withington—and bought the Owl Café and Theater, a venue in Mexicali that boasted 100 prostitutes and the longest bar in the world. Frank and his wife, Blanche (pictured), settled in San Ysidro, along Hall Avenue, in 1918. They both ran a jewelry store and pawnshop. They also bought a ranch, bred horses, and raised Guernsey cows on a dairy farm. (Both, San Ysidro Public Library.)

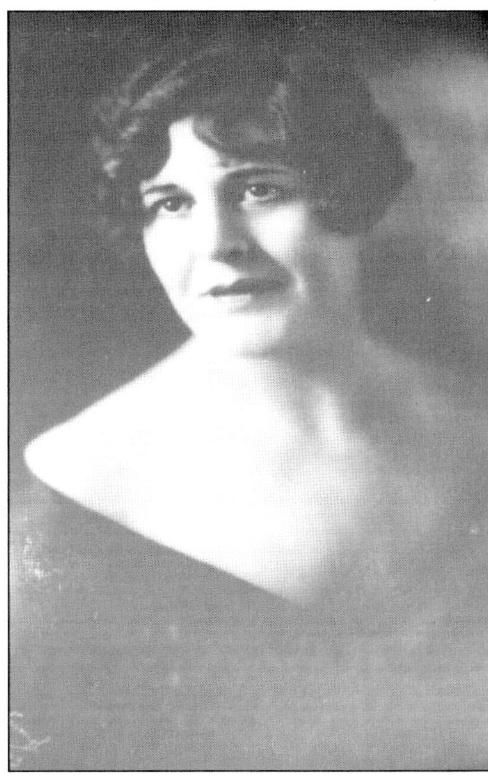

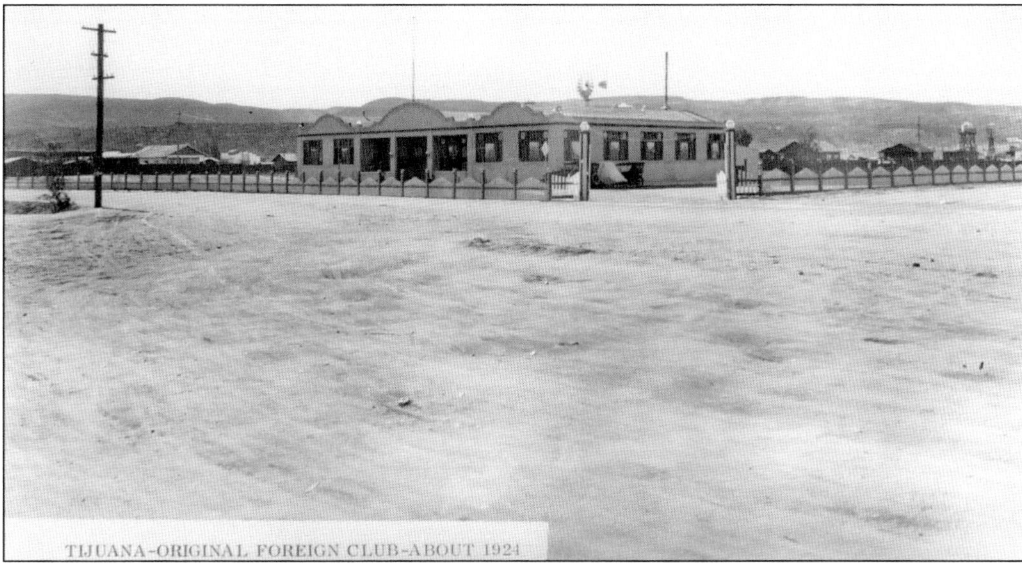

By 1917, Frank Beyer, Marvin Allen, and Carl Withington owned the finest casinos and cantinas in Tijuana, including the Tivoli Bar and the Foreign Club. In 1920, the group added the Sunset Inn and Racetrack, along with the Monte Carlo Casino. Beyer, alongside California gambling promoters such as James W. "Sunny Jim" Coffroth and Baron H. Long (owners of the Lower California Jockey Club built in 1916), became a "border baron" responsible for the "vice industry" of Tijuana. From 1920 to 1932, the men found immense wealth across the border thanks to Prohibition. They generally hired Americans, particularly at management levels. Beyer was said to spend most of his time at the racetrack wearing a rumpled gray suit with a black hat tucked under his arm. He also boasted about drinking one bottle of whiskey per day. (Both, Evelyn Sevel.)

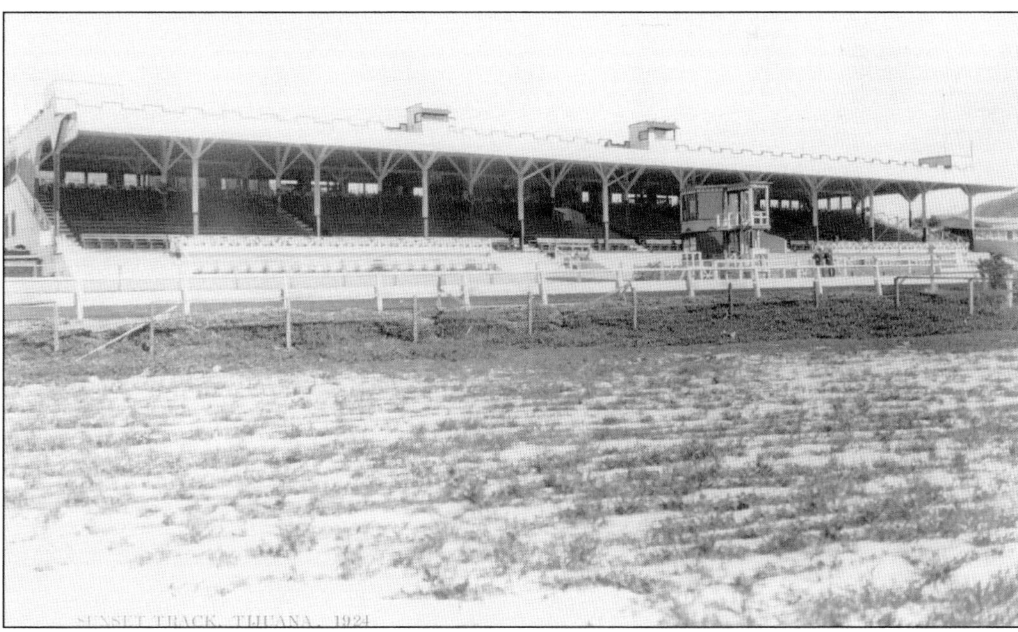

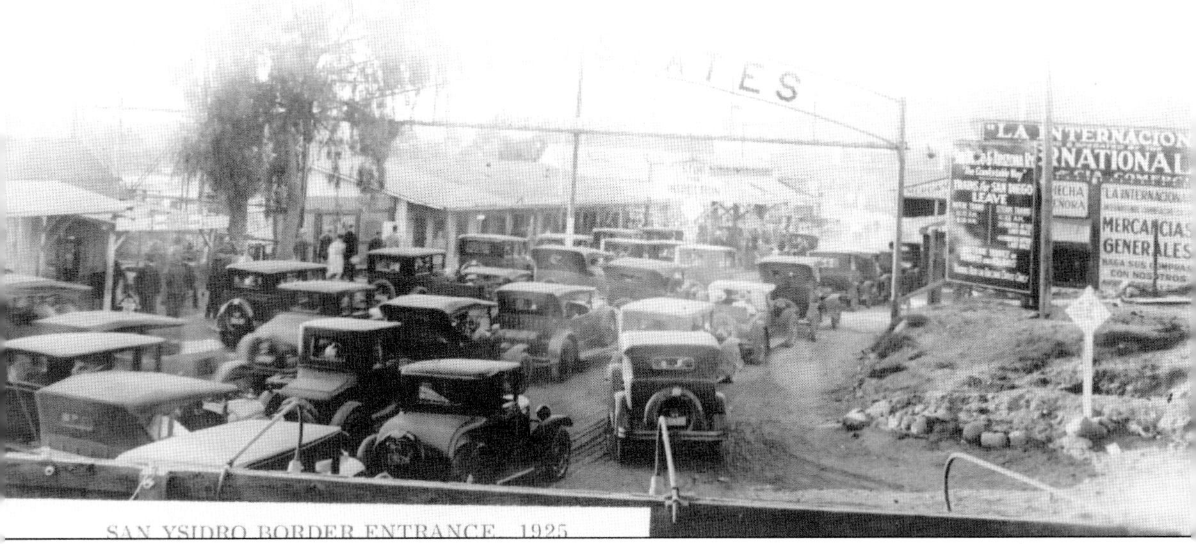

The "border barons"—Frank Beyer, Marvin Allen, and Carl Withington—promoted Vice City and successfully brought an estimated 180,000 people across the border and into Tijuana each year. Visitors enjoyed saloons, casinos, brothels, and opium dens—all of which were illegal in the United States. With the increase in border traffic, customs agents, immigration officials, and Prohibition, officers found it difficult to work together to enforce laws. Meanwhile, American employees of the racetracks, casinos, saloons, and hotels lived in San Ysidro. Even Mexican and US customs officials moved to the town. By 1928, the population was estimated at 1,200. The town began to focus more on ties to commercial interests in Tijuana and started establishing businesses that catered to tourists. (SDPHA.)

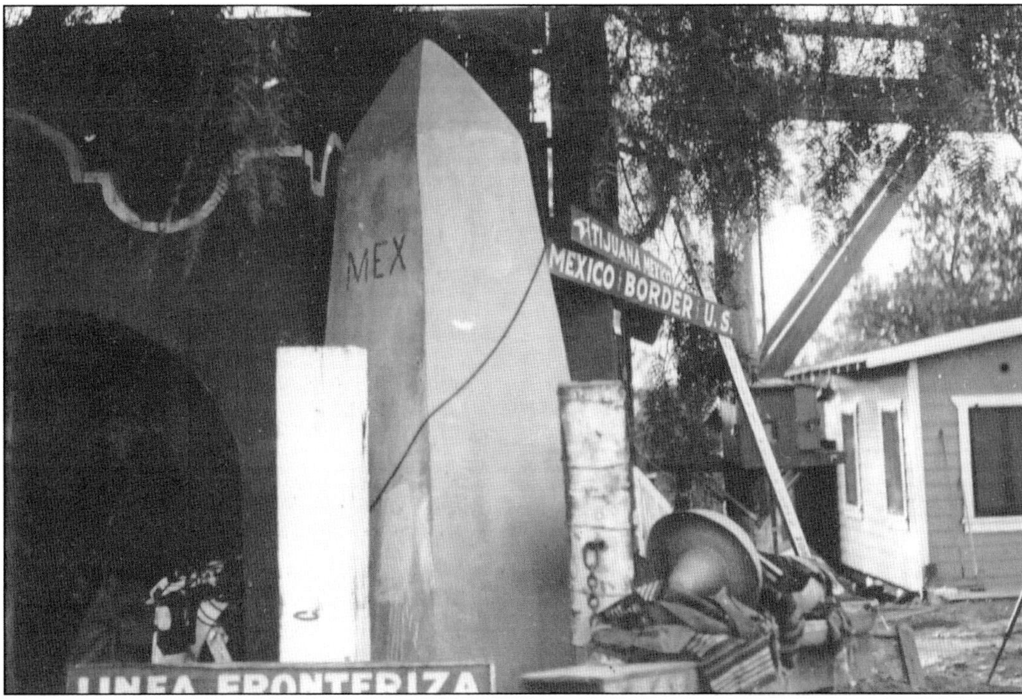

Smuggling became rampant along the border. People often carried liquor through the mountains on horseback and cut the international fence at many locations. American moralists demanded border curfews, which were instituted in 1926 and again in 1931. In response, American tourists cut large holes in the eight-mile-long border wires in order to enter Tijuana illegally and return home after hours. This picture from around the 1930s depicts an unpatrolled border area in disarray. (Miguel Guerrero, Joyce Hettich Collection.)

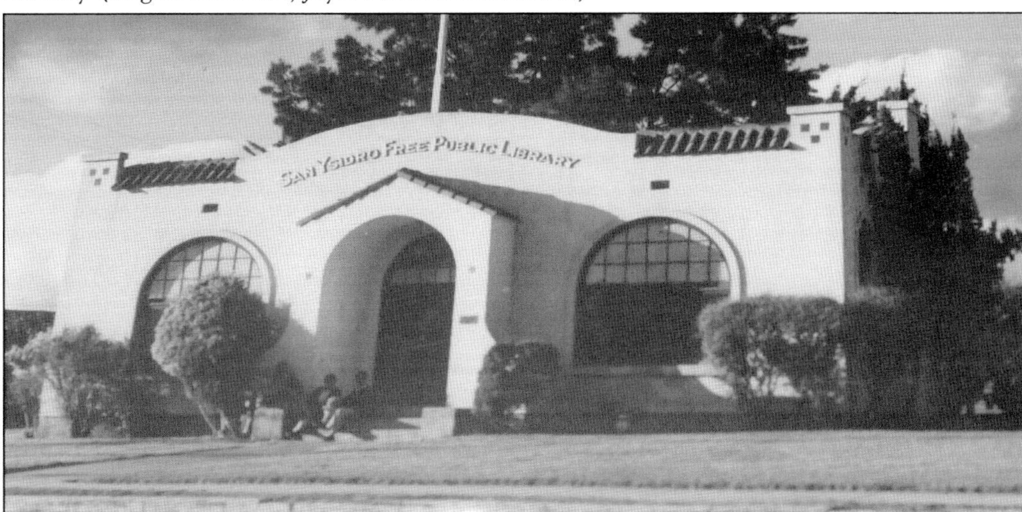

In 1924, Frank Beyer donated $7,000 for a library in the place where the Little Landers Park once stood in the small town of San Ysidro. He bought over $500-worth of books and wanted the library to have copies of the *Police Gazette*, a racy magazine, available in a men's smoking room. The library added a spittoon for tobacco-chewing and installed portraits of Beyer and his wife that still remain today. (San Ysidro Public Library.)

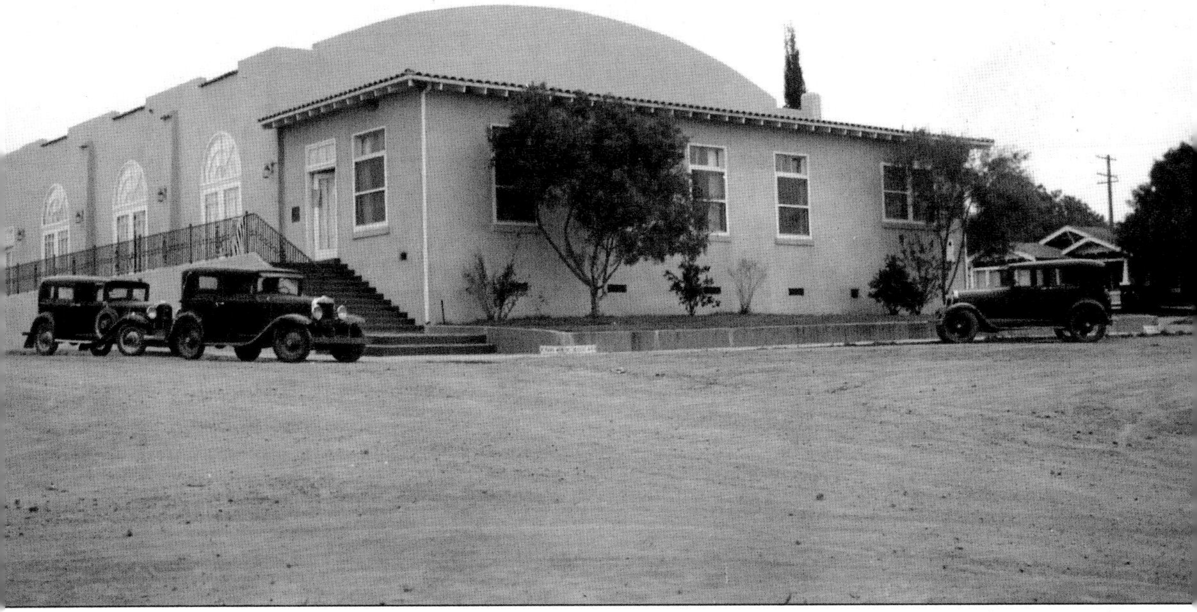

In 1925, Beyer donated funds for the town to build a civic center on Hall Avenue. The San Ysidro Women's Club used the site for many festivities. Nearby, the "border barons"—Frank Beyer, Marvin Allen, and Carl Withington—set up a bank where they could "wash" (launder) their earnings from Tijuana before bringing the money to banks in Los Angeles. (CSDDP.)

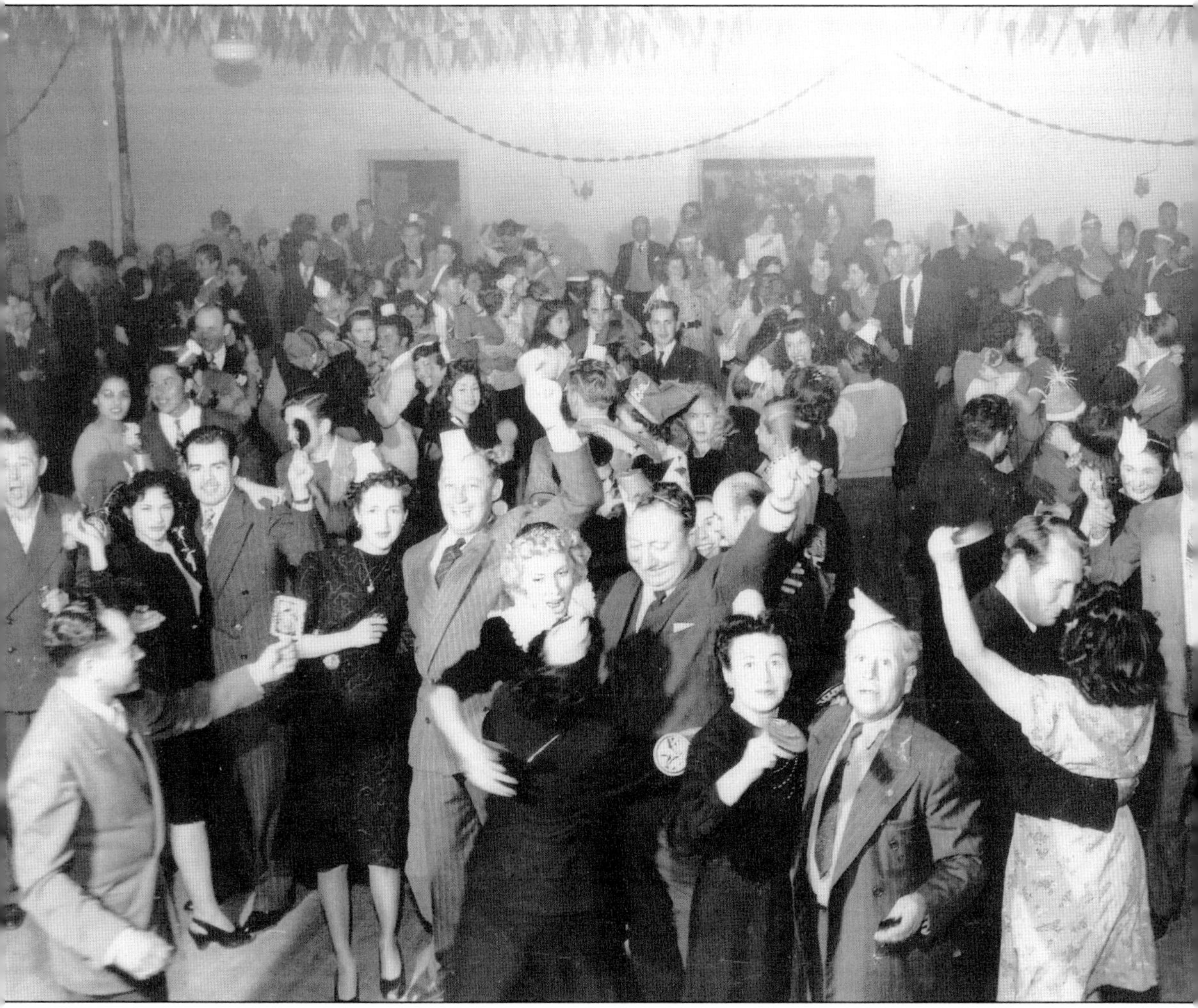

This picture shows the civic center during a New Year's celebration in the 1940s. The couple at the farthest left are Al Velasquez and Kitty Leal. Al Velasquez worked at an auto-supply store in San Diego. His brother Jose Velasquez was a cook's helper at the Agua Caliente casino in Tijuana. The civic center still stands today. (Charlie Velazquez.)

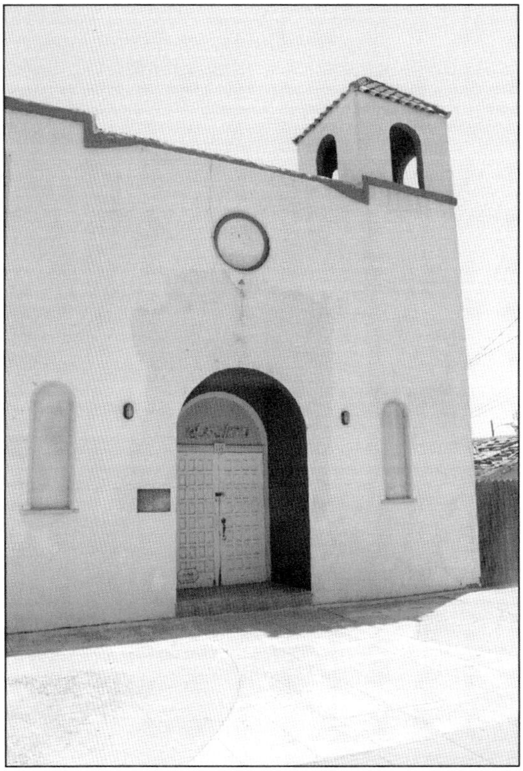

Frank Beyer also donated land and $1,000 for the construction of the Our Lady of Mount Carmel Church. Louis Gill built the church—the first Catholic church in San Ysidro—in a Mission Revival style. Fr. Seville Alloero, originally from Tijuana, gave the first service on Easter Sunday in 1927. The building has undergone renovations and is still standing. (Author.)

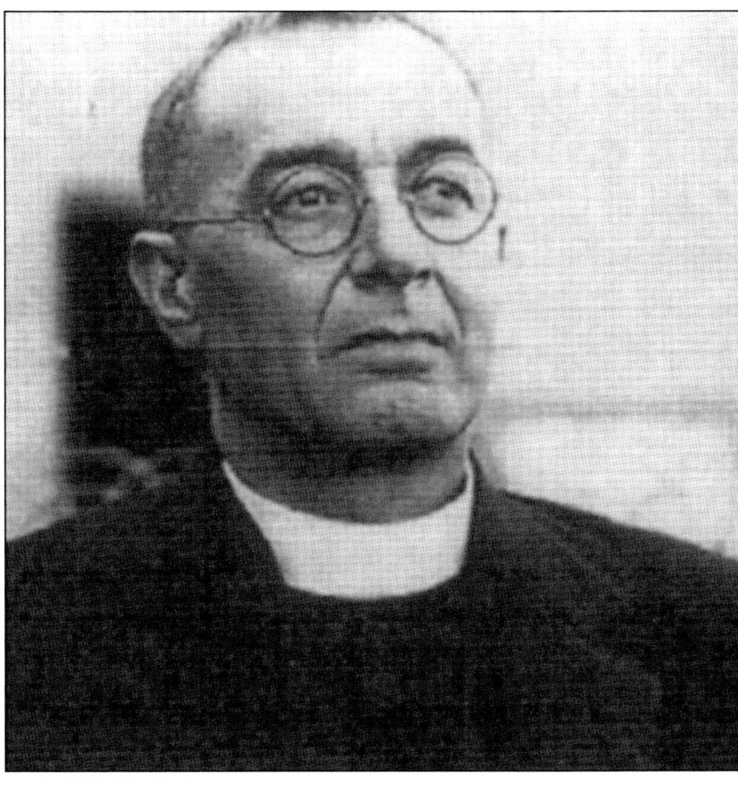

Fr. Seville Alloero remained a priest at the church from 1928 to 1932, ministering to worshippers who came across the border each Sunday. In his first two years, the Mexican government persecuted clergy and Catholics, who were not allowed to practice their faith in public. Alloero also crossed into Tijuana to perform baptisms and other services in private homes. (Mike Strange.)

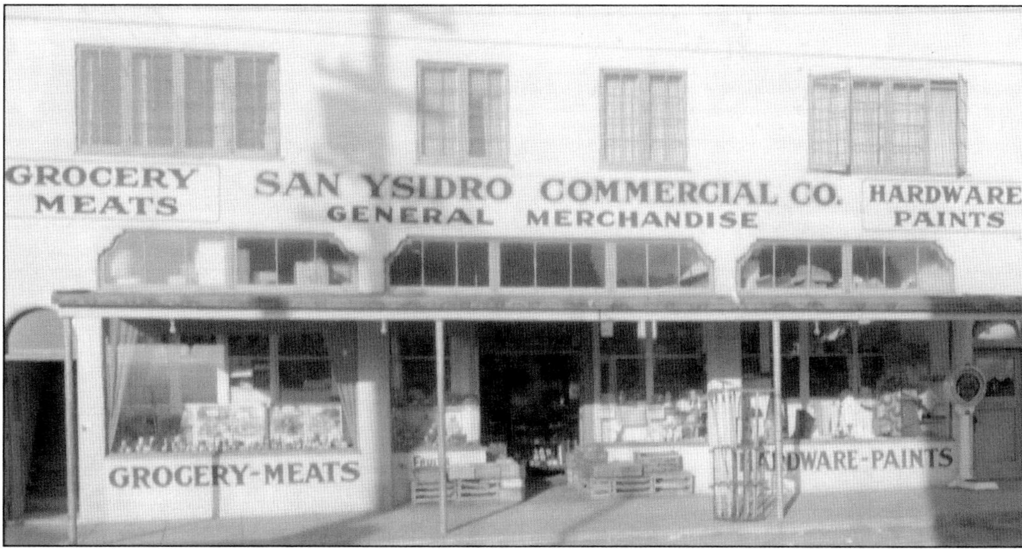

Louis Gill, the nephew of Irving Gill, designed this building for the San Ysidro Commercial Company, which was established in 1927. Josie Velasquez and Harold Burgie bought and owned this store during the 1940s, 1950s, and 1960s. Since the store sold almost everything (clothing, feed, hardware, meat), its motto was: "If we don't have it, you don't need it." (Miguel Guerrero, Joyce Hettich Collection.)

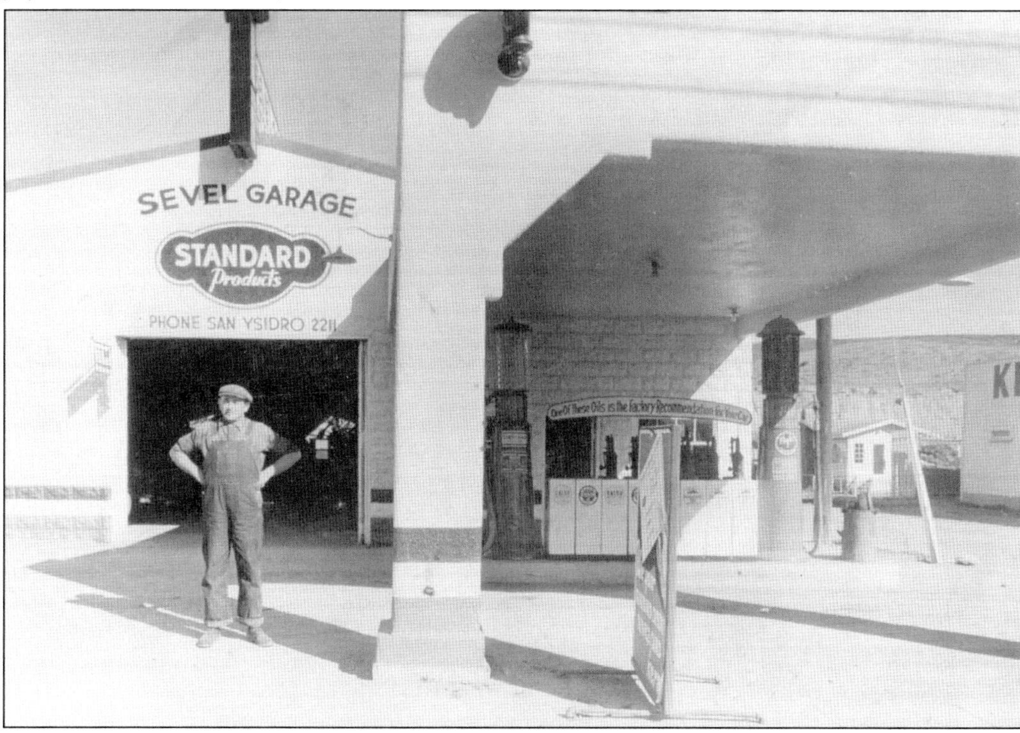

In 1918, Harry Sevel (pictured) came to San Ysidro. Born in Lithuania, his family escaped anti-Semitism and fled to South Africa while he was a young child. At age 16, Sevel jumped a freighter ship set for the United States. He ended up in San Ysidro and, by 1927, opened Sevel Garage, a gas station and towing service along San Ysidro Boulevard. (Evelyn Sevel.)

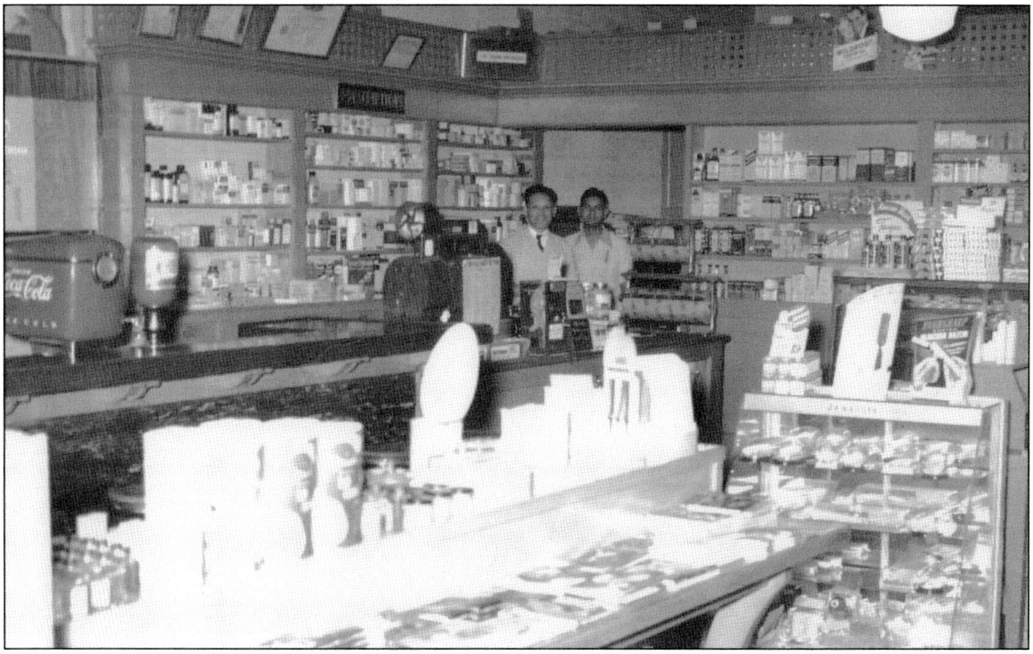

Cesar Soto (left) opened the San Ysidro Pharmacy in 1930. His brother Eddie (right) often worked as the soda jerk, fixing malts and other drinks. Cesar provided prescription medications as well as magazines, comic books, and candy. Staying in business for 35 years, he was one of the last drugstores to sell Coke's for a nickel and have a soda fountain with a marble counter. (Evelyn Sevel.)

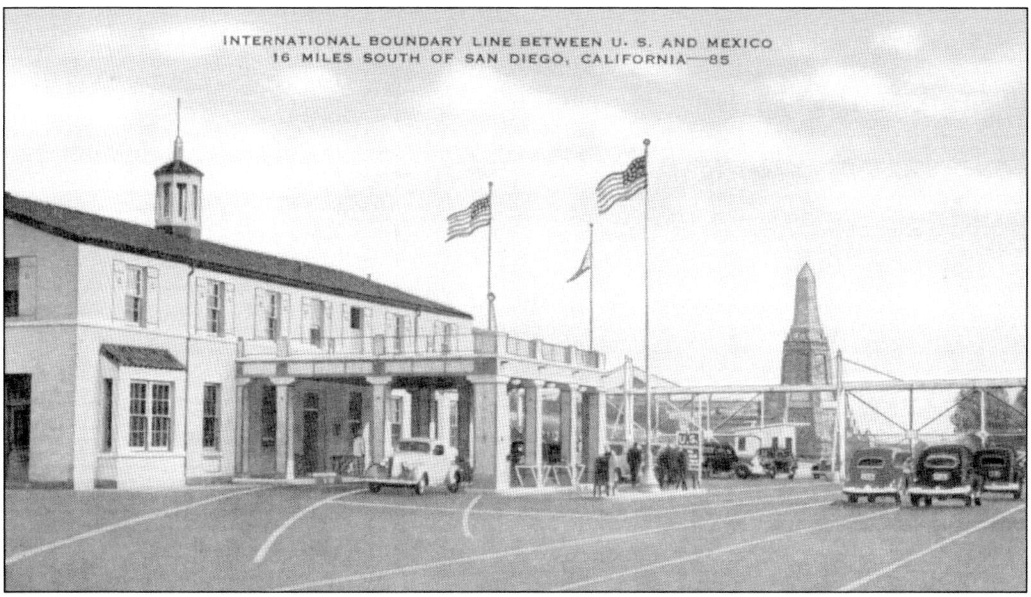

In 1932, the repeal of Prohibition by the United States, along with Mexico's nationalization of foreign-owned properties, affected American investments in Tijuana. However, Mexican politicians then turned Tijuana, Mexicali, and Ensenada into "free zones" for receiving American goods without charging customs taxes. As a result, San Ysidro's port of entry became popular and was listed second in annual traffic volume (behind Detroit) in 1932. A new US Customs House was constructed that same year, pictured here. (CSDDP.)

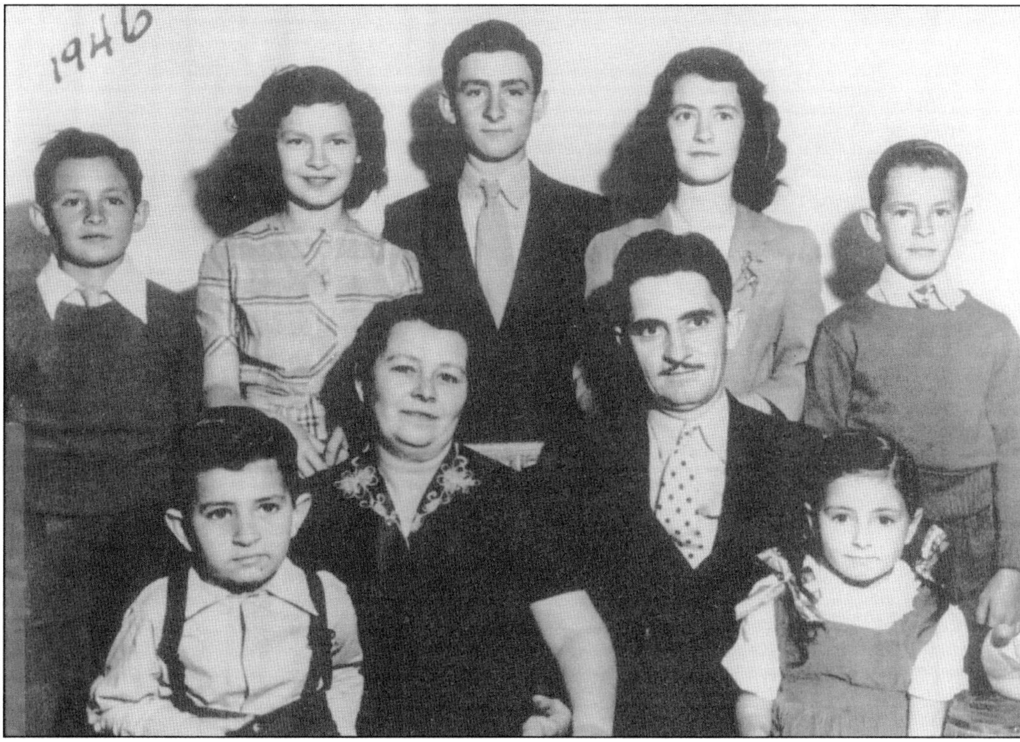

Opportunity brought many residents of Mexican and mixed decent to San Ysidro, including Joseph Villacusa Cuen, born in Las Prietas in Sonora, Mexico. While working in a copper mine in Nogales, Arizona, he met and married Virginia Mannion, a full-blooded Irish woman. They had eight children. Pictured, from left to right, are (first row) Tommy, Virginia, Joseph, Eleanor; (second row) Fred, Sarah, Joseph, Olga, and Edward. (Fred Cuen.)

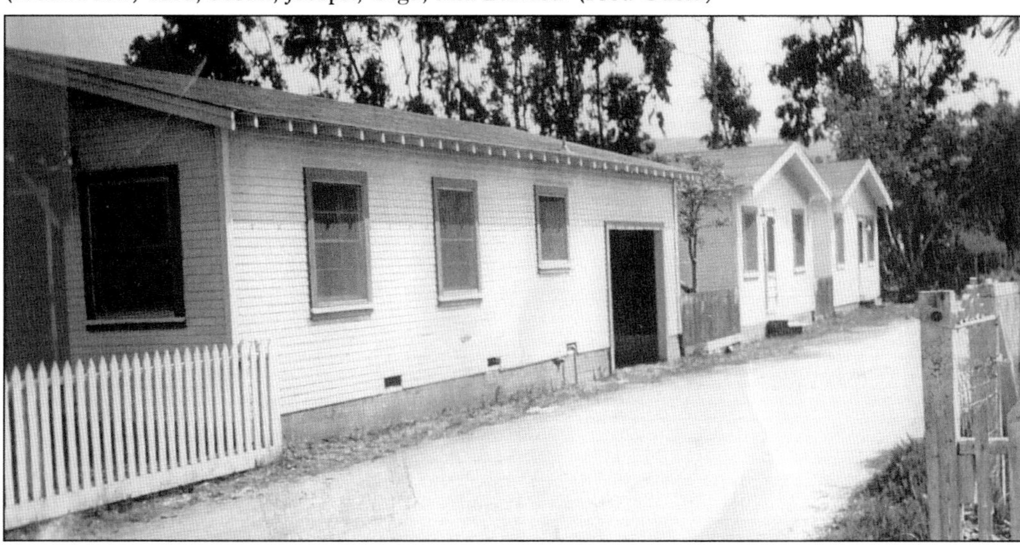

Joseph and Virginia left Arizona and first settled in Tijuana where Joseph found work at a bakery. However, he wanted to find work in the United States and landed a job at Ryder & Sons Feed Store in Chula Vista. Virginia became "Rosie the Riveter" for Convair Aircraft. They bought a house along San Ysidro Boulevard and built three homes in the backyard, pictured here. (Fred Cuen.)

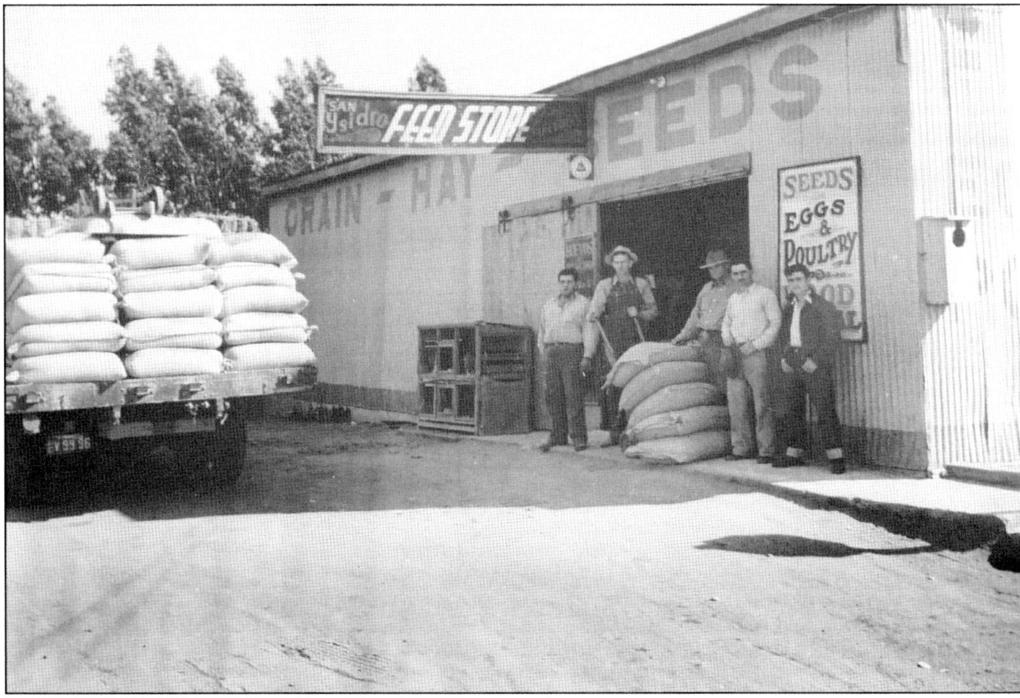

In 1940, Joseph and Virginia Cuen bought the feed store next to their home. Thereafter, they owned the only feed store 50 miles in any direction and served wealthy ranch owners in San Ysidro and the Tijuana River Valley. The Cuens' entire property contained three to four acres and included horses, cows, and rabbits. Joseph Cuen is second from the right and his son Joe is farthest on the right. (Fred Cuen.)

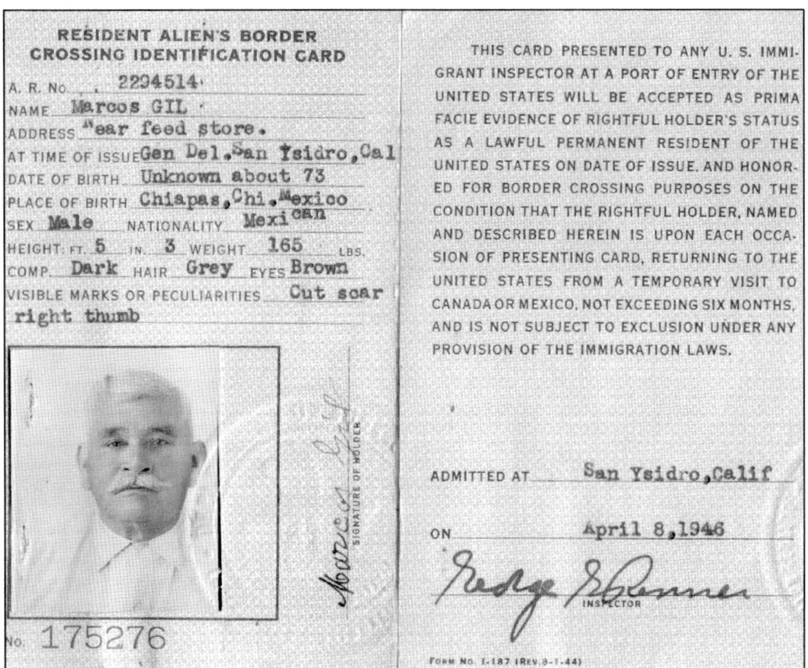

RESIDENT ALIEN'S BORDER CROSSING IDENTIFICATION CARD

A. R. No. 2294514
NAME Marcos GIL
ADDRESS Near feed store.
AT TIME OF ISSUE Gen Del.San Ysidro,Cal
DATE OF BIRTH Unknown about 73
PLACE OF BIRTH Chiapas,Chi.Mexico
SEX Male NATIONALITY Mexican
HEIGHT: FT. 5 IN. 3 WEIGHT 165 LBS.
COMP. Dark HAIR Grey EYES Brown
VISIBLE MARKS OR PECULIARITIES Cut scar right thumb

Marcos Gil
SIGNATURE OF HOLDER

No. 175276

THIS CARD PRESENTED TO ANY U. S. IMMIGRANT INSPECTOR AT A PORT OF ENTRY OF THE UNITED STATES WILL BE ACCEPTED AS PRIMA FACIE EVIDENCE OF RIGHTFUL HOLDER'S STATUS AS A LAWFUL PERMANENT RESIDENT OF THE UNITED STATES ON DATE OF ISSUE, AND HONORED FOR BORDER CROSSING PURPOSES ON THE CONDITION THAT THE RIGHTFUL HOLDER, NAMED AND DESCRIBED HEREIN IS UPON EACH OCCASION OF PRESENTING CARD, RETURNING TO THE UNITED STATES FROM A TEMPORARY VISIT TO CANADA OR MEXICO, NOT EXCEEDING SIX MONTHS, AND IS NOT SUBJECT TO EXCLUSION UNDER ANY PROVISION OF THE IMMIGRATION LAWS.

ADMITTED AT San Ysidro,Calif
ON April 8,1946
INSPECTOR

FORM NO. I-187 (REV. 8-1-44)

When Fred Cuen started school, his family sent him to live with Marcos Gil. This image shows a resident card that was given to Mexicans. Fred lived with Gil from 1939 to 1943. During that time, he worked at the dairy farms or went over to the feed store to tend the 100 rabbits. When Gil died, Fred returned to live with his parents. (Fred Cuen.)

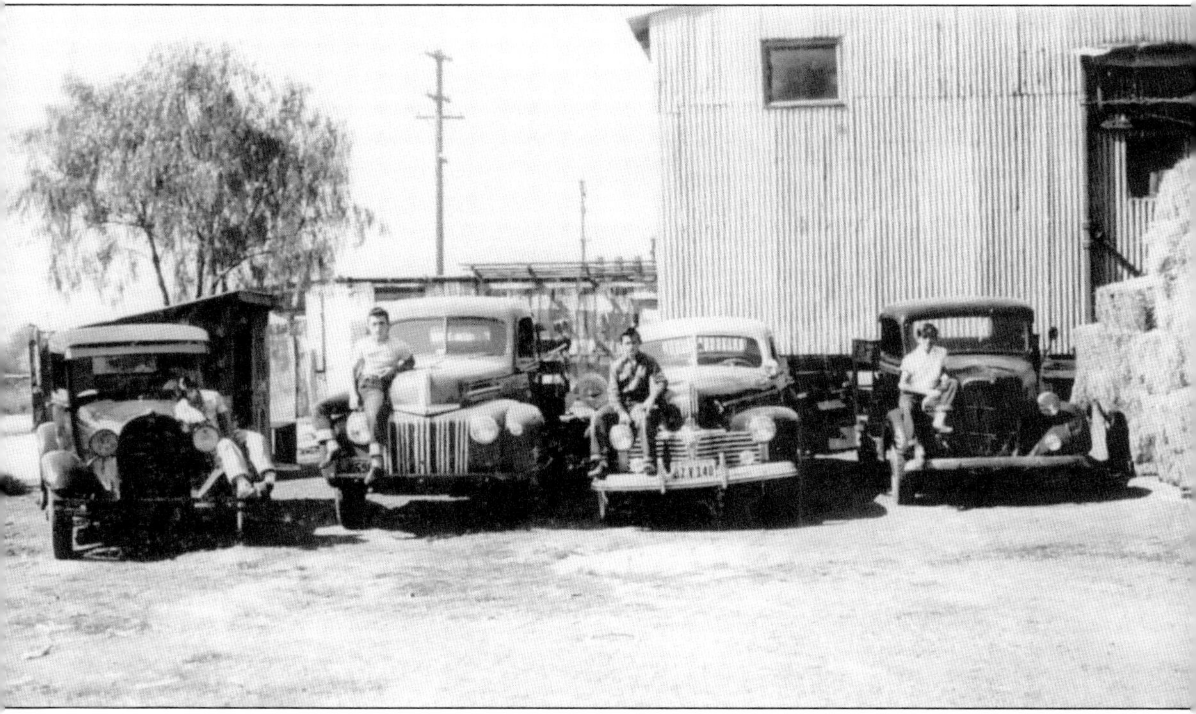

Three nights per week, Fred Cuen would drive—without a driver's license—to Imperial Valley, 115 miles away, in his feed delivery truck to pick up 28 tons of hay. He worked most of the night filling the hay barn, then got up for school. Cuen is second from right in this image that shows the feed store's delivery trucks. (Fred Cuen.)

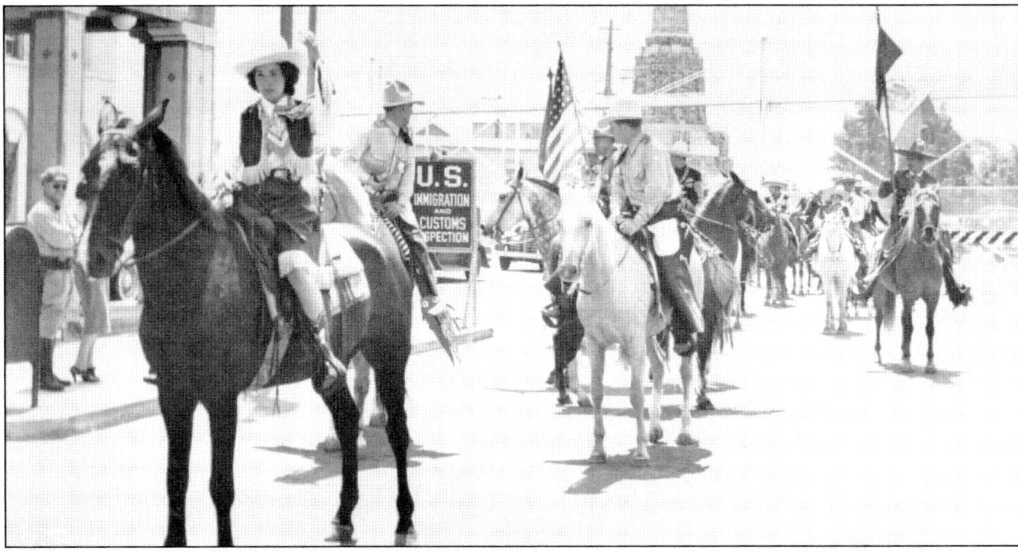

A Fourth of July parade has been held every year in San Ysidro. These two pictures from 1940 show horses passing through the San Ysidro border entry with the monument in the background (above) and San Ysidro Boulevard filled with residents (below). The Safeway Store and the hardware store are visible in the below image. Hotel San Ysidro, which existed from the time of Little Landers (1909), is at the end of the street. Although the community remained predominantly Anglo-American, Spanish surnames became more common. Before Prohibition, both San Ysidro and the town called Tia Juana sat side-by-side on the US side of the border. With the population boom, however, the two towns eventually merged. The American Tia Juana ceased to exist, leaving the second city—Tijuana—exclusively on the Mexican side. (Both, Evelyn Sevel.)

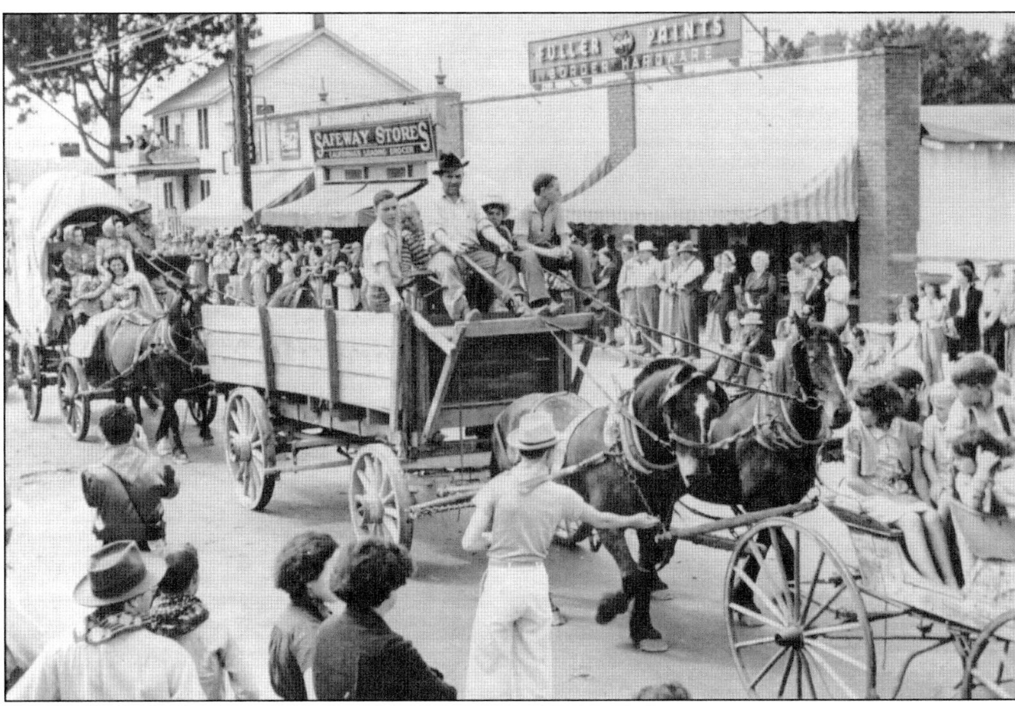

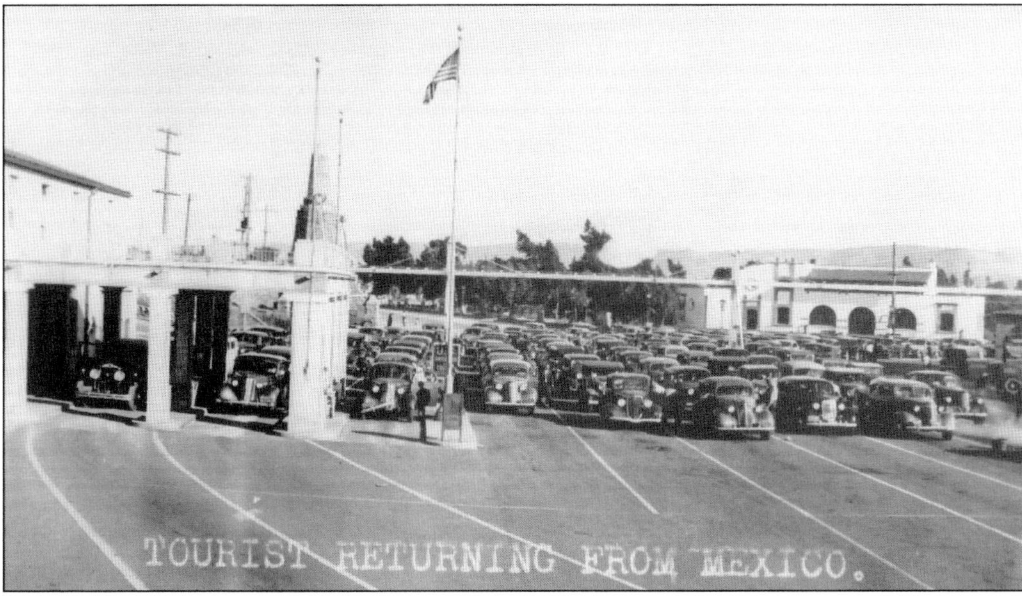

On the weekends, Fred Cuen would go down to the Tijuana racetrack at 3:00 a.m. and exercise 70 or 80 horses for $1 per horse. According to Cuen, the border in those days had a vehicular queue on the American side stretching for several miles with cars wanting to enter Mexico. No wait existed for those coming into the United States. (SDPHA.)

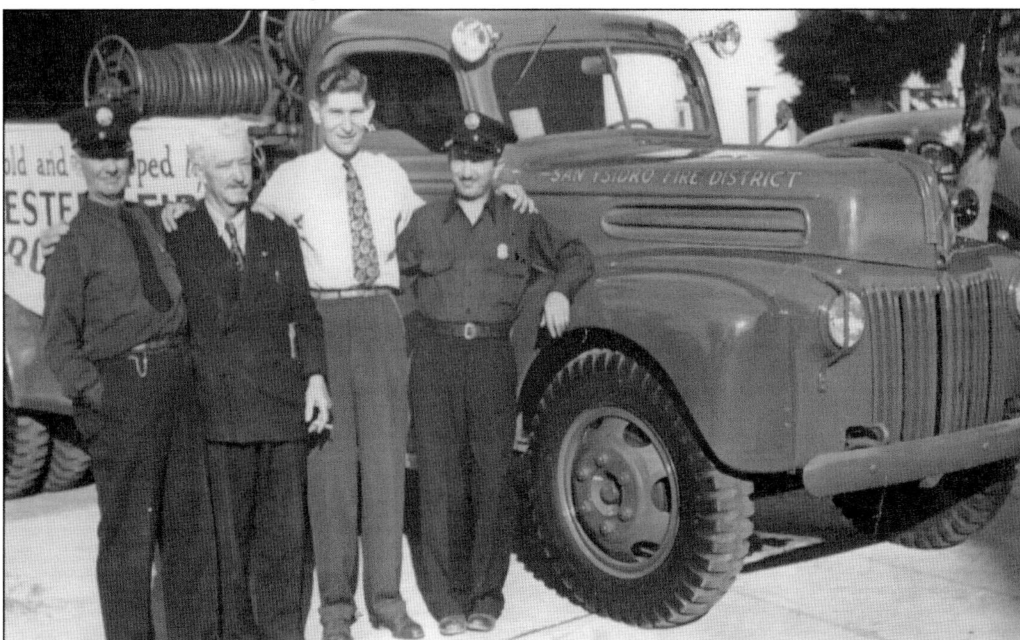

A lack of funds meant that no police station existed in San Ysidro, only a sheriff who knew everyone by name, as well as a volunteer fire station. In 1946, the San Ysidro Volunteer Fire Department moved to a new location on San Ysidro Boulevard. Residents raised funds, and members of the department constructed the building. Cesar Soto, owner of the pharmacy, was the fire commissioner. Eugene Cordeau (second to right) was the San Ysidro Fire Commissioner. Herbert Bibo is the man farthest to the left. (Miguel Guerrero, Joyce Hettich Collection.)

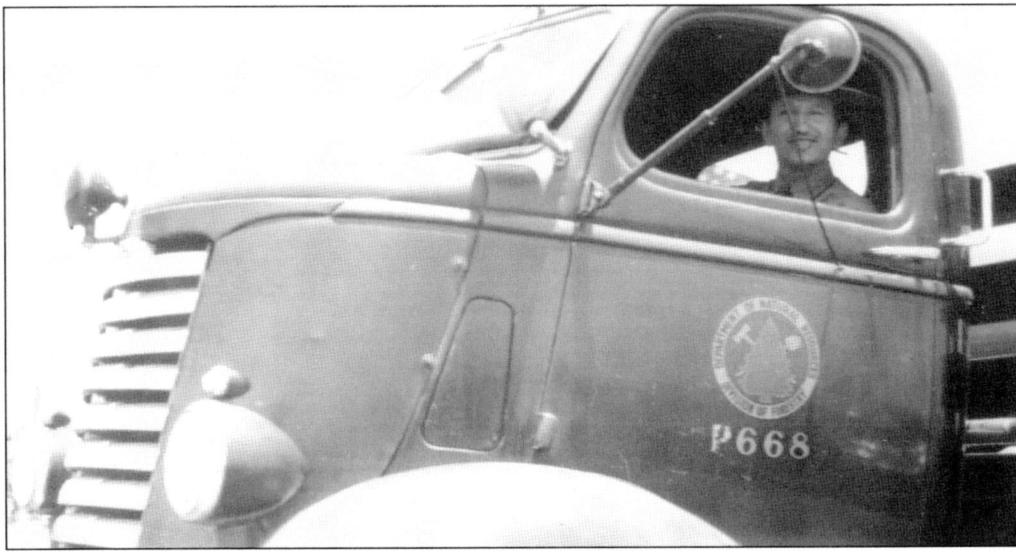

This picture features volunteer fire chief Herbert Bibo. A member of the community with a strong sense of service, Bibo also collected clothing from residents to send to Europeans in need after World War II. Here, he sits in a 1944 Ford with a pumping capacity of 500 gallons per minute. The vehicle was built for the Army but never used and then bought by San Ysidrans for their fire house. (Charlie Velazquez.)

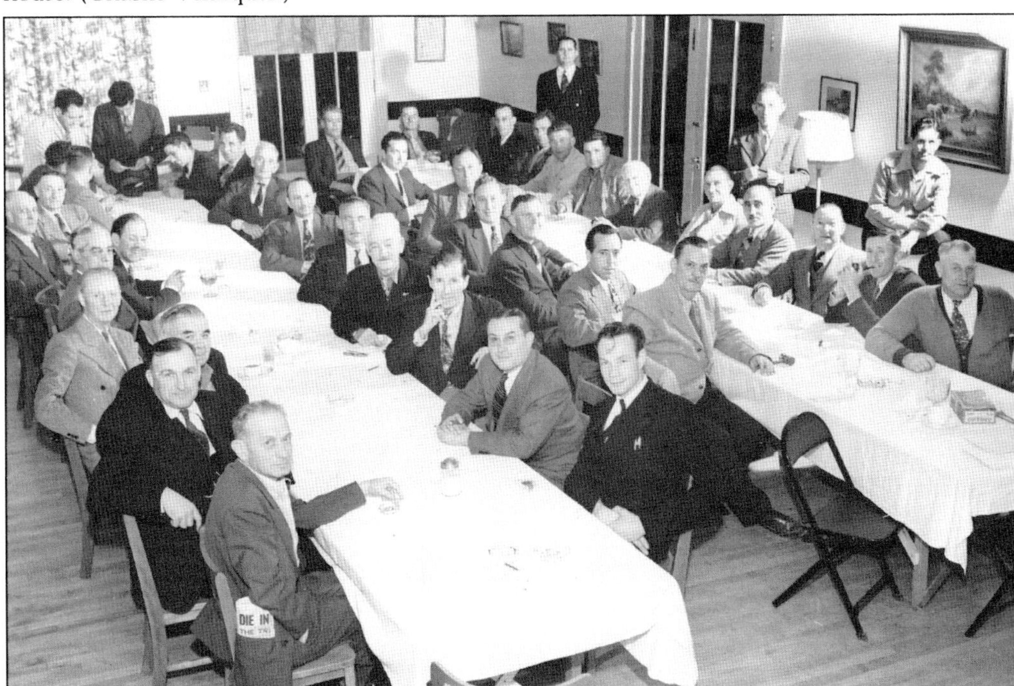

Members of the San Ysidro Chamber of Commerce pictured here in the late 1940s include fire chief Herbert Bibo (sixth from the front in the second row from the left). The chamber of commerce formed in the 1920s and was often featured on the front page of the *San Ysidro Border Press* newspaper. The group members concerned themselves with issues such as how to enforce traffic laws along San Ysidro Boulevard. (Evelyn Sevel.)

This World War II memorial once stood in front of the public library but was destroyed at an unknown date. The marble commemoration honored San Ysidro residents who fought in the war. Two names included Alfredo Velazquez, who fought in the European theater, and Adolfo Velazquez, who died in 1942 during maneuvers in Texas. (Charlie Velazquez.)

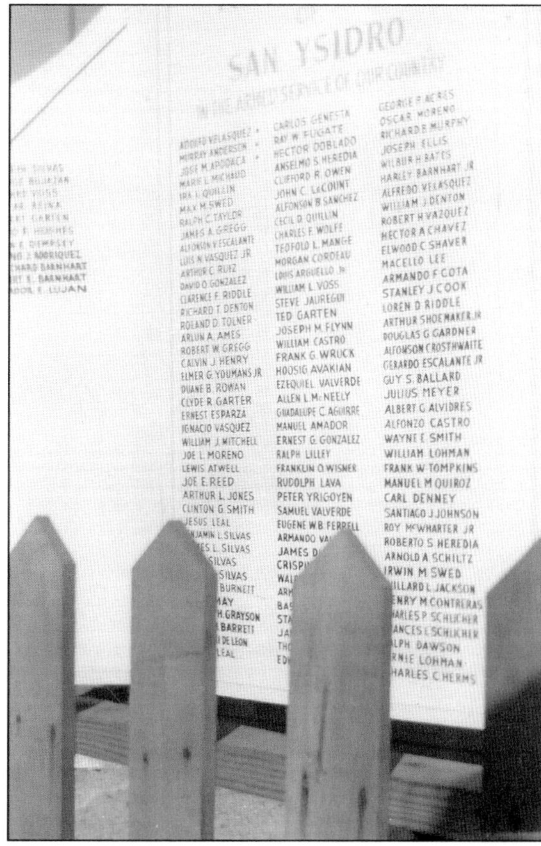

In 1949, the San Ysidro Merchants baseball team played in the minor leagues with teams such as the Navy. Pictured here are, from left to right, (first row) Francis Gregg, Bernardo Armas, Ray Doblado, Gilbert Leal, Jim Sanchez, and bat boy "Bobby" Sanchez; (second row) Bob Gonzalez, Erwin Wylie, "Red" Ballard, Genaro Valezquez, and Charlie Velazquez. (Charlie Velazquez.)

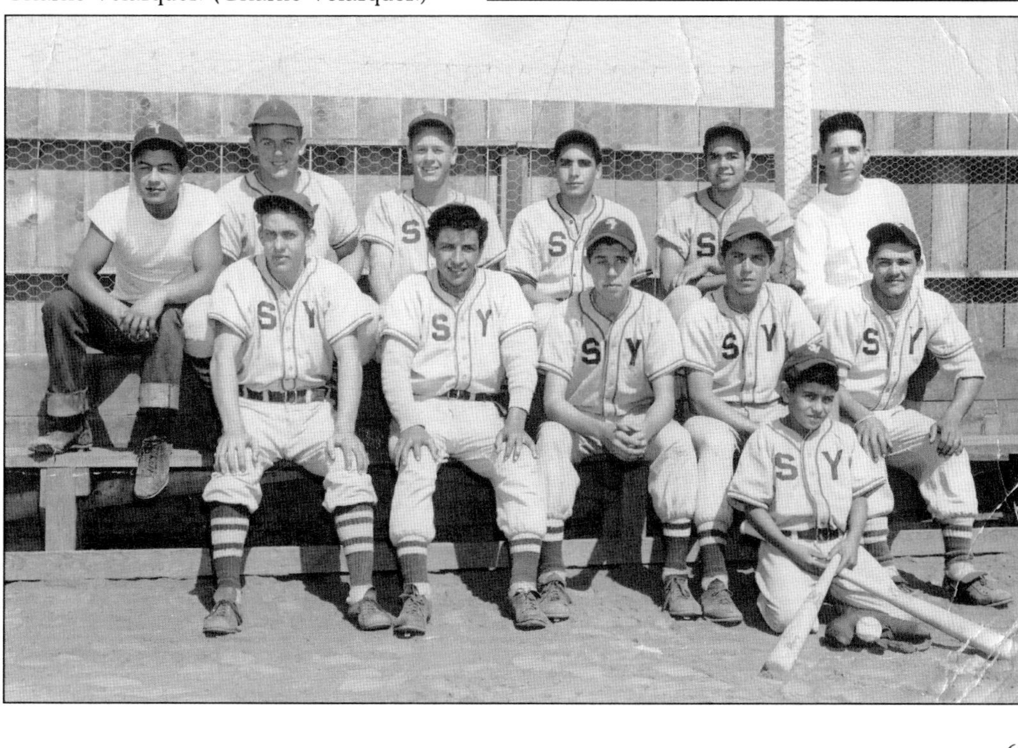

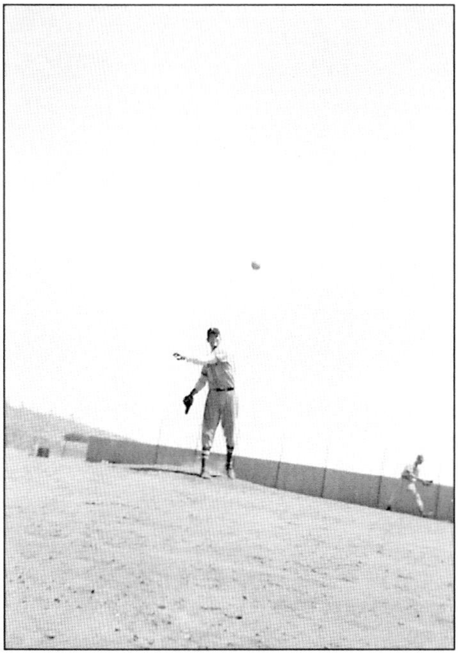

Dr. Michael Bajo was a pitcher on the San Ysidro Merchants baseball team. Born in Indiana to Slovak parents, he was drafted as a left-handed pitcher by the Chicago White Sox in 1941, but he quit to study medicine. In 1948, he moved to San Ysidro and served as the town's only doctor for several decades. He delivered more than 11,000 babies, often accepting chickens or produce as payment. (Jack Gechter.)

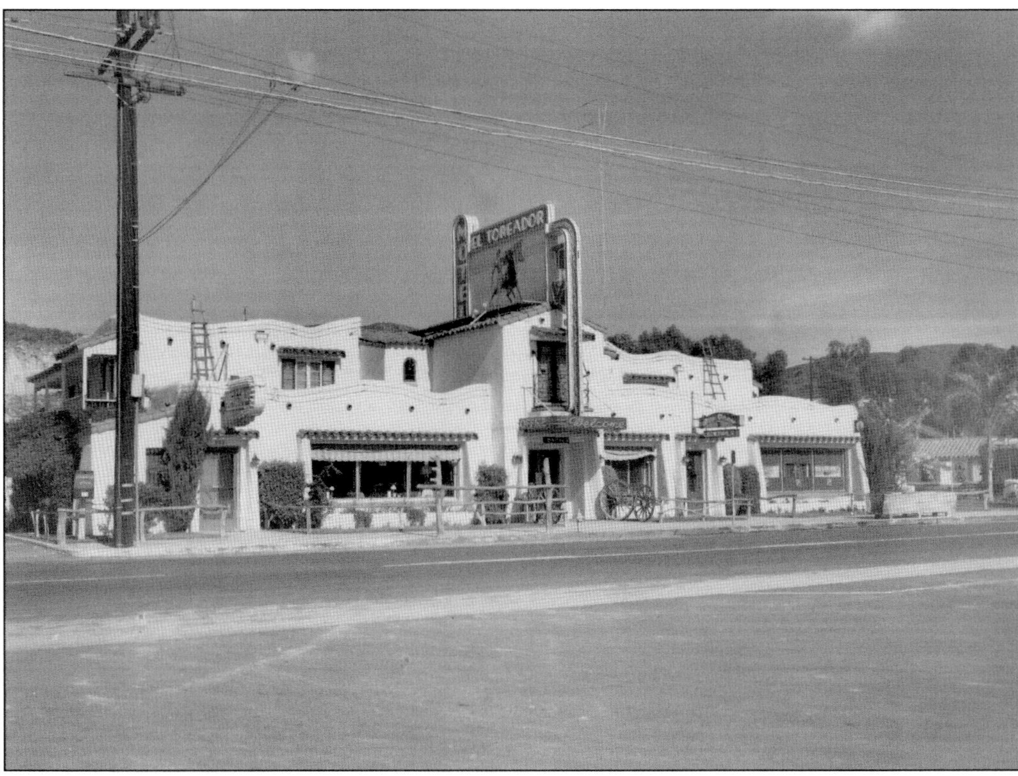

The small town of San Ysidro became renowned thanks to the El Toreador Motel, built in 1948 by a Portuguese contractor. This Spanish-style motel often served as a stopping place for celebrities, including Buster Keaton, John Wayne, and Jay Silverhills ("Tonto" in *The Lone Ranger* series), who also boarded horses in the Tijuana River Valley during the early 1950s. (SDHC.)

Six

The Farming Community

While movie stars stopped in San Ysidro on their way to "Vice City," the last five miles of the Tijuana River along the American side provided rich and fertile soil for farming. The mild weather meant that farmers could grow year-round crops and more than 100 varieties of fruits and vegetables. In the early 1900s, dairy farmers already existed in the region, and soon farmers of Japanese and Swiss extraction sought their livelihood in the area. Robert Egger's property housed both a dairy and a vegetable farm starting in the 1930s. However, Egger and other farmers in the river bottom faced many challenges, including floods and government encroachment upon their livelihoods.

During World War II, Japanese-American farmers were removed to internment camps. Next, Cal American Water Company diverted water from the Tijuana River to naval ships in Coronado. Consequently, the soil became too salty to grow vegetables, and many farmers left.

Robert Egger did not give up. He tilled every parcel of land he bought, and when the soil became too salty, he dug a 1,500-foot well. At the height of his prosperity, he employed between 200 and 300 people, including Mexicans who legally came to the United States through the bracero program. His farming enterprise did so well that he was able to donate land for a recreation center, a Catholic church, and a school, as well as for the Swiss Club.

Dairy farmers continued operating despite the new suburban development of the 1960s and 1970s. During the dairy surplus of the 1980s, the government paid farmers to slaughter cows or sell them abroad, and it was then that much of the farming in the region came to an end.

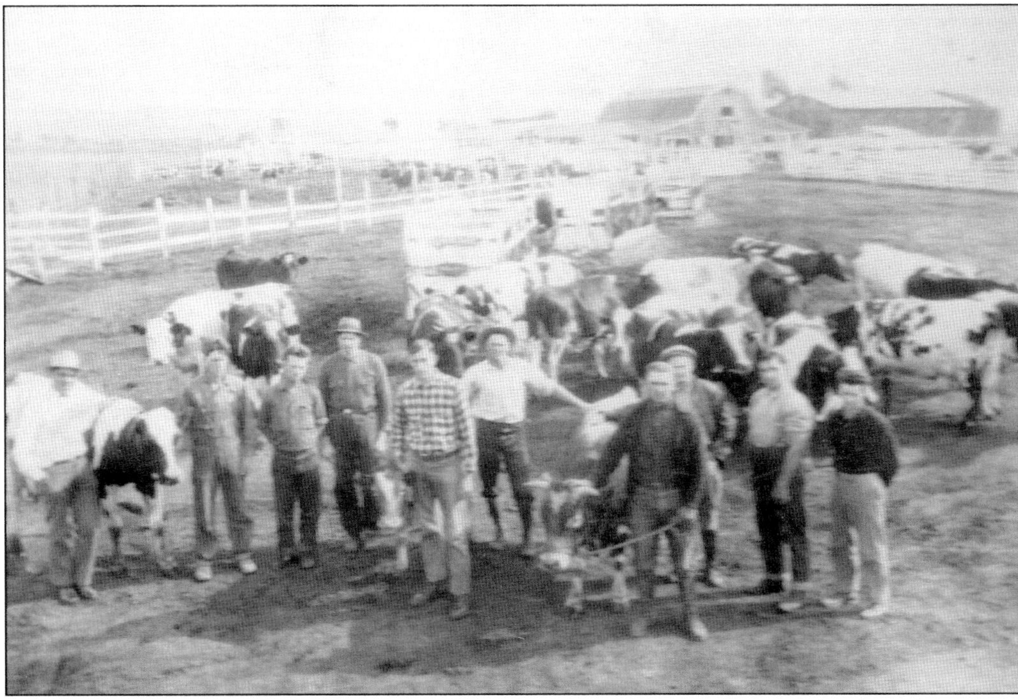

The Tijuana River Valley provided fertile soil thanks to many underground wells. This picture shows workers at Henry Schnell's Dairy Mart Farms in the late 1930s. (Robert Egger is the second man from the right.) August M. Schnell started Schnell dairy in 1888, selling milk to the Hotel del Coronado. His son Henry continued within his father's profession, merging with Arden Dairy in 1927 and then forming Dairy Mart Farms in 1937. (Egger family.)

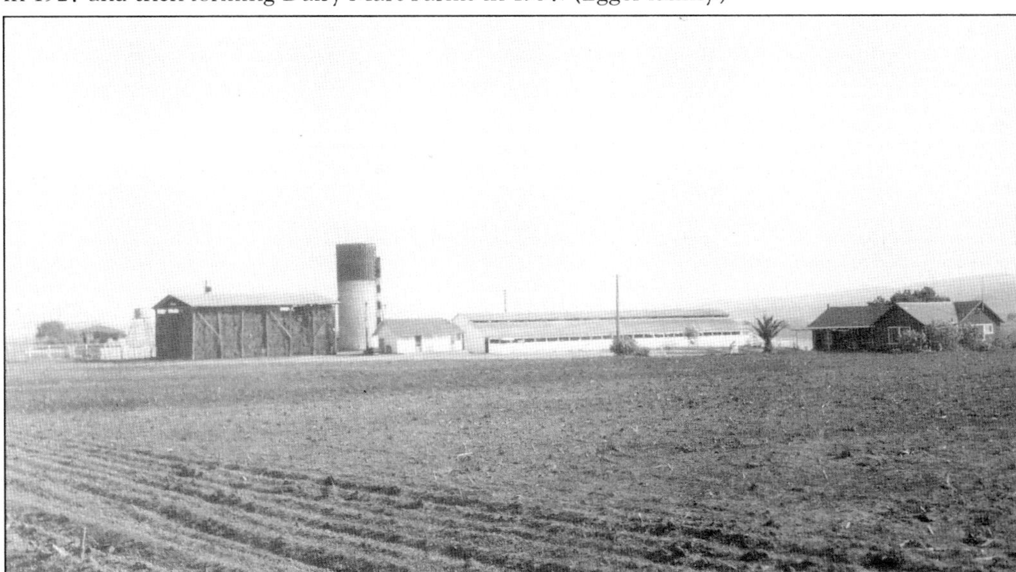

Schnell sold part of his property to Robert Egger, who began his own dairy farm on approximately 60 acres of land. As shown in this 1931 picture of Robert Egger's farm, the property included a large barn, a silo, and plowed fields. Egger quickly extended his operations to include vegetable farming. (Egger family.)

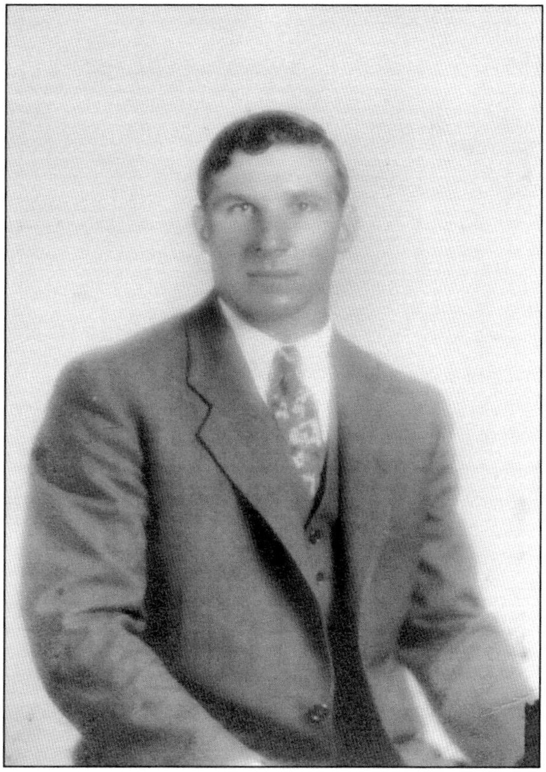

Robert Egger (1900–1978) was born in Kerns, Kanton Obwalden, Switzerland. At age 26, he left for economic reasons and first landed in San Francisco, but the abysmal fog sent him south. He started working at the Zumstein Dairy Farm, located in Imperial Valley, but he disliked the hot weather there. Next, he worked at a meatpacking plant in San Diego before coming to Schnells Dairy Mart in the river bottom. There, Egger worked for Harold Gray, who ran the day-to-day operations. In 1936, Egger purchased the land, buildings, equipment and cattle of a second ranch (Ranch 2) for $46,891.06. The picture below shows a receipt of items Egger purchased in 1931. Schnell listed his original cost and the depreciation value of the items. After his first purchase from Schnells, whenever a piece of property came open, he purchased it for the exclusive purpose of farming the land. (Both, Egger family.)

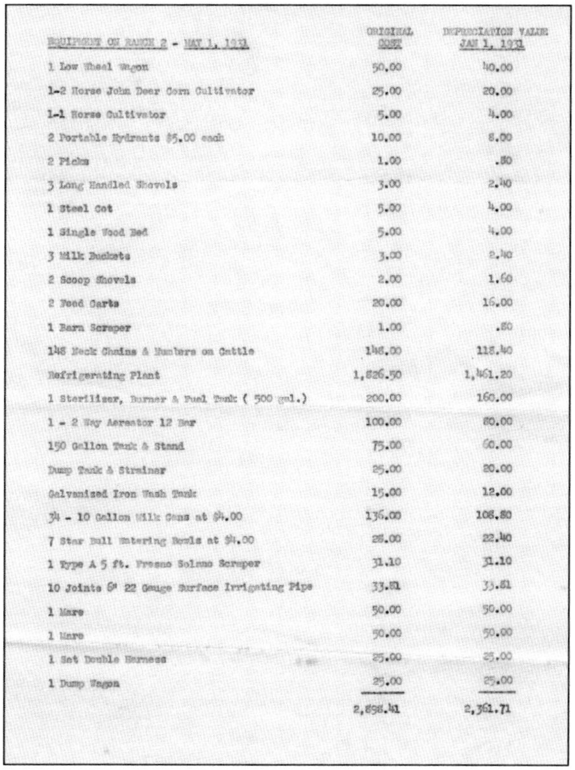

EQUIPMENT ON RANCH 2 - MAY 1, 1931	ORIGINAL COST	DEPRECIATION VALUE JAN 1, 1931
1 Low Wheel Wagon	50.00	40.00
1-2 Horse John Deer Corn Cultivator	25.00	20.00
1-1 Horse Cultivator	5.00	4.00
2 Portable Hydrants $5.00 each	10.00	8.00
2 Picks	1.00	.80
3 Long Handled Shovels	3.00	2.40
1 Steel Cot	5.00	4.00
1 Single Wood Bed	5.00	4.00
3 Milk Buckets	3.00	2.40
2 Scoop Shovels	2.00	1.60
2 Feed Carts	20.00	16.00
1 Barn Scraper	1.00	.80
148 Neck Chains & Numbers on Cattle	148.00	118.40
Refrigerating Plant	1,826.50	1,461.20
1 Sterilizer, Burner & Fuel Tank (500 gal.)	200.00	160.00
1 - 2 Way Aerator 12 Bar	100.00	80.00
150 Gallon Tank & Stand	75.00	60.00
Dump Tank & Strainer	25.00	20.00
Galvanized Iron Wash Tank	15.00	12.00
34 - 10 Gallon Milk Cans at $4.00	136.00	108.80
7 Star Bull Watering Bowls at $4.00	28.00	22.40
1 Type A 5 ft. Fresno Solano Scraper	31.10	31.10
10 Joints 6" 22 Gauge Surface Irrigating Pipe	33.81	33.81
1 Mare	50.00	50.00
1 Mare	50.00	50.00
1 Set Double Harness	25.00	25.00
1 Dump Wagon	25.00	25.00
	2,898.41	2,361.71

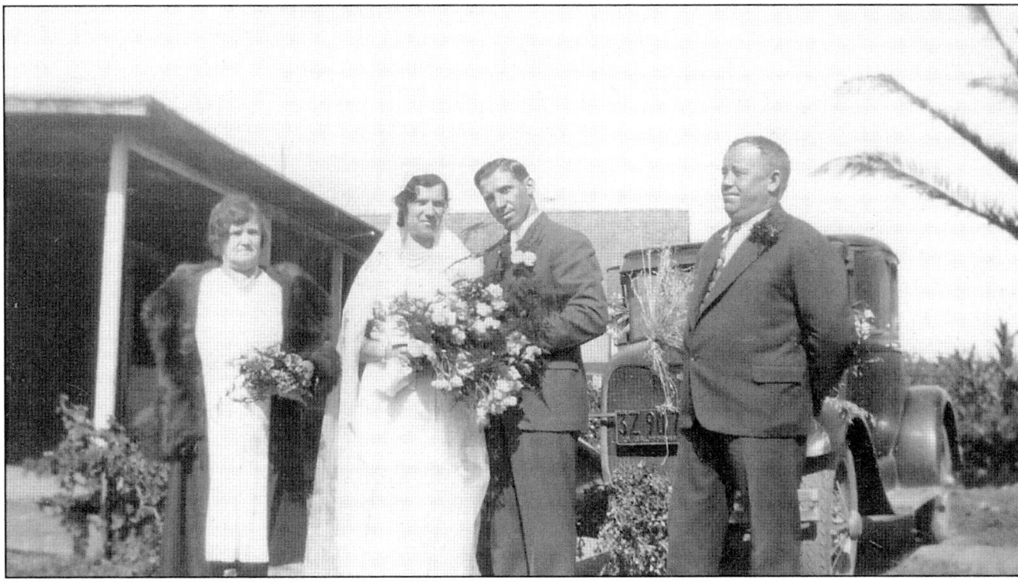

Emma Studer was born in the Swiss town of Ober-Frick in Kanton Aargau. She left Switzerland and found work in Imperial Valley in 1929. She then switched jobs, working in Point Loma. While there, she frequented a church, where she met Robert Egger. They married in San Ysidro on July 8, 1932. (Egger family.)

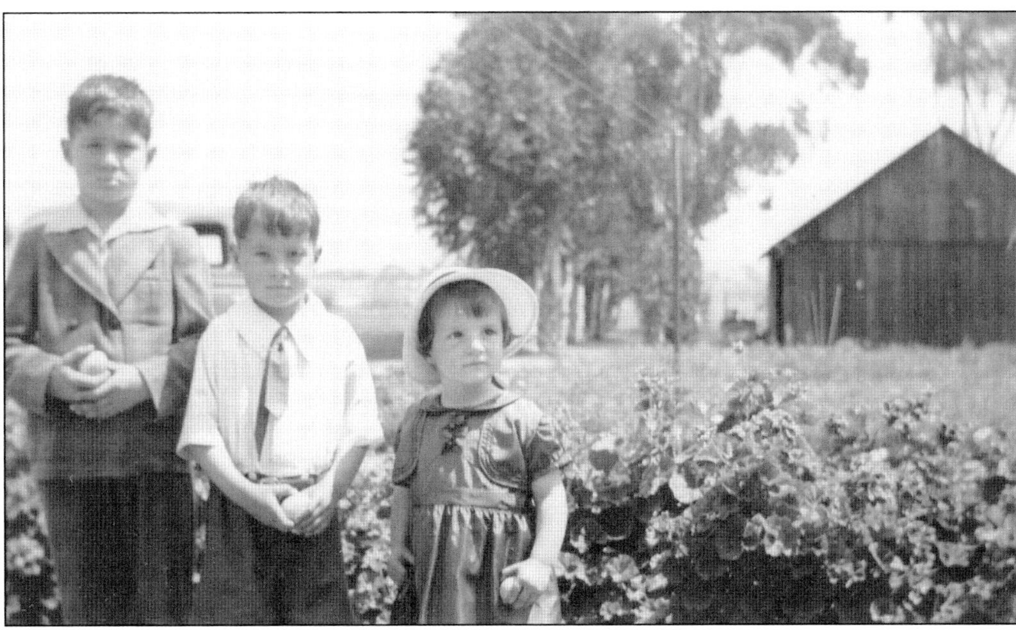

Robert and Emma Egger had three children: (from left to right) Robert Jr., Walter, and Mary. The children began working on the farm at an early age. Mary, born in 1937, remembers that she started driving a pick-up on the farm when she was six years old. This picture was taken in 1939. (Egger family.)

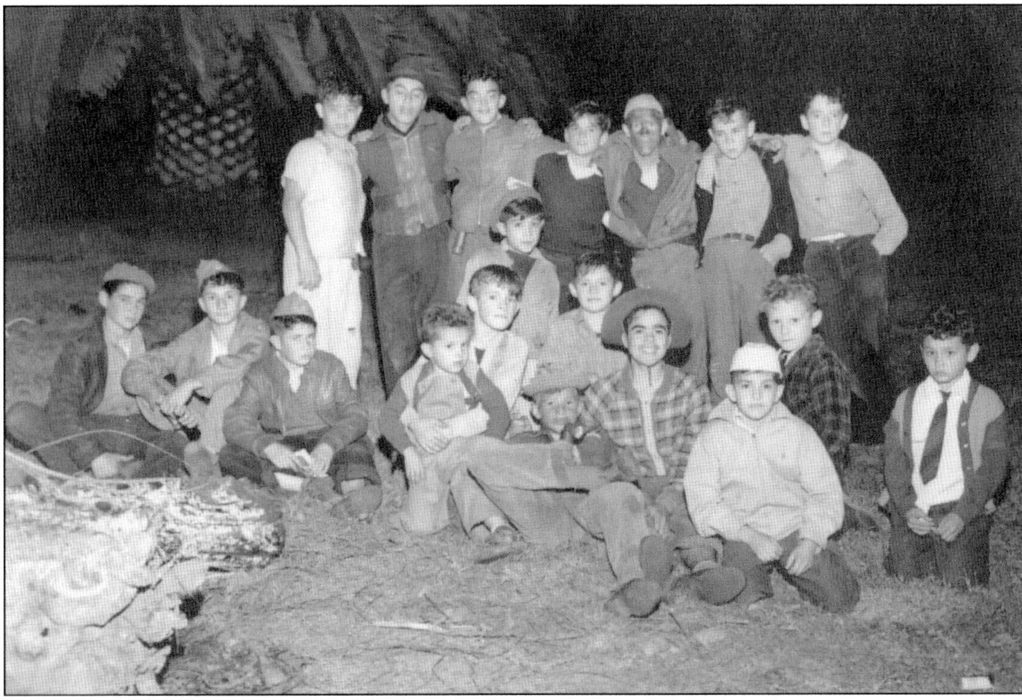

San Ysidro and the Tijuana River Valley had a small-town feel, as if everybody knew everyone. Here, Bobby Egger is pictured during a Halloween party in 1946 with many children from other farms and the town of San Ysidro, including the Cuens. (Emilio "Emo" Noriega.)

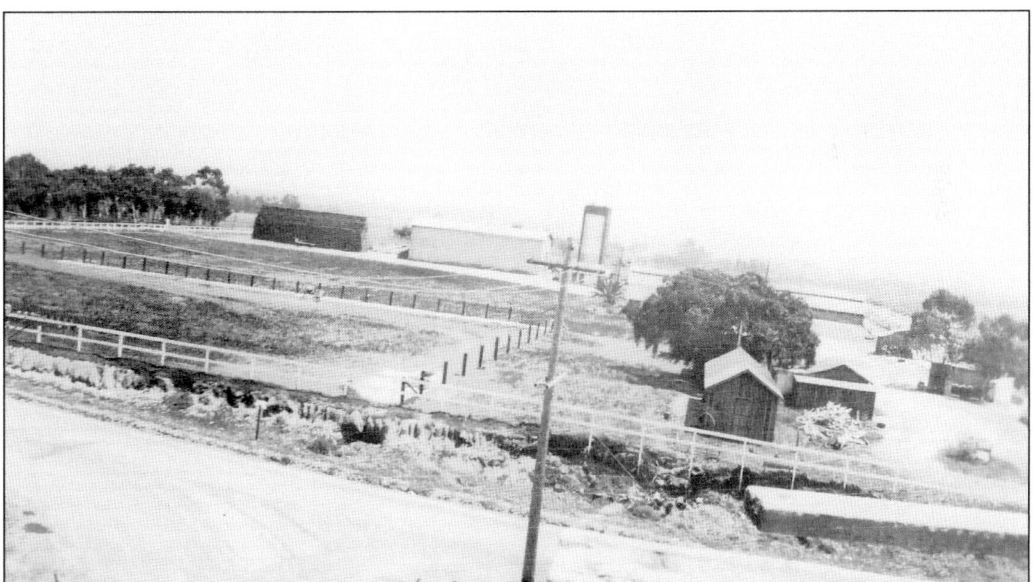

Two other notable Swiss families, the Zumsteins and the Hofers, owned farms in Imperial Valley and in Pacific Beach. Robert Egger called the Zumstein family over to the valley and encouraged them to buy dairies to get out of the heat. By the 1940s, the Hofers and the Zumsteins owned dairy farms alongside the Eggers. This picture shows the growing Egger property around the 1940s. (Egger family.)

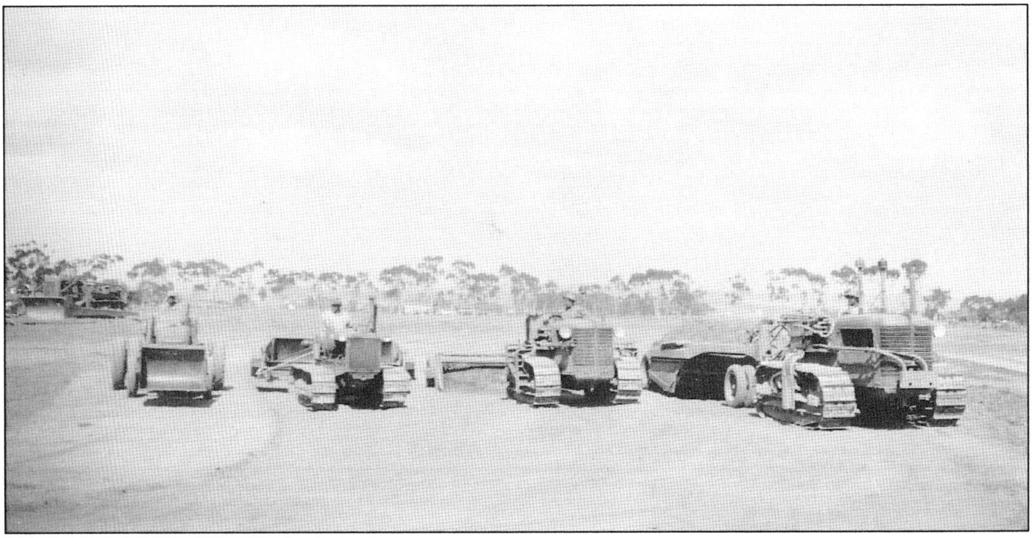

Robert Egger farmed every tract of land he bought. In some areas, he dynamited the eucalyptus trees and used a skip loader to haul off the rocks and debris in order to make way for farming. At first, he grew vegetables, including celery, tomatoes, and green beans, and later added lettuce and romaine. His tomatoes were shipped as far away as New York, and his celery was distributed all over the country. (Egger family.)

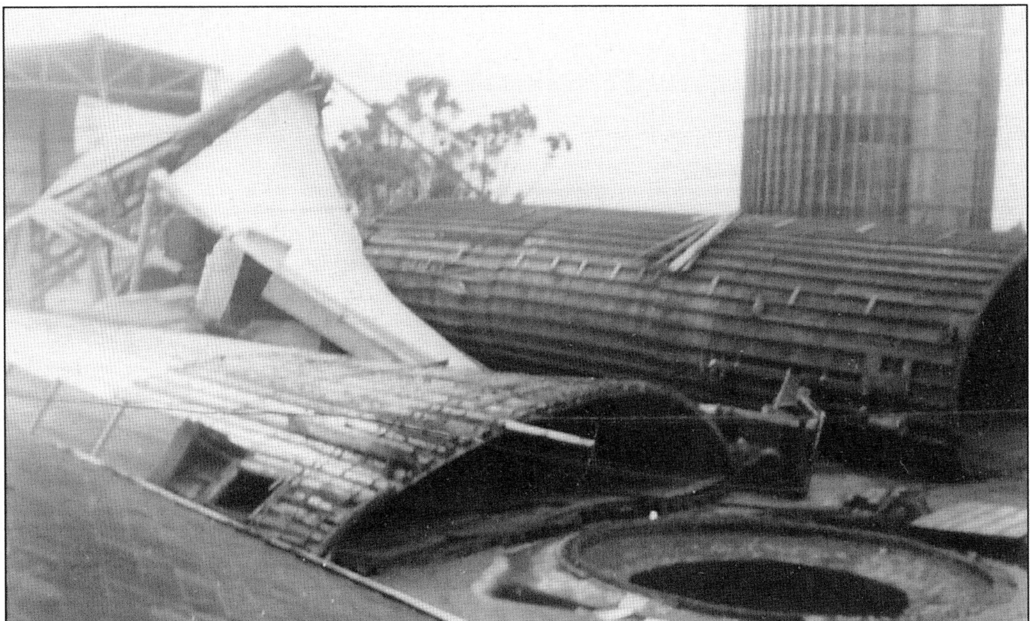

The weather in the Tijuana River Valley was not good for curing hay, so Robert Egger purchased it from El Centro. The corn and alfalfa silage was then stored in three 55-foot-tall silos. Not only was the river bottom prone to floods, but in 1938, a windstorm blew down one of Egger's silos and destroyed it. (Egger family.)

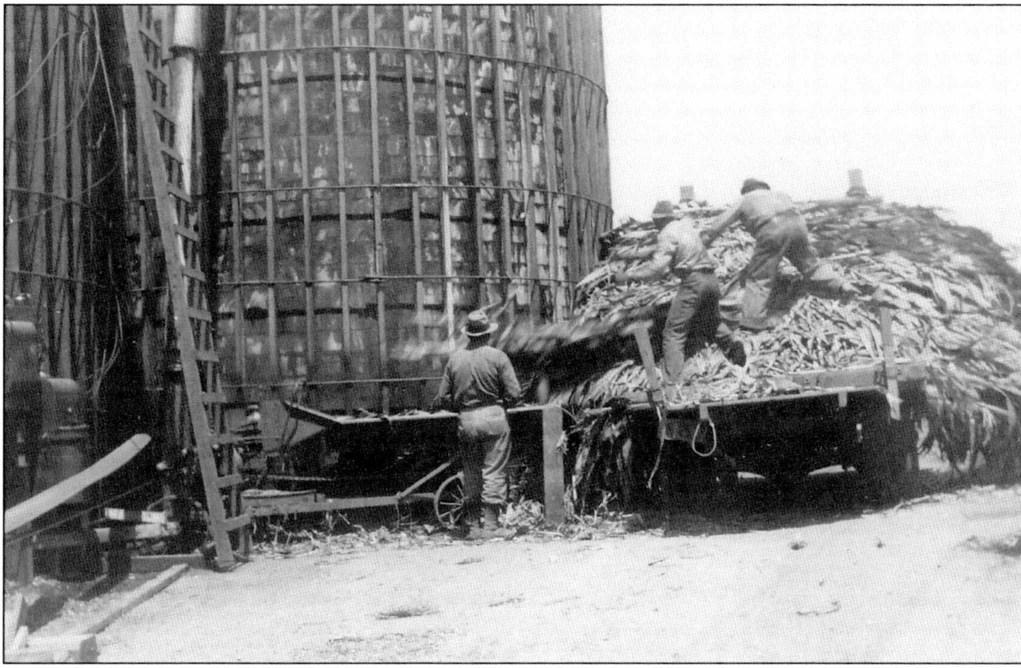

The Egger farm used primarily corn and alfalfa silage. Farm workers would first cut the silage, then dump it into one of three silos. Silage (aka "green feed") would also be fed directly to the cows. This picture shows the intense labor required to farm the Egger property. (Egger family.)

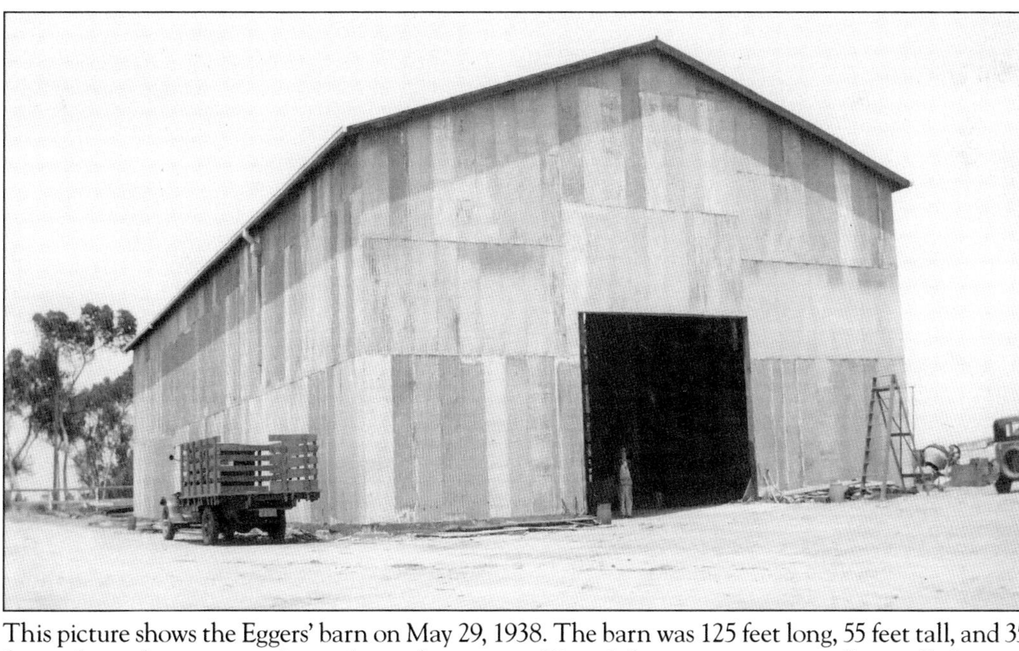

This picture shows the Eggers' barn on May 29, 1938. The barn was 125 feet long, 55 feet tall, and 35 feet wide, and its mammoth size shows the extent of Egger's farming operations. Originally located off Leon Street, the barn was moved a half-mile down the hill in the 1950s. (Egger family.)

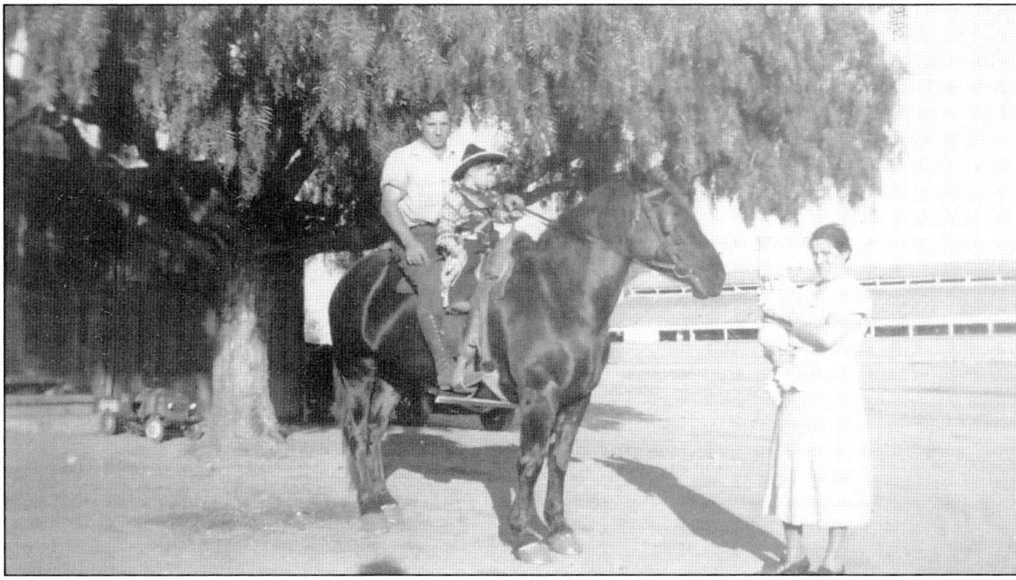

This 1938 picture shows Robert Egger Jr. on a horse with his father. The family owned many horses that were used to pull hay wagons. Egger owned and used these horses up until the early 1940s. In the background, the dairy is visible, and the family's house is behind the horse at the left. Mary, born in 1937, is the baby Emma Egger holds in her arms. (Egger family.)

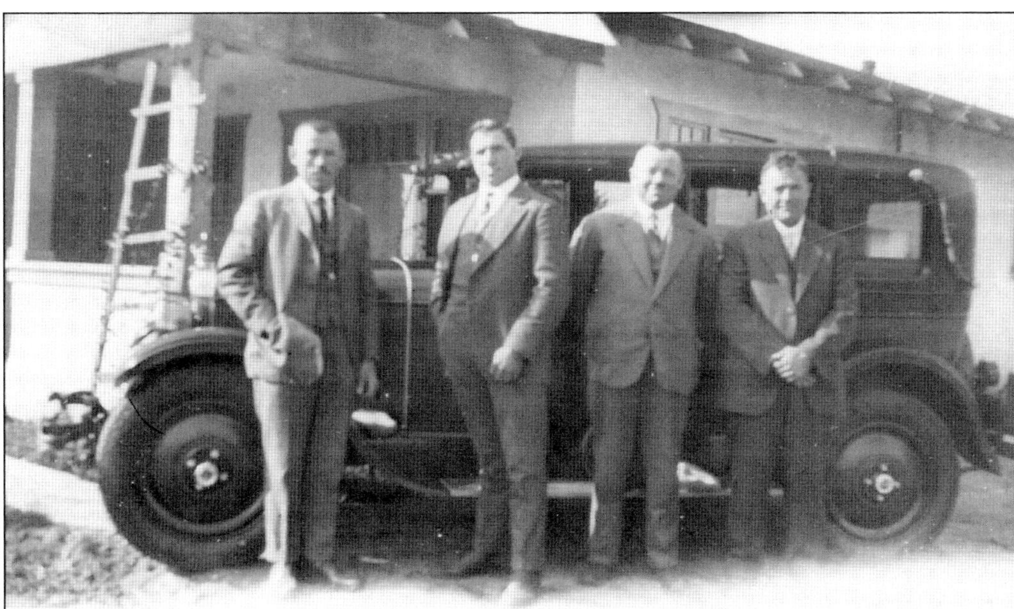

Robert Egger maintained ties to his Swiss heritage via many Swiss friends and as one of the founders of the Swiss Club, which formed in 1939. By 1949, the organization held its first "Schwingen Fest," also known as Swiss wrestling. Egger donated land for the Swiss Club in 1953, and in 1957, the members were able to build a great hall. Due to the expansion of Interstate 5, however, the hall had to be relocated in 1970. (Egger family.)

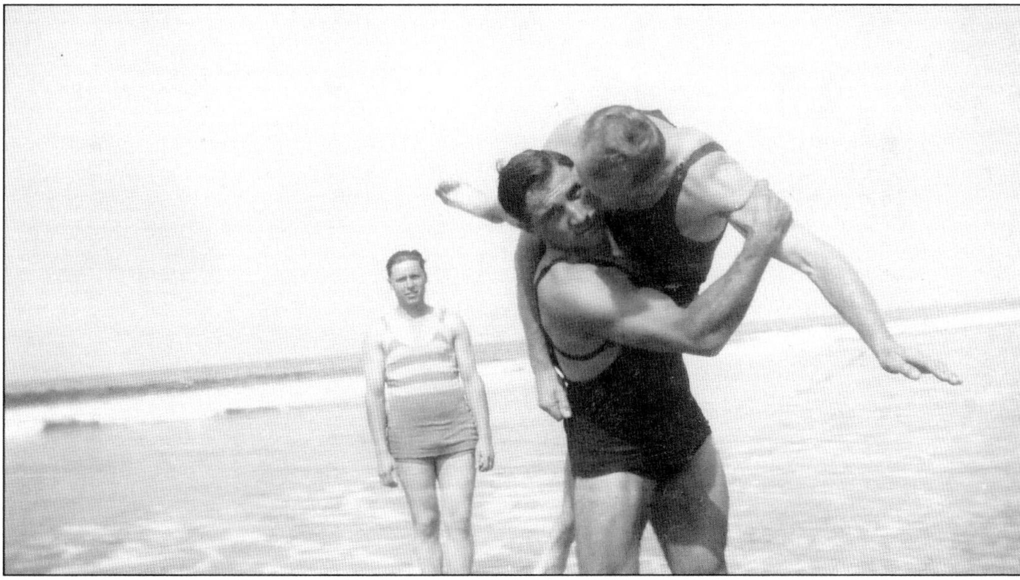

Here, Egger is at the beach with an unidentified friend enjoying the national pastime of the German-speaking part of Switzerland—Schwingen. In this wrestling sport, throws and trips are part of the game, in which the first competitor to pin his opponent's shoulders to the ground wins. (Egger family.)

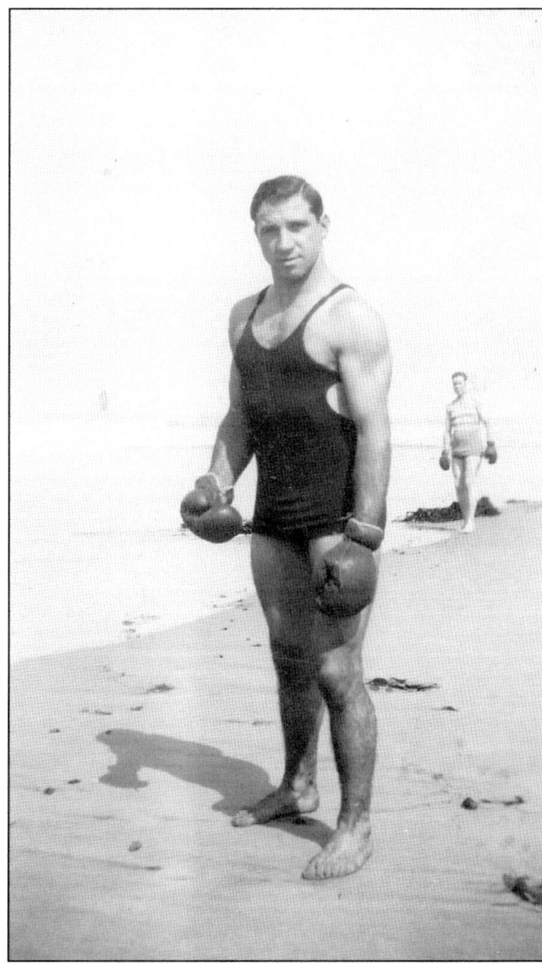

Robert Egger is pictured here in his Schwingen outfit. The mission of the Swiss Club was to pass the Swiss community's traditions and heritage to future generations in the San Diego area. Egger remained close to his roots in this way. Although he is at the beach in this image, farm life was usually so intense that he had very little time for entertainments. (Egger family.)

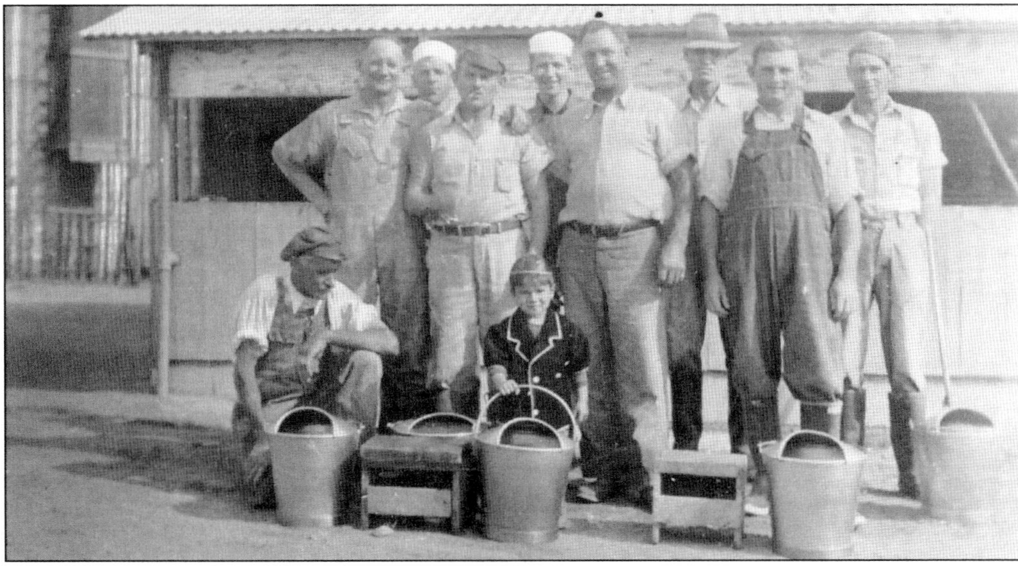

At one point, Robert Egger employed between 200 and 300 people. He created Quonset huts for many of his employees. When the United States initiated the bracero program in 1942, Egger hired farm workers from Mexico who received permits to work in the United States for six months, after which they had to return to Mexico. Egger supplied his Mexican employees with meat from the dairy farm and lent them a 10-acre plot to farm. (Egger family.)

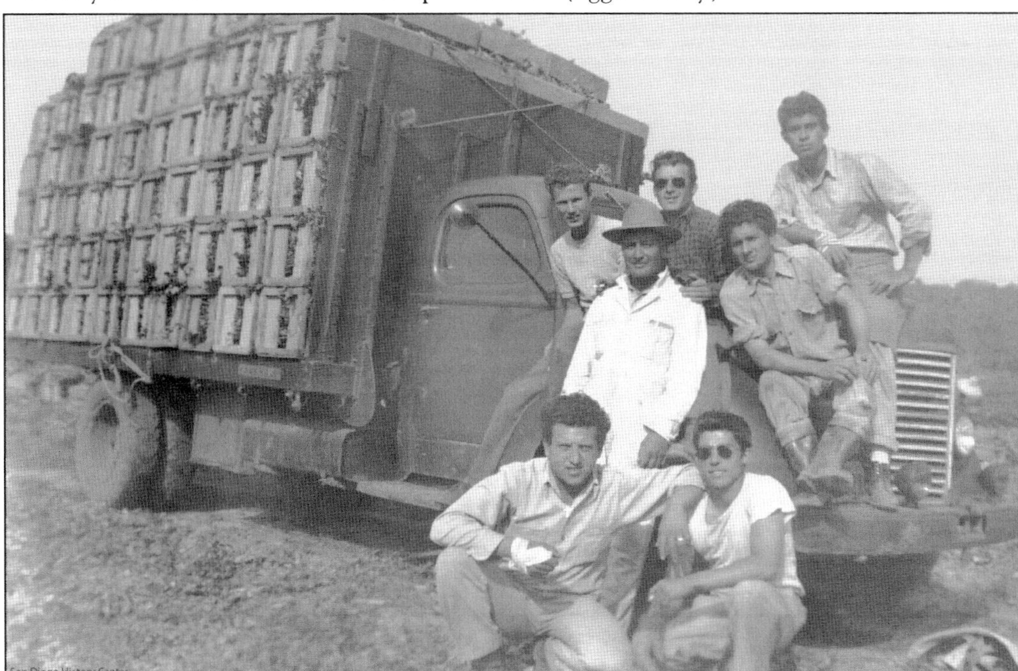

The bracero program was instituted when the United States experienced severe labor shortages during World War II. The program allowed Mexican laborers to enter the United States legally and work for growers and ranchers. From 1942 to 1964, more than four million Mexican laborers worked in fields across the United States, including throughout the Tijuana River Valley. In this picture from the Alicia Valadez collection, field workers paused to pose for a photograph in 1948. (SDHC.)

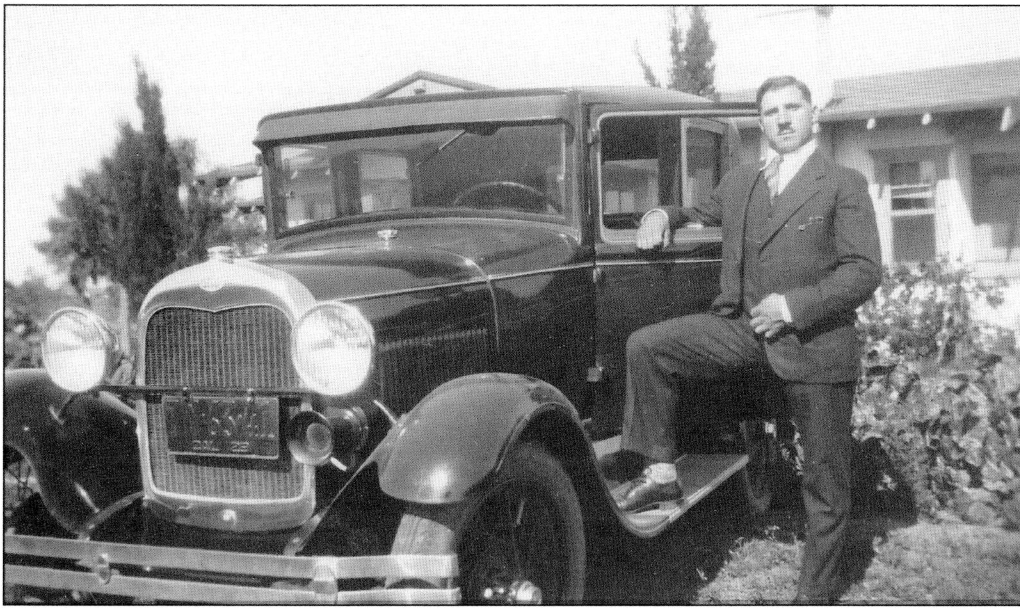

Over time, Robert Egger owned property that stretched north to Chula Vista, south to the border, east covering much of Otay Mesa, and bordering Ream Field at the Pacific Ocean. He was the only farmer in the area who grew vegetables along with owning a dairy. Here, the self-made man stands in front of his car. (Egger family.)

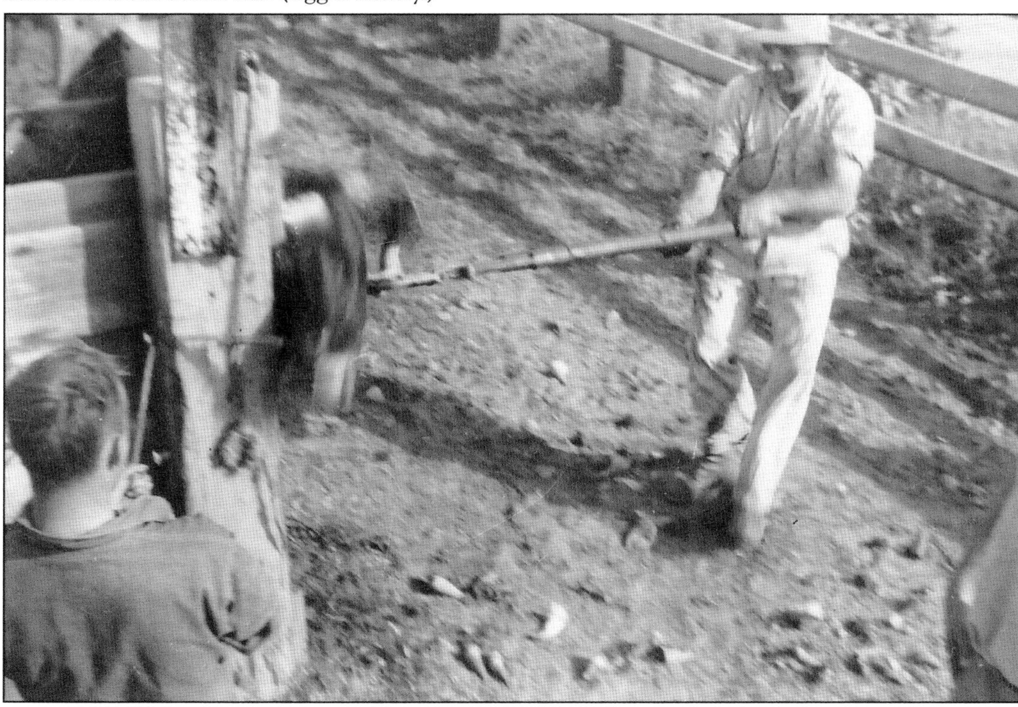

During World War II, the Cal American Water Company began to divert water from the Tijuana River Valley to naval ships in Coronado. As a consequence, irrigation water became salty, and most vegetable farmers left the area. Egger, however, dug a 1,500-foot well. At the bottom, he found 97-degree water that was 10,000 years old. This well still exists today. (Egger family.)

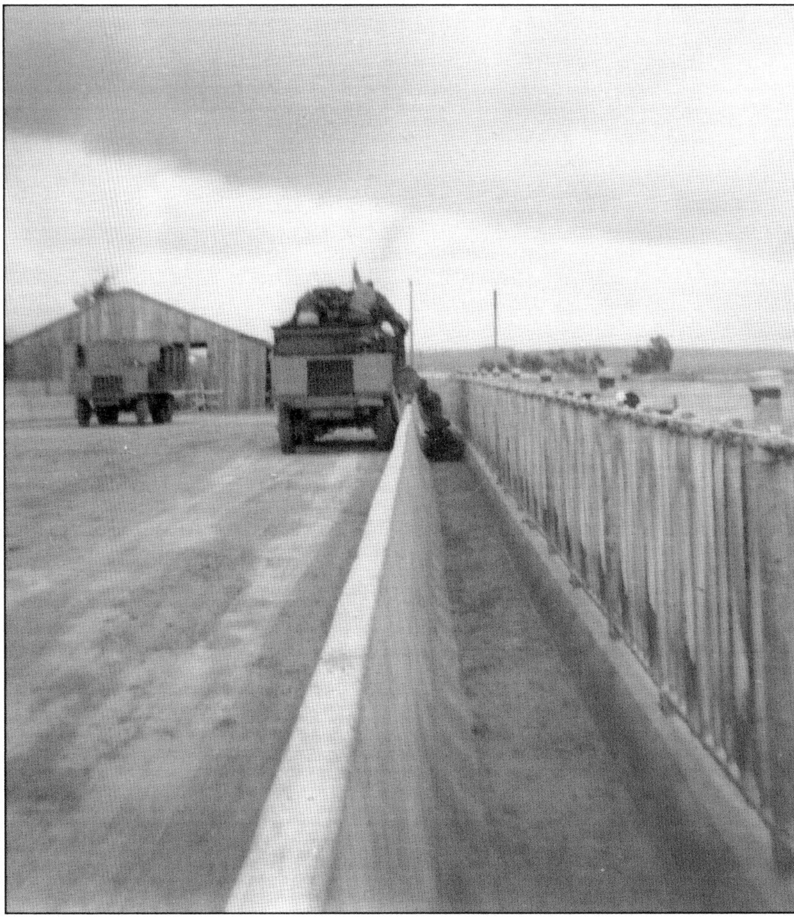

World War II affected the Egger farm in another way as well, as Robert Egger bought surplus military supplies, such as this half-track, from auctions. Usually used for troop transfers, the half-track still had gun turrets on the front upon purchase. The Eggers used it for corn and alfalfa. This half-track is dumping green chop (alfalfa or corn) into the manger for the cows. (Egger family.)

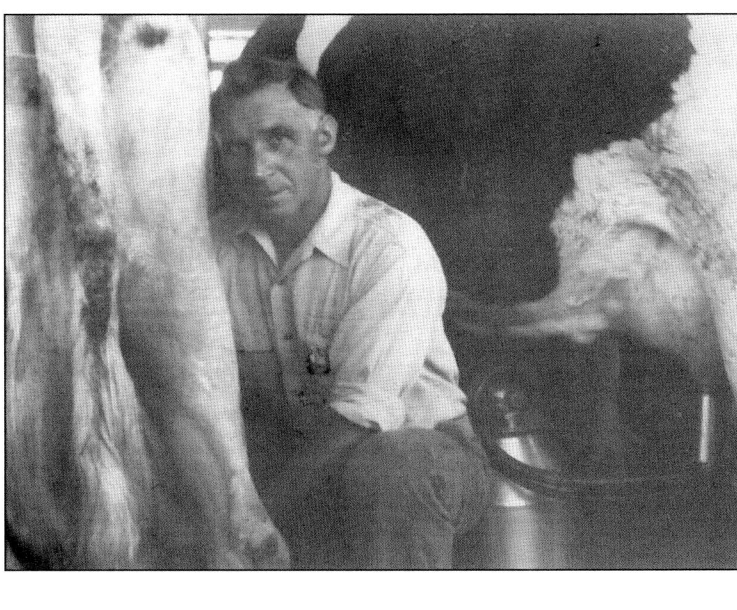

During the war, Robert Egger had more than 1,000 cows. They were milked by hand around the clock, which meant Egger had to work 20 hours per day managing the operation. He thrived during the war alongside other dairy farmers who all sent milk to Dairy Mart, which had a large tanker truck that came around to buy the farmers' milk supplies. (Egger family.)

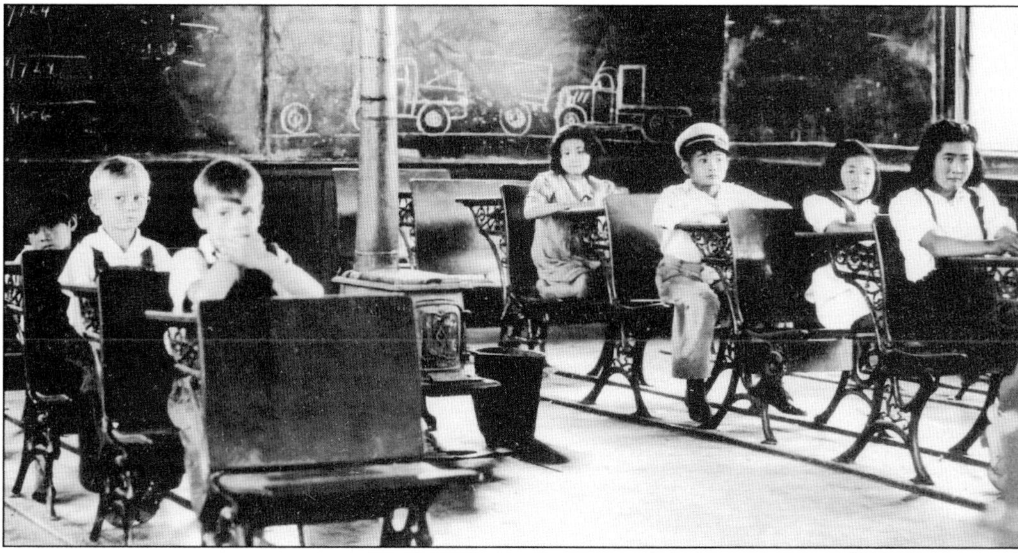

Ten to twelve Japanese farmers also lived in the Tijuana River Valley, including the Yanos, the Segawas, and truck farmers Imaizumi Jimpei and Tahibama Chikammi. They and their children integrated seamlessly into the community, as shown in this picture of Japanese-American children at the Monument City School. (Evelyn Sevel.)

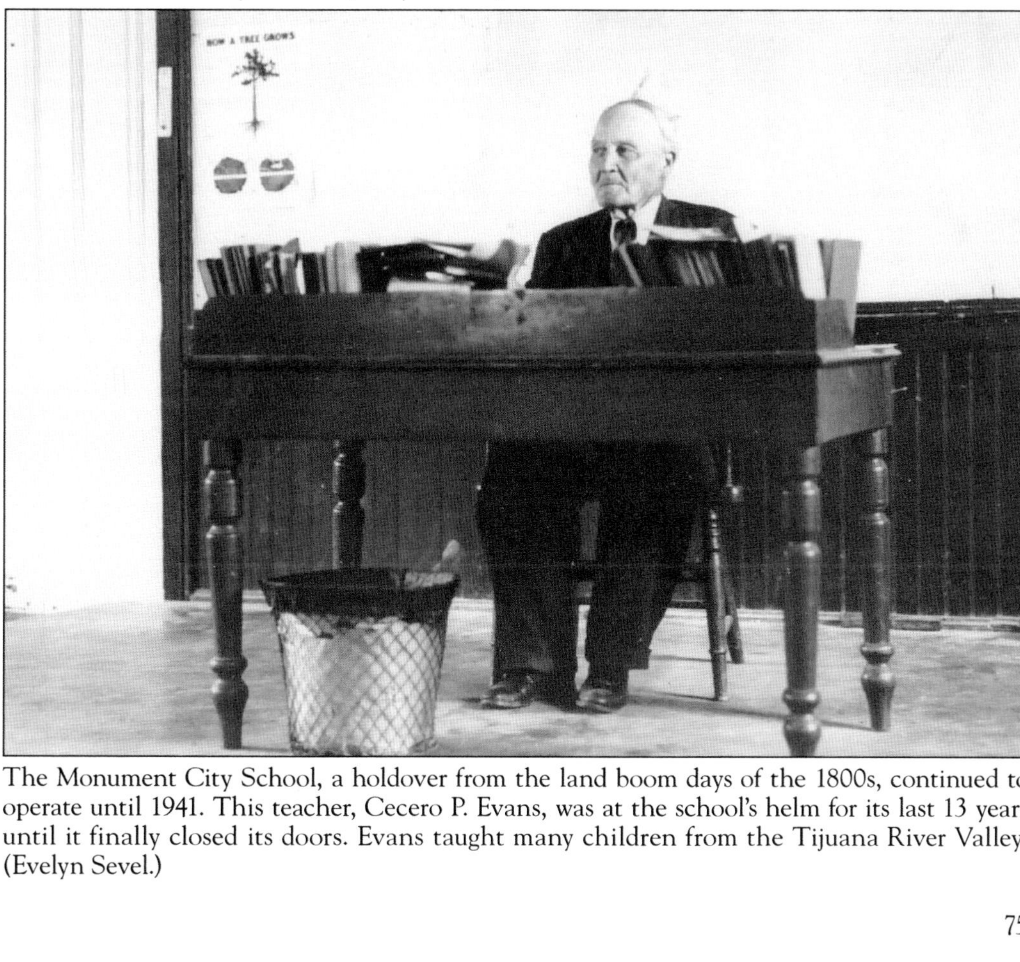

The Monument City School, a holdover from the land boom days of the 1800s, continued to operate until 1941. This teacher, Cecero P. Evans, was at the school's helm for its last 13 years until it finally closed its doors. Evans taught many children from the Tijuana River Valley. (Evelyn Sevel.)

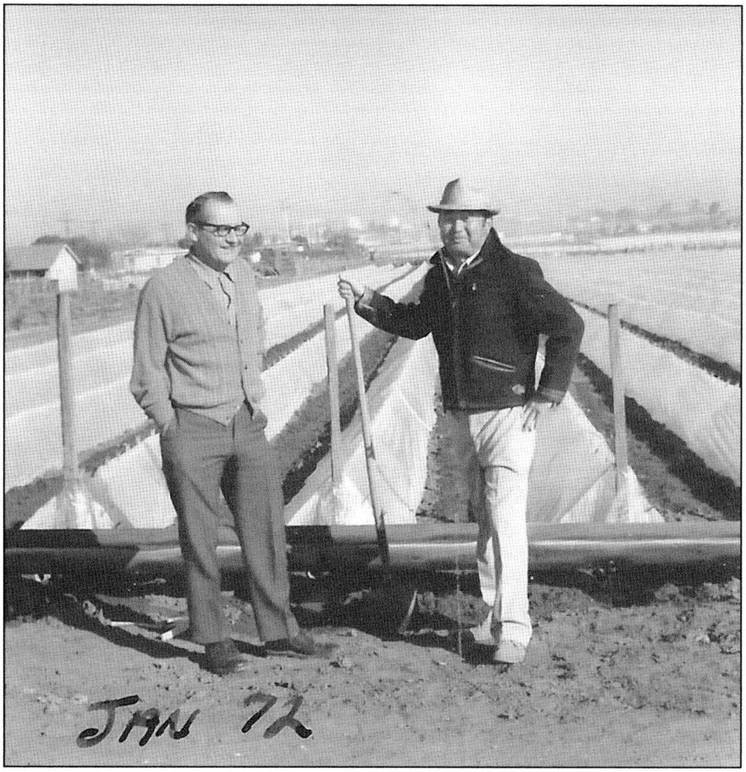

In 1941, all Japanese-American farmers were given 10 days notice before being carted off by the FBI to internment camps for the duration of World War II. When farmers returned to their homesteads after 1945, many found they had lost everything. In this January 1972 picture, Toki Yano (right), who grew up in the Tijuana River Valley until he was forced into an internment camp, stands at this new farm in Imperial Valley. (Japanese-American Historical Association.)

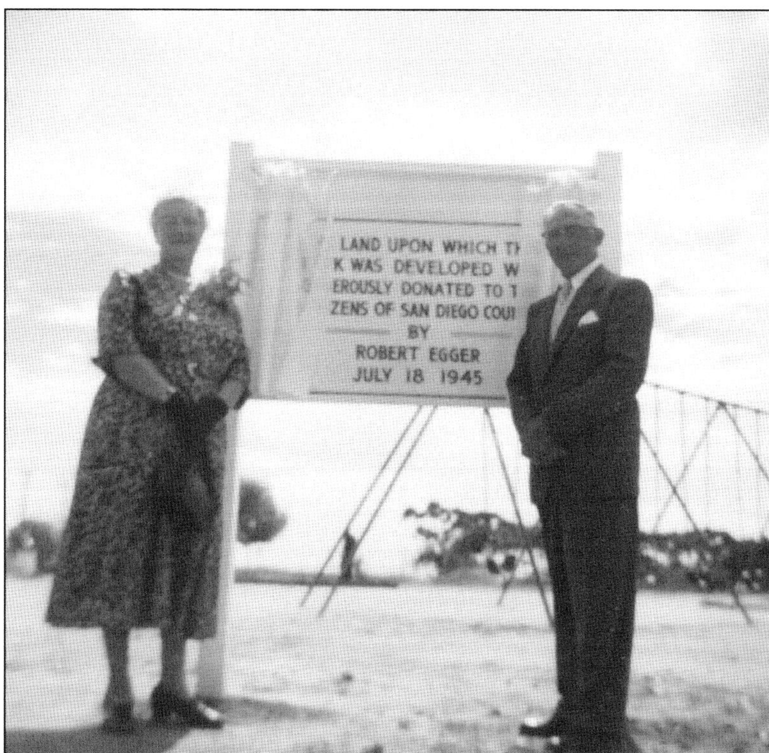

On June 27, 1946, Robert Egger presented the county board of supervisors with a deed to a five-acre plot of ground for the citizens of the South Bay district for use as a community park. The recreation center and park created in Egger's name still exist today, although at different locations due to the building of the Interstate 5 freeway. Here, he is pictured with his wife, Emma. (Egger family.)

In 1947, Robert Egger donated land for St. Charles Catholic Church. In this picture, the Most Reverend Charles F. Buddy (middle), bishop of the San Diego diocese, stands with Egger (left). A lifelong Catholic, Egger devoted himself to community service. He was also an active member of the larger community; the *San Ysidro Border Press* reported his presence at chamber of commerce functions and others. (Egger family.)

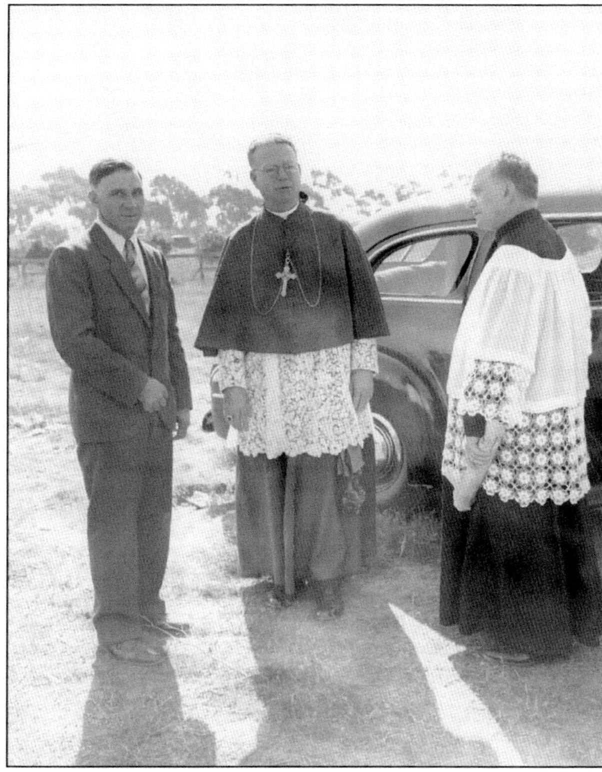

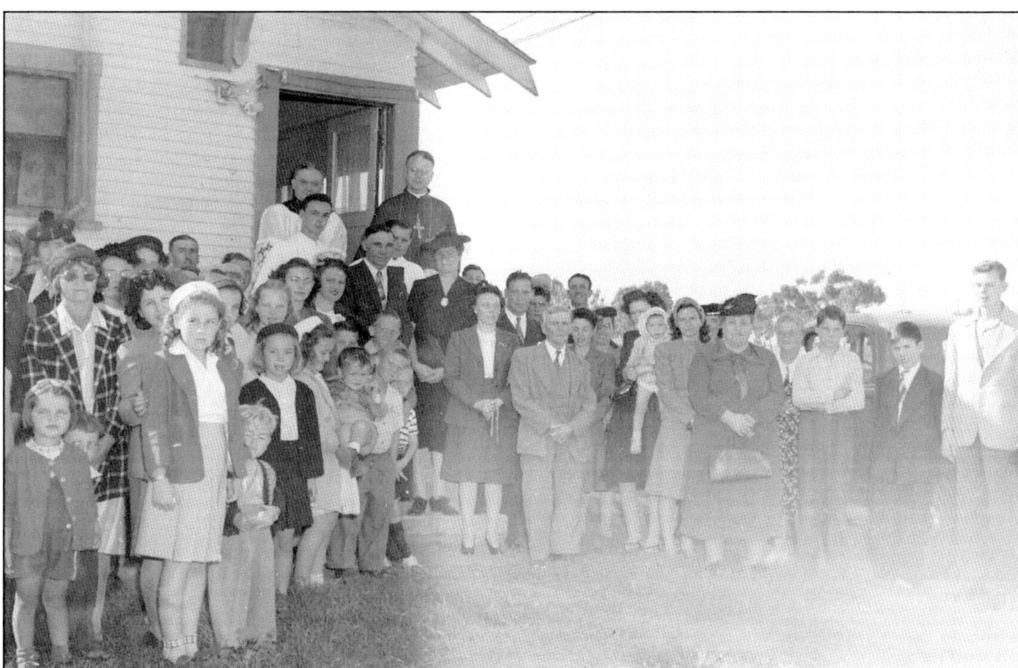

Robert Egger also donated land for a church school. In this picture, Bishop Buddy (back center), Robert and Emma (front center) pose with the children and some of their parents. Egger additionally donated land for Marian Catholic High School in 1960. (Egger family.)

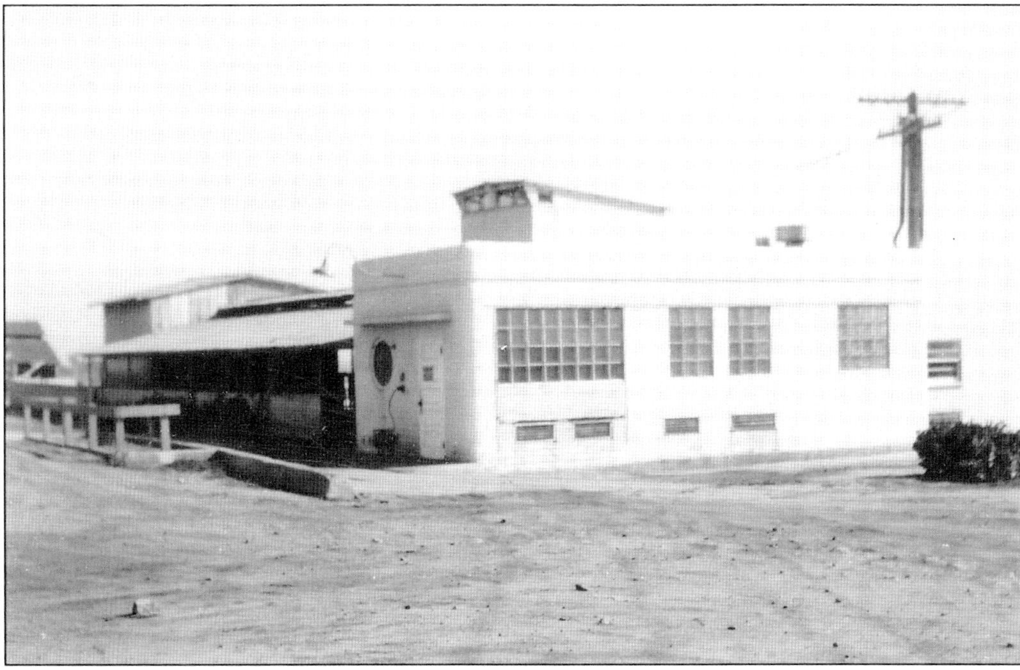

In 1959, Robert Egger purchased another dairy barn with a 2,000-gallon tank to store milk. He sold his product to Dairy Mart farms. Dairy Mart employees would pick up the milk every morning, take it down to the creamery, bottle the milk, and make ice cream, butter, and other products. In the picture below, Robert Egger (left) stands with employee Ernie Ambort in front of the new dairy building. (Both, Egger family.)

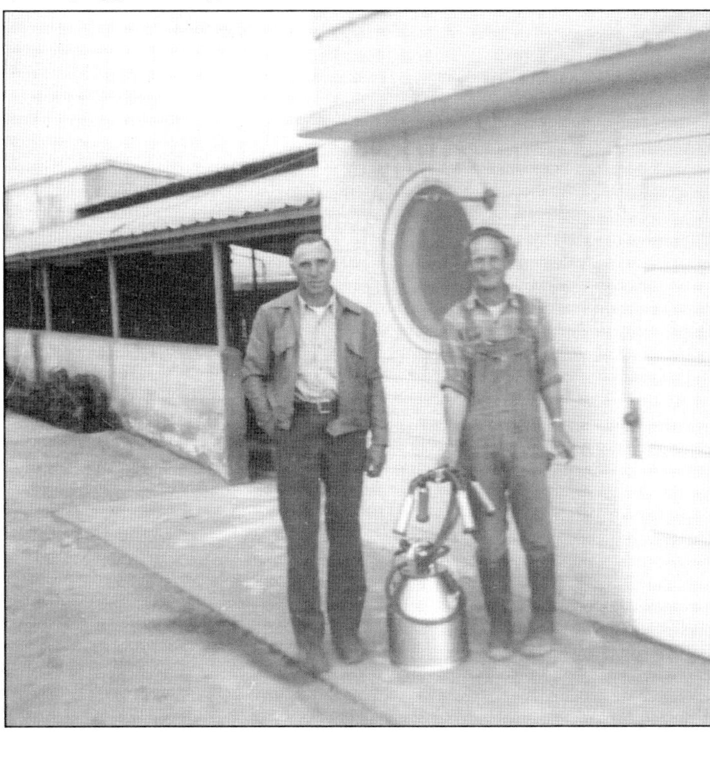

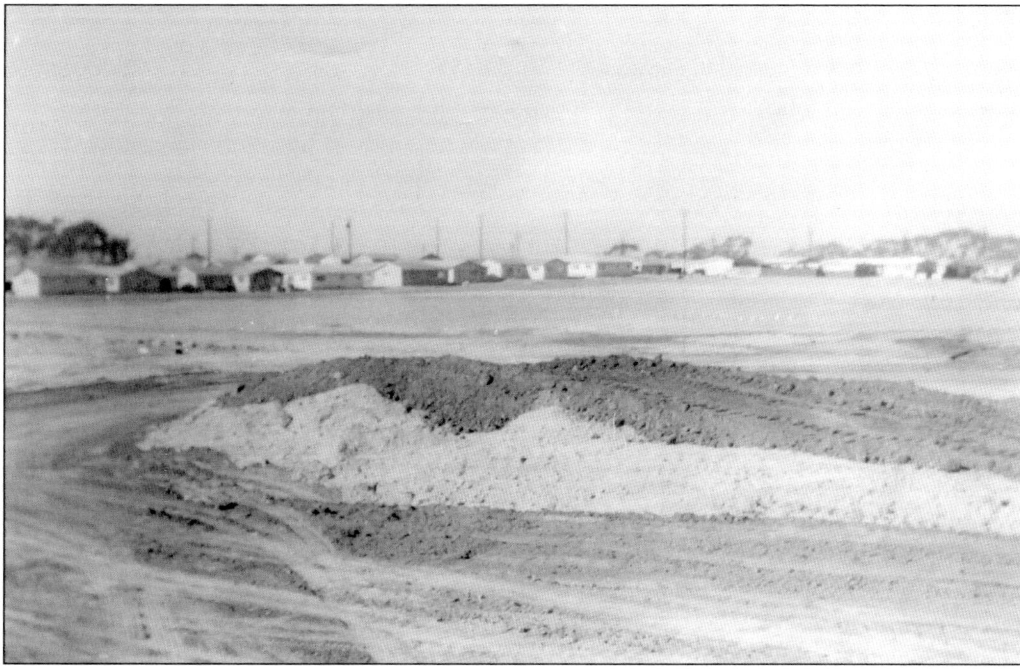

Farming in the Tijuana River Valley started to decline during the 1960s. In this picture from January 1960, suburban development is visible alongside the Egger property. As residential units replaced farmland, property taxes began to be assessed differently, and taxes for farmers skyrocketed; the Eggers subsequently began to sell their land. (Egger family.)

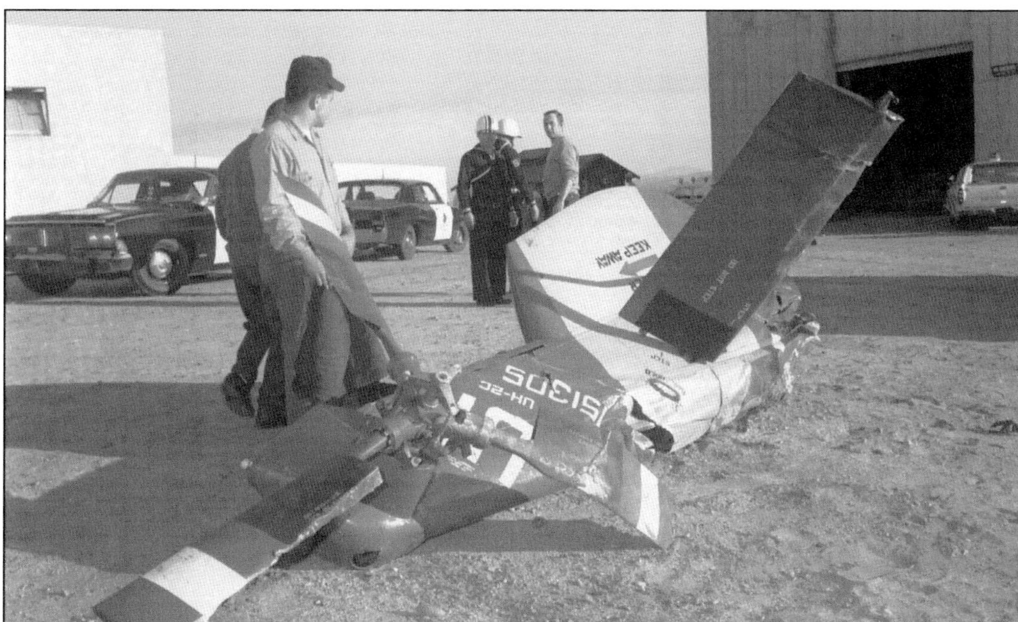

On December 23, 1968, a Navy helicopter crashed into a corral on the Egger property. The pilot, Lt. Thomas A. Matthews, and two enlisted crewmen were killed. Concerned about liability issues, the Navy soon approached Robert Egger about buying some of his farmland. He had to agree and then lease the land back from the Navy in order to continue farming. (SDHC.)

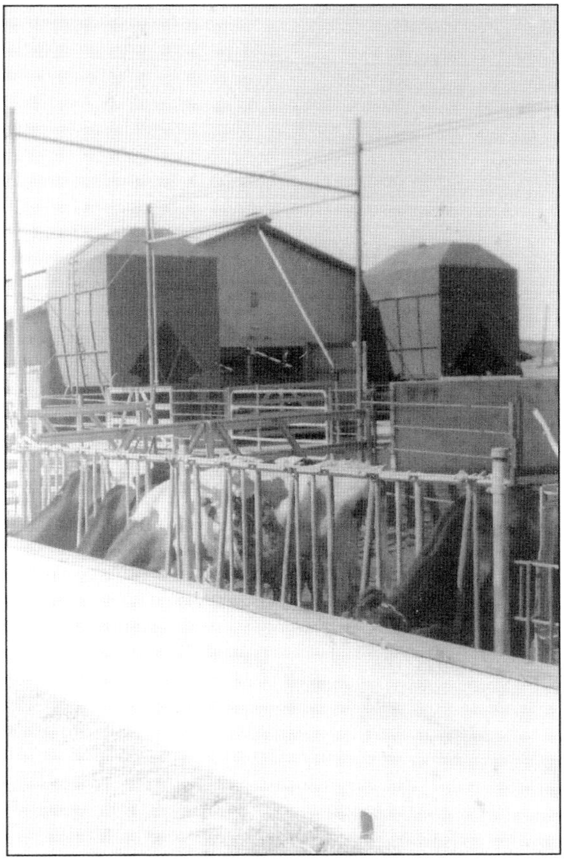

Even with so many cows, the Eggers realized that the more milk they sold to one entity, the larger discount that entity received, so the Eggers felt they were giving away their profits. In 1965, they created their own creamery called Swiss Farms. For a time, all the local elementary schools served Swiss Farms milk. A decade later, the government—which subsidized the dairy industry—had a surplus of dairy products and began to pay dairymen to quit their farms. The State of California offered Robert Egger's son Walter (who was then owner of the farm) money to get rid of his cows by butchering them or selling them out of the country. The Egger dairy closed in 1985, and dairy farmers soon abandoned the Tijuana River Valley altogether. (Both, Egger family.)

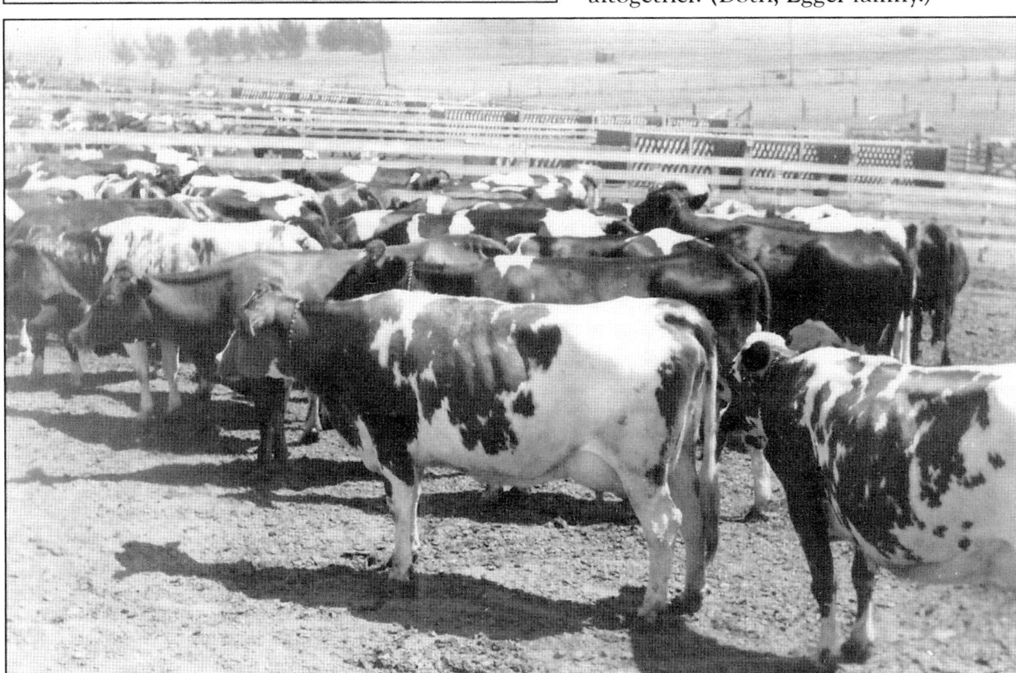

Seven

The Military Base

While the Tijuana River Valley remained predominantly farmland throughout the first half of the 20th century, large naval bases existed within the region, including Ream Field to the north, Brown Field to the east, and, starting in 1926, the Border Field area.

Tijuana, on the Mexican side of the border, now sat 300 feet above sea level surrounded by a natural watershed. During heavy rains, the city's runoff would flow down through the Tijuana River and into the Pacific Ocean. Although the Navy noted that the environment was unsuitable for expansive building due to these drainage problems, World War II created a pressing need for a military presence by the border.

In 1946, the Border Field base was deactivated for a time, but the escalation of the Cold War reopened military operations. Although the Army completely left, the Navy took over its property, and, in 1951, turned Border Field into an outlying field attached to Ream Field. The base was then used for dive-bombing practice and became a launch site for drone airplanes.

By 1961, Border Field once again became inactive. The Naval Electronics Laboratory remained for a time to operate a testing facility for its work in underwater radio communication experiments. During that time, some of the land was leased for use as an exercise track for racehorses.

In 1971, the federal government transferred the land to the State of California for use as a park. The newly established Border Field State Park welcomed visitors to a property that included the marble obelisk on the border. For the first time in decades, the historic site was again open to tourists.

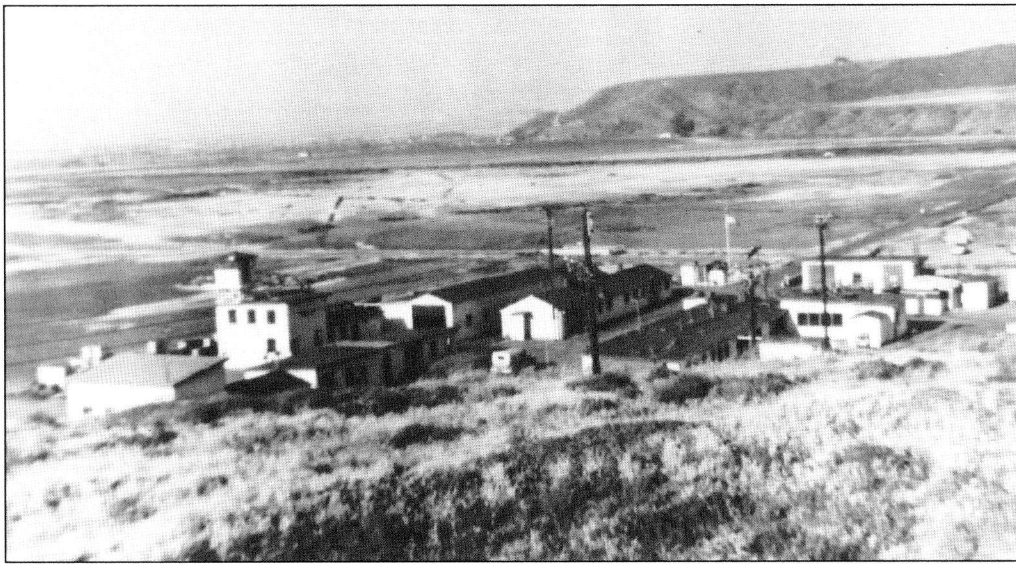

In July 1929, the US Navy began leasing approximately 98 acres of land that stretched to the Mexican-American boundary line. Fenced-in boundary monument No. 258 was located on the base and was all but forgotten. By 1942, the Navy turned the auxiliary airfield into a machine gun and bombing training center for pilots preparing for combat against the Japanese. They built about 35 temporary structures, including offices, barracks, a galley, ammunition storage facilities, and shops. In these pictures, the observer tower is visible to the left. The building next to it on the left is the metal shop, and the small buildings behind the tower are power plant shops. One of the long buildings in the center is a parachute shop. There is also a machine shop and a galley. Out of view are the barracks, a club, and an avionics shop. (Both, California State Parks.)

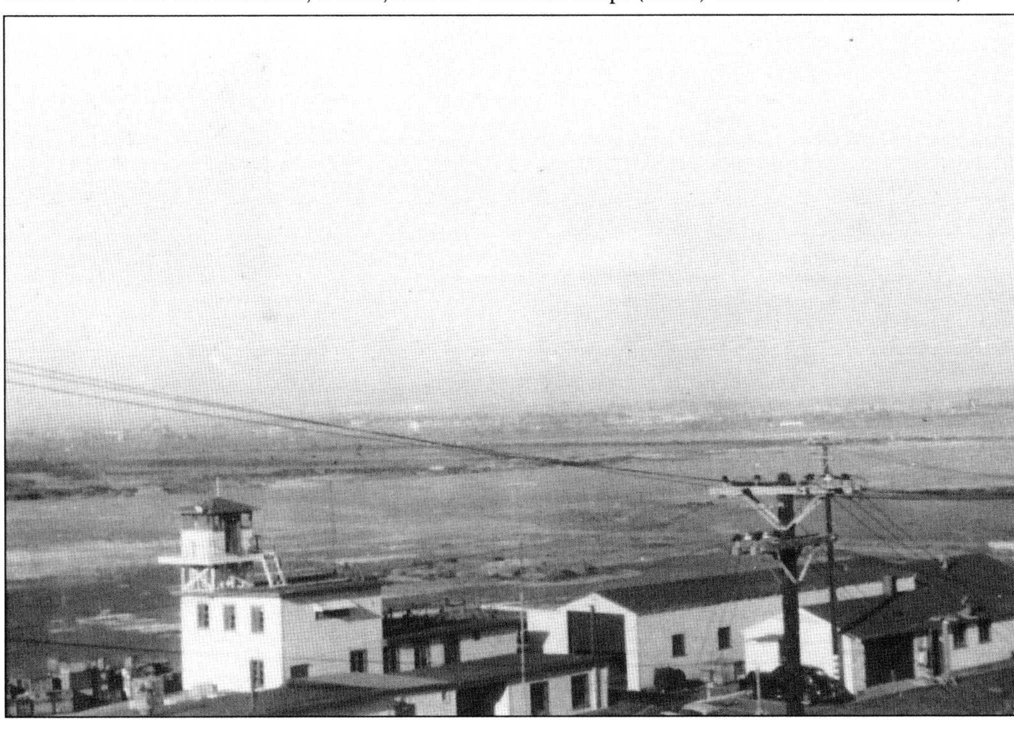

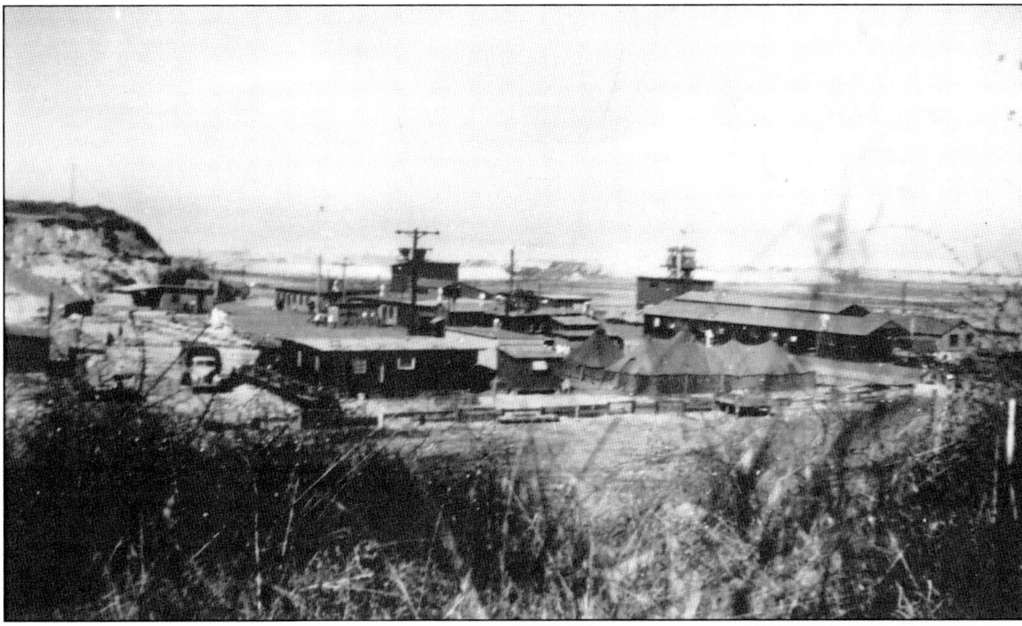

In 1942, the Army also bought about 28 acres of land in the same area, purchased the largest portion from then-owner Russell V. Grant. They built this fire control station that jutted up against the boundary line. Forty-three soldiers were stationed at the site. The Army then set up bunkers, temporary huts, a railroad spur, and more. They also placed long-range artillery guns there. (California State Parks.)

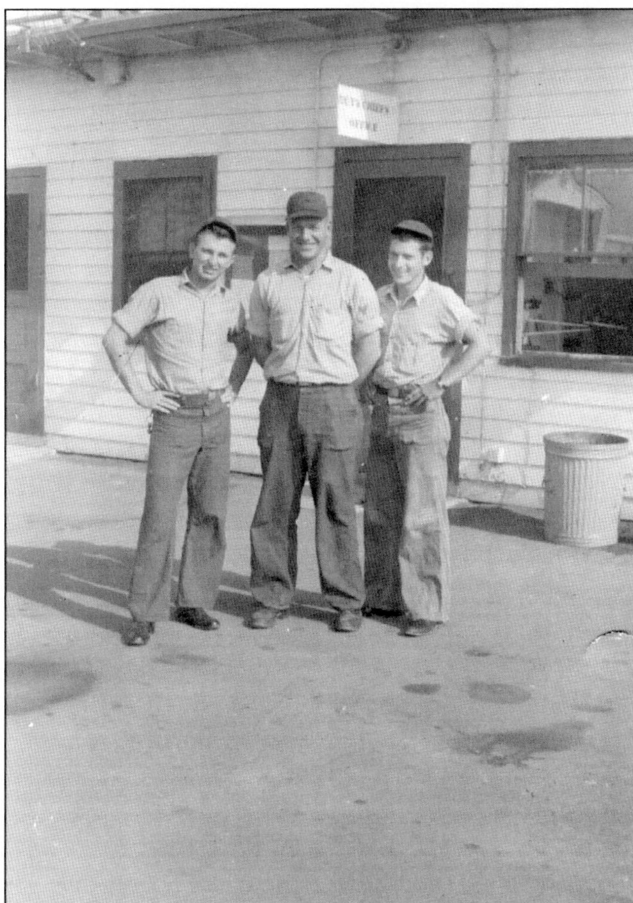

Next to it, Border Field grew during the war to contain an auxiliary training airfield, a gunnery range, a bombing target, air-to-air gunnery, a machine gunner–training center, and an emergency landing field. Navy personnel moved into the barracks and lived on base. In this picture, three "salts" pose for the camera: (from left to right) Dennis Walters, Jack Gann, and John Purdue. (California State Parks.)

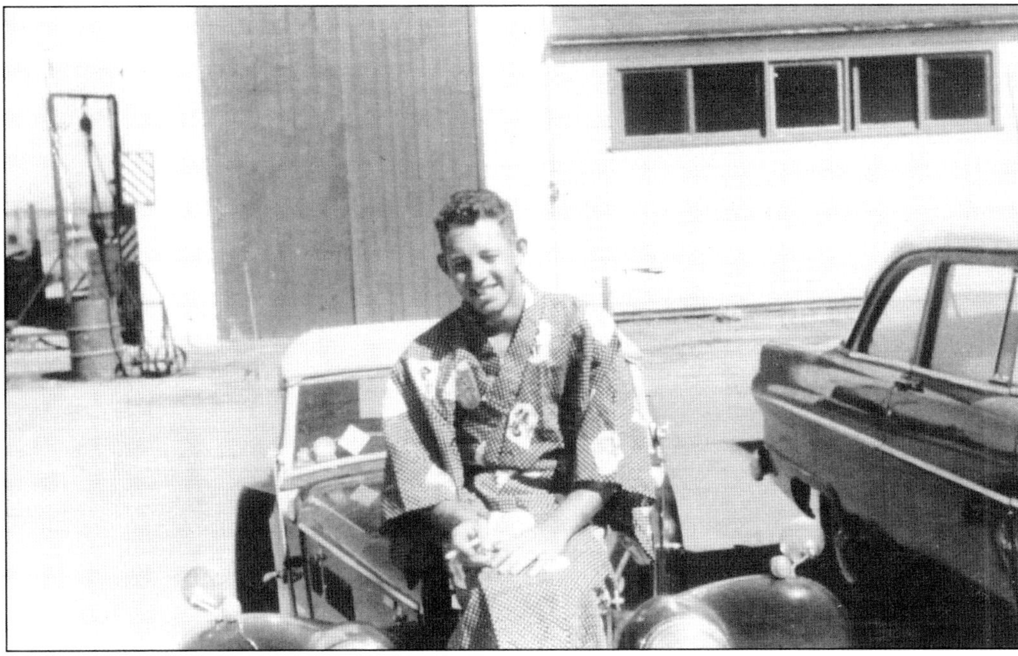

This picture shows Darrel "The Kid" Clark in front of the metal shop. In 1942, the Navy continued to construct more buildings, including a hangar, a storehouse, barracks, a mess hall, a post office, and a bachelor officers' quarters. In 1943 and 1944, the base expanded to cover between 180 and 230 acres. (California State Parks.)

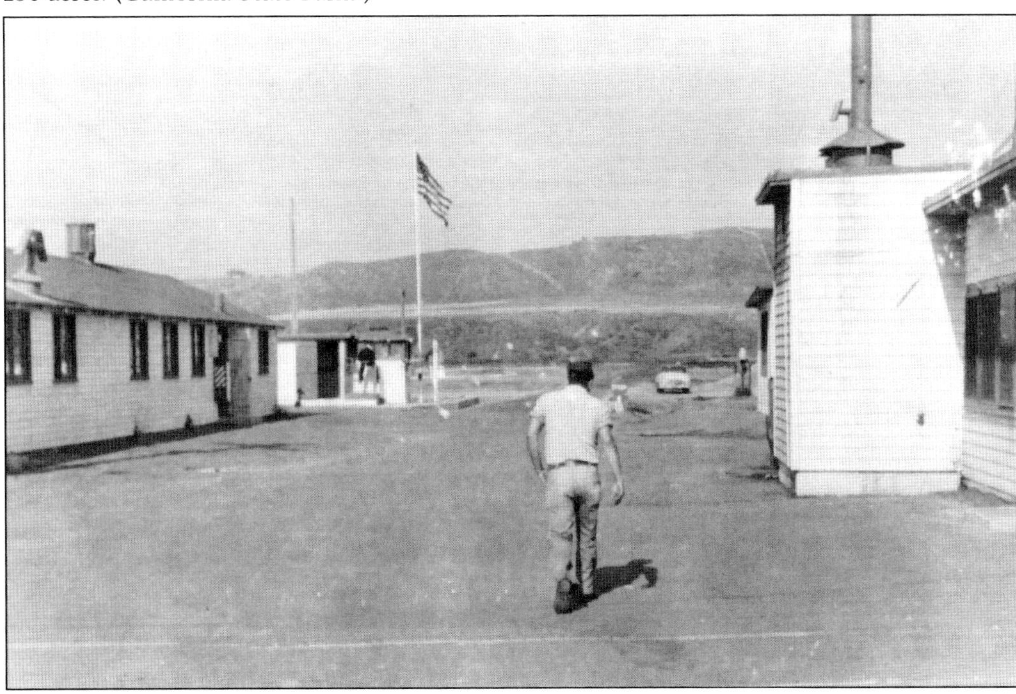

By the end of the war, the Navy decided that it did not want to expand its operations due to the region's drainage problems. In this picture, the parachute loft is to the left, a galley is to the right, and in the far left background is a watch shack with a flag. (California State Parks.)

In the 1950s, due to the Cold War and, in particular, hostilities with Korea, the Navy bought approximately 28 more acres of property to the east. Border Field already contained an airstrip, and flight operations continued to expand. Both aircraft squadron and helicopter units were stationed at the field during different periods. This picture shows the avionics shop in the foreground. (California State Parks.)

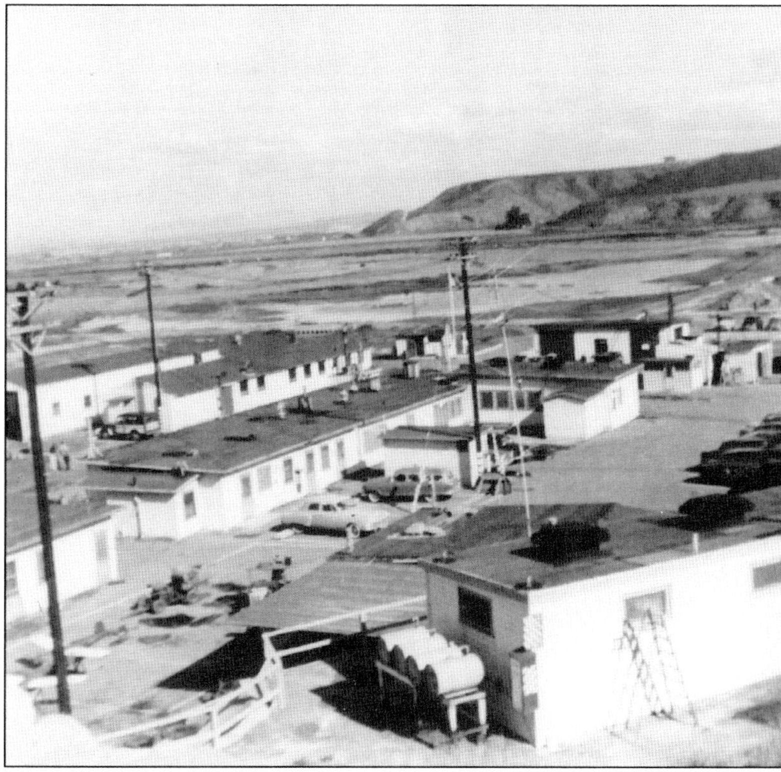

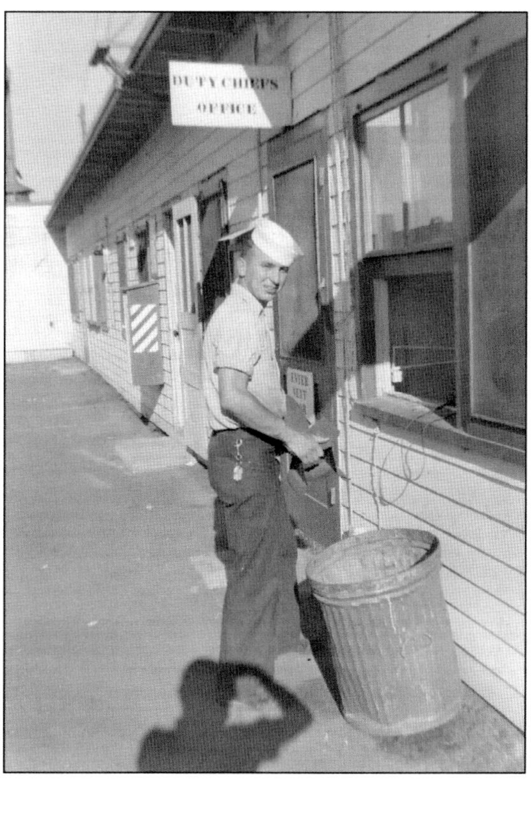

The aircraft industry in San Diego boomed both during and after the war. Companies that provided massive employment in the region included Consolidated Aircraft Corporation, Rohr Aircraft, Solar Aircraft, and Ryan Aeronautical. In addition, Border Field offered employment plus room and board for many young sailors willing to enlist in the Navy. In this picture, Dennis Walters stands in front of the duty chief's office. The galley is at the end of the office building. (California State Parks.)

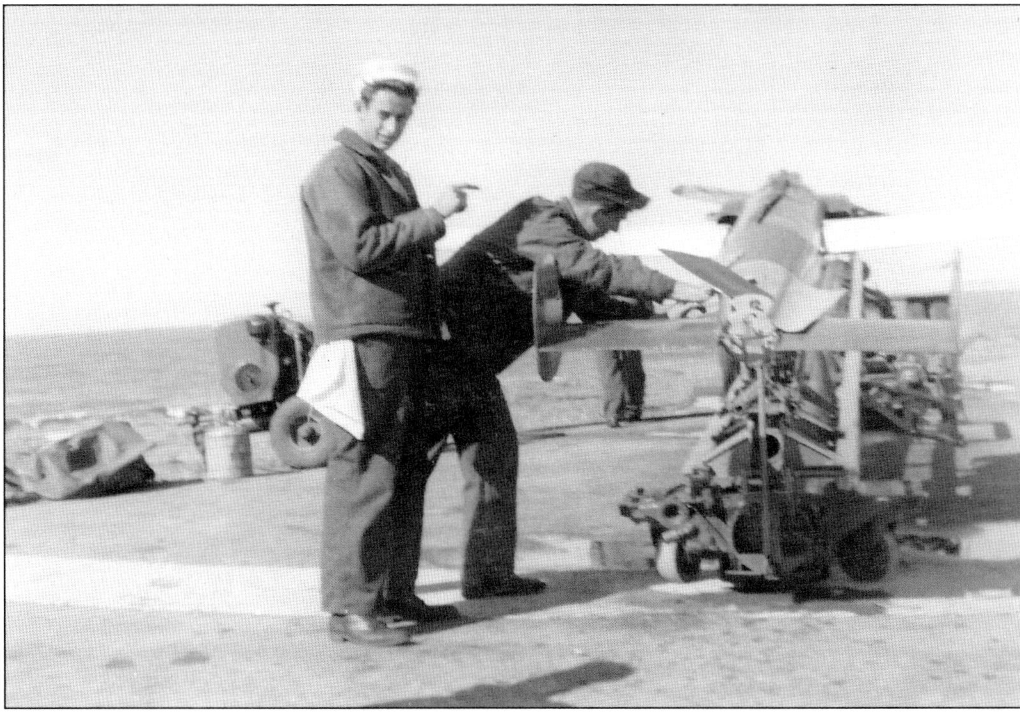

Border Field became a naval auxiliary air station under the administrative control of Ream Field. The base served as a launch site for pilotless drone airplanes, and fleet combat squadrons used the airstrips for target practice. In the picture above, servicemember John Purdue (left) and Dennis Walters (right) work on a drone. In the image below, the drone is in the middle of a launch on top of a hill. The drone was launched out over the ocean, but these target practices were not without danger. The *San Diego Union* reported in 1953 that a runaway drone from nearby Ream Field crashed into the barn of Arthur Shoemaker in Otay Mesa. The plane crash dragged one horse through a chicken house and garage. Three famous horses who had won awards at Tanforan and Caliente race tracks died. The incident put an end to these activities. (Both, California State Parks.)

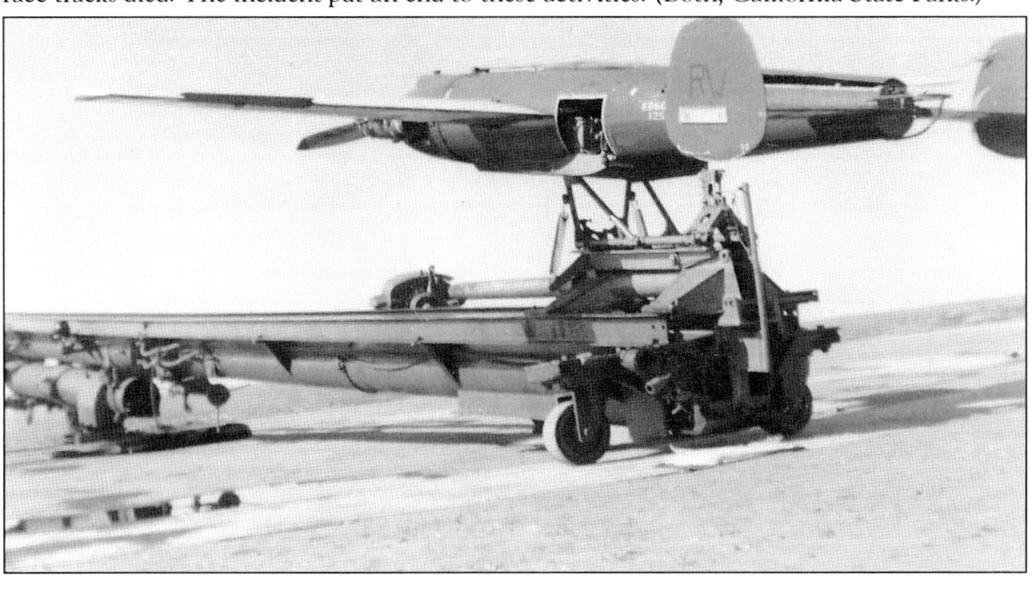

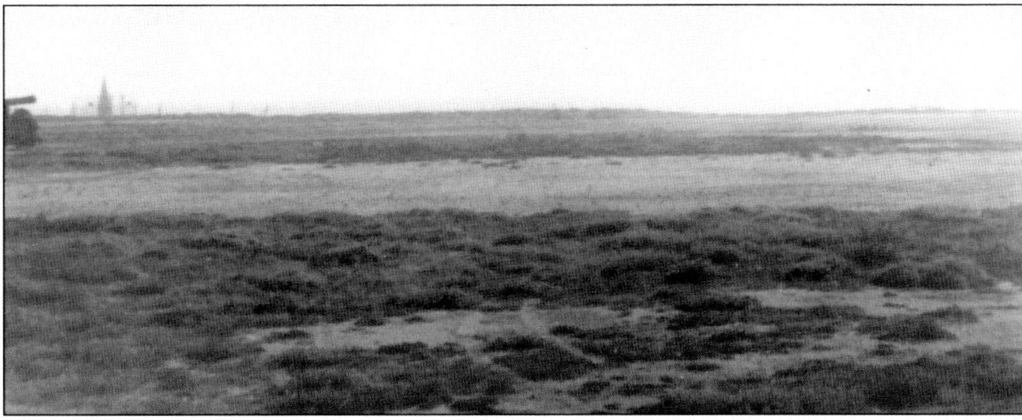

This 1957 photograph shows boundary monument No. 258 surrounded by its steel fence in the far left background. Left of the obelisk is the nose of a catapult. The area leased by the Navy also included the boundary monument near the Pacific Ocean. Since the base was off-limits to civilians starting in 1929, tourists could not visit the historic site. (California State Parks.)

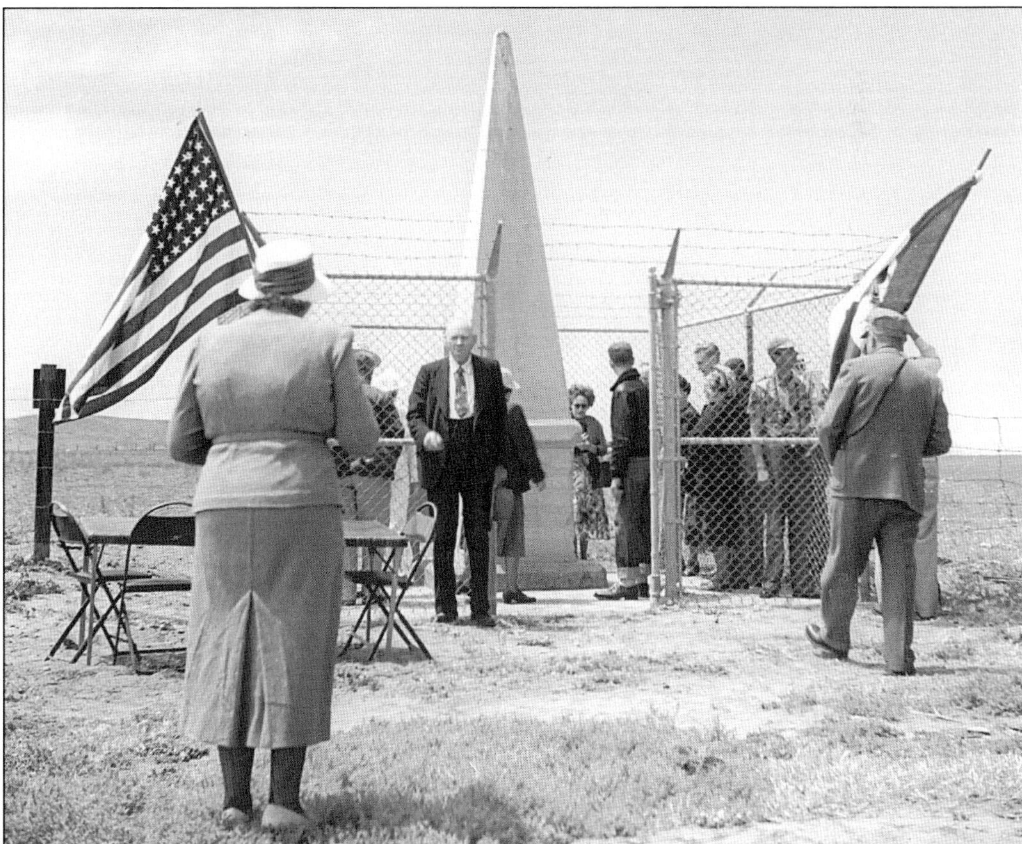

On July 17, 1951, the San Diego Historical Society held a 100th anniversary celebration to honor boundary monument No. 258 along the Pacific Ocean. The Navy gave the historical society permission to host the event. Participants were encouraged to swim in the ocean back and forth between the two countries. San Diego Historical Museum director John Davidson stands in front of the gate. (CSDDP.)

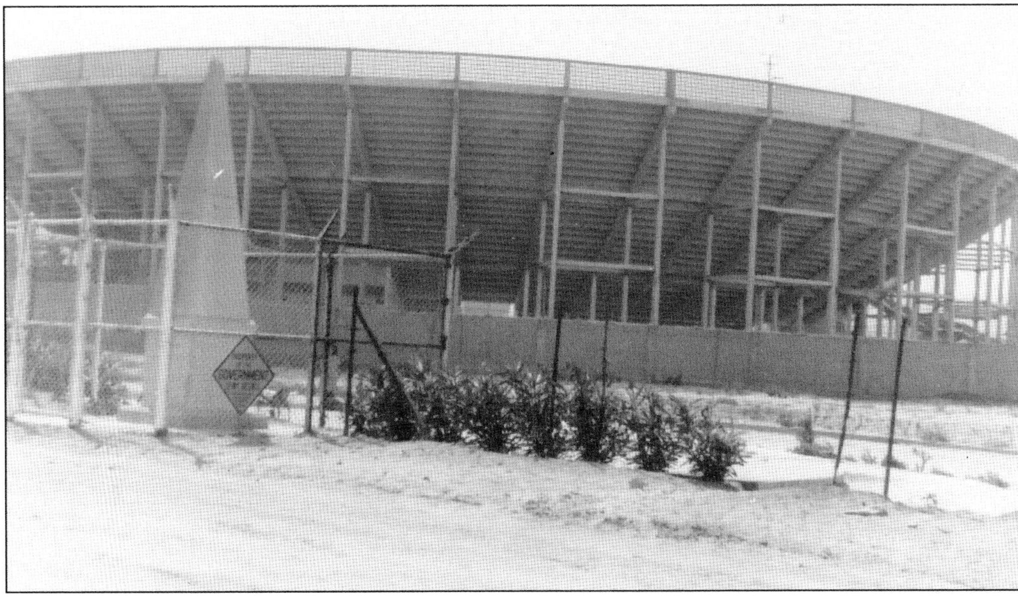

In 1961, Border Field was deactivated as a naval base. One year before, Tijuana mayor J. Salvador Lopez-Hurtado helped initiate construction on the Plaza de Toros Monumental de Tijuana, or Bullring by the Sea. The stadium, which held 21,621 spectators and stood only 60 meters away from the boundary monument, was built in 116 days. The stadium, which became the second largest bullring in Mexico, was inaugurated on June 26, 1961, and today is used for bull-fighting, concerts, and other events. (California State Parks.)

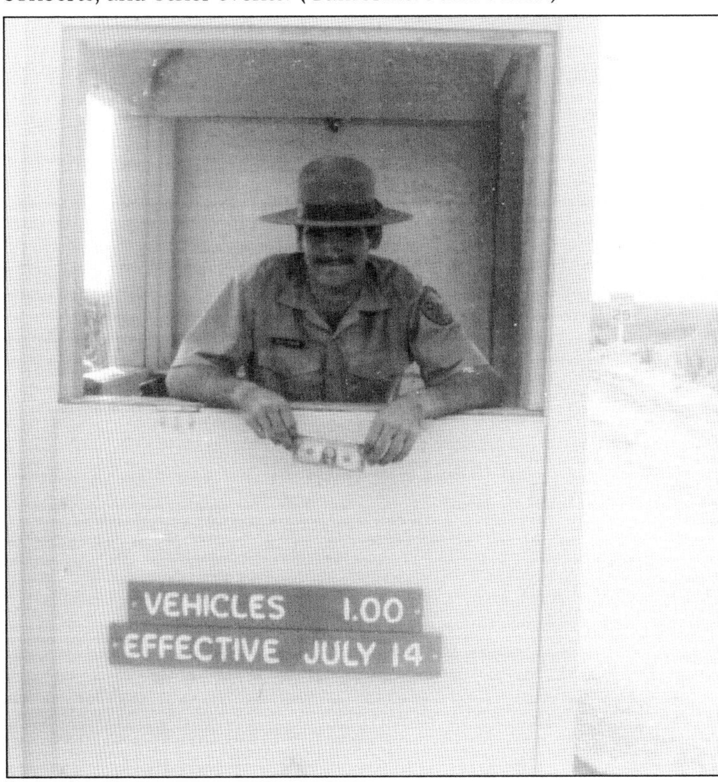

In 1971, the Navy turned Border Field over to the California State Parks and Recreation Department. In this picture, park aide Mike Hudson poses with the first dollar received at Border Field State Beach on July 14, 1973. It took six years for the park to be prepared for visitors. Thereafter, the obelisk was accessible to visitors again after several decades behind Navy boundaries. (California State Parks.)

Eight

Grassroots Movements

Throughout the 1940s and 1950s, prices skyrocketed for the San Ysidro Irrigation District. Operating costs were high, and the town was in constant debt. In 1957, several San Ysidro community leaders obtained the required signatures from 25 percent of residents, and then the San Diego City Council voted to annex the town. According to some, developers wanted San Ysidro annexed in order to construct residential units on open farmland. Others maintained that San Ysidro's taxes were not able to cover the costs of a police station, a fire station, and other municipal services. Ultimately, most agreed that the town could not meet the increased demand for water, so they sought help from San Diego.

San Ysidro was not linked to San Diego by land; the distance between the two cities was 17 miles, with Chula Vista and National City between them. At first, annexation seemed to have little effect upon the small-town community. Then, in 1964, when the federal government ended the bracero program, illegal immigrants began to cross the border in larger numbers and remained in America permanently. Spanish-speakers became the majority in San Ysidro, which, according to many residents, coincided with fewer services provided by the City of San Diego. Grassroots movements arose to address these issues.

By the 1970s, developers once again took an interest in boundary monument No. 258; they hoped to build an upscale marina around the Pacific Ocean and the Tijuana River Valley. Biologists and environmentalists protested the potential ecological destruction, and after a decade of fighting, they managed to preserve what is now the largest coastal wetland in Southern California.

However, fragmentation still marked this period due to the construction of major freeways, which cut through the town and split the community—San Ysidro was no longer a "Mayberry." The devaluation of the peso in the 1980s sent San Ysidro into a severe economic crisis. Then, in 1984, San Ysidro was forever affected by a tragic massacre in a McDonald's that, at the time, was the largest mass shooting by a lone gunman in history.

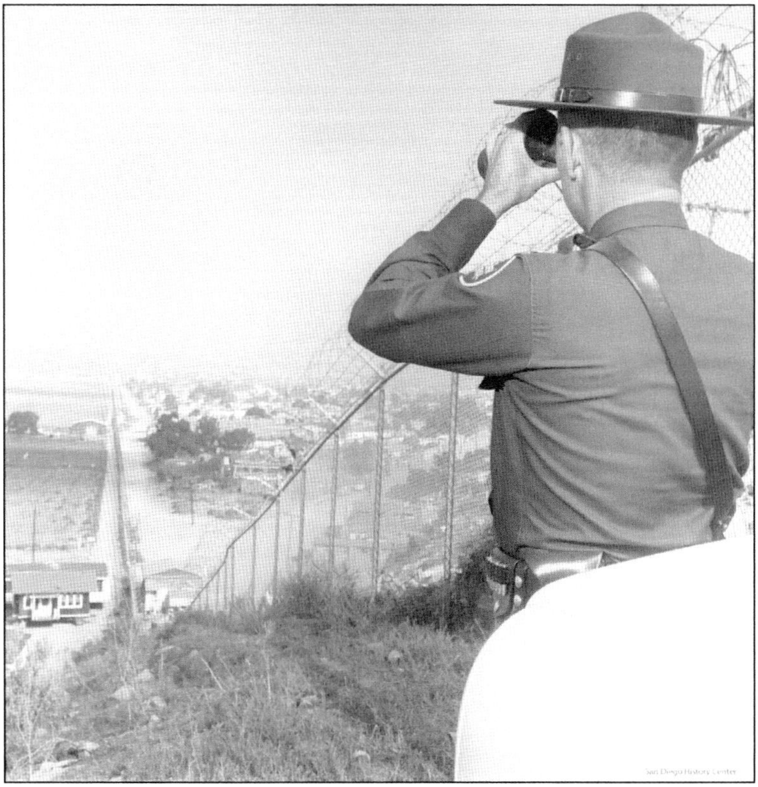

On July 7, 1955, *Bay Cities Press* reported that a 22,000-foot-long chain-link fence was being erected at the border to protect unauthorized crossings from Mexico into the United States (and vice versa). The fence was 14 feet high, with eight strands of concertina wire on top. Eventually, the report said, the fence would extend to the Pacific Ocean. This picture shows the border fence in 1962. (SDHC.)

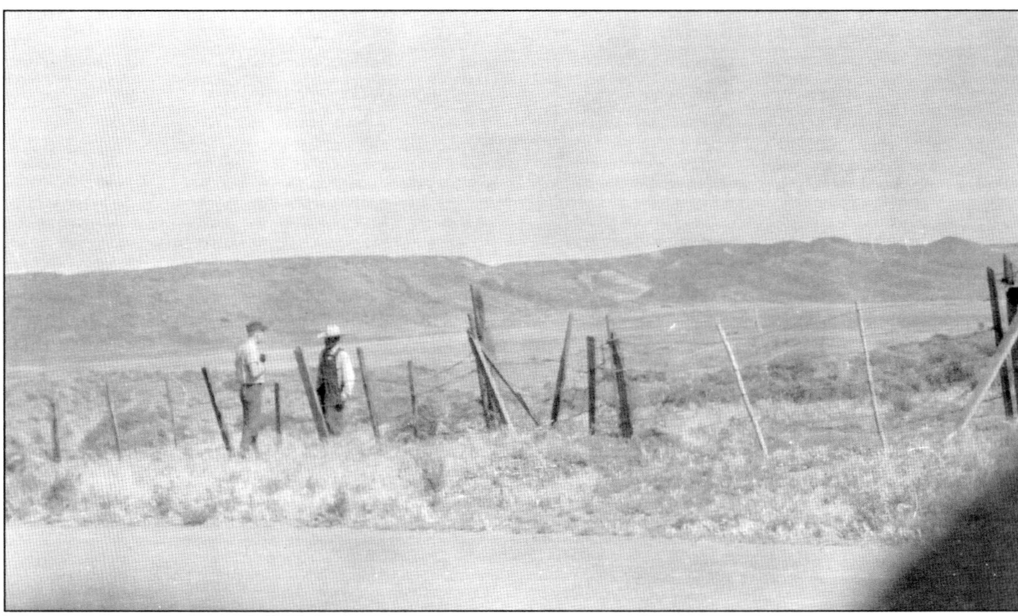

The fence near the marble obelisk still remained composed of only five strands of wire connected together by steel posts. In these areas, the boundary fence was the same as it had been since 1911, when customs officials complained about animals crossing the international line. In this 1957 photograph, a sailor talks to a Mexican farmer across the border fence in the Tijuana River Valley. (California State Parks.)

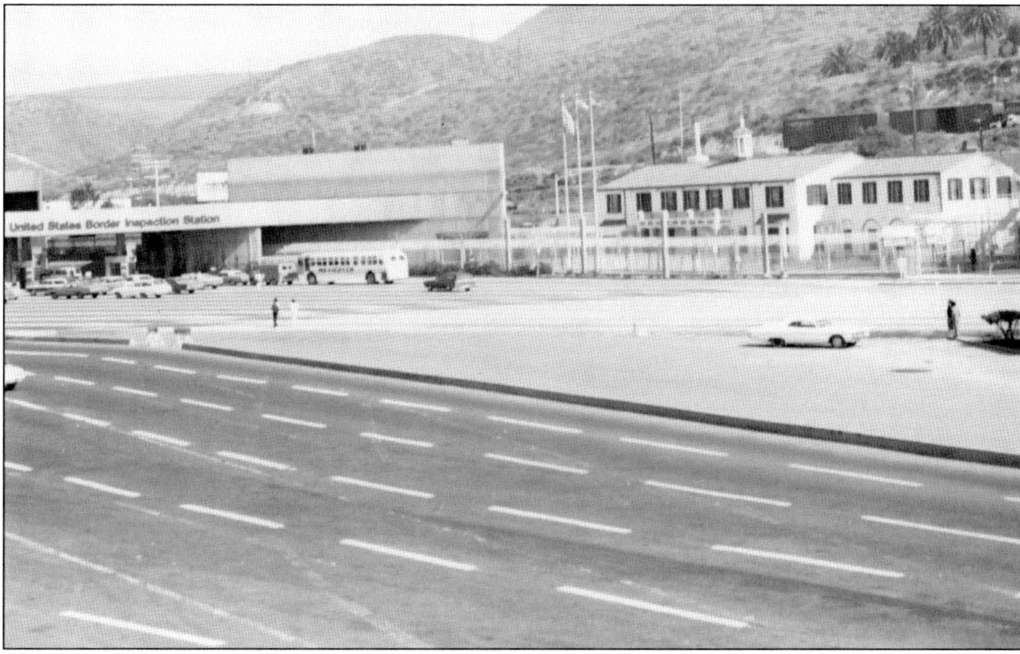

In 1957, the city of San Diego annexed San Ysidro. At first, very little changed in the daily lives of residents. The US Customs Port of Entry at San Ysidro officially became part of the Port of San Diego. In this picture, the old customhouse is at right. The customhouse is now listed in the National Register of Historic Places. (Miguel Guerrero, Joyce Hettich Collection.)

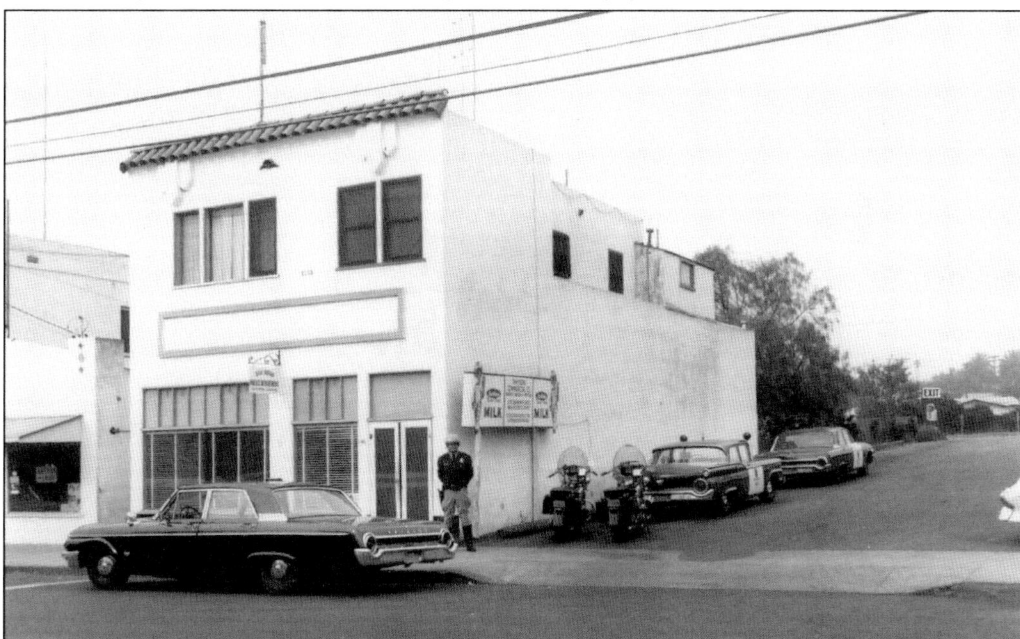

Annexation meant that instead of a local sheriff who knew everyone in town, the San Diego Police now protected and served San Ysidro residents. In this 1962 picture, the first southern division police station has already been constructed in the center of town at 141 West San Ysidro Boulevard. (SDPHA.)

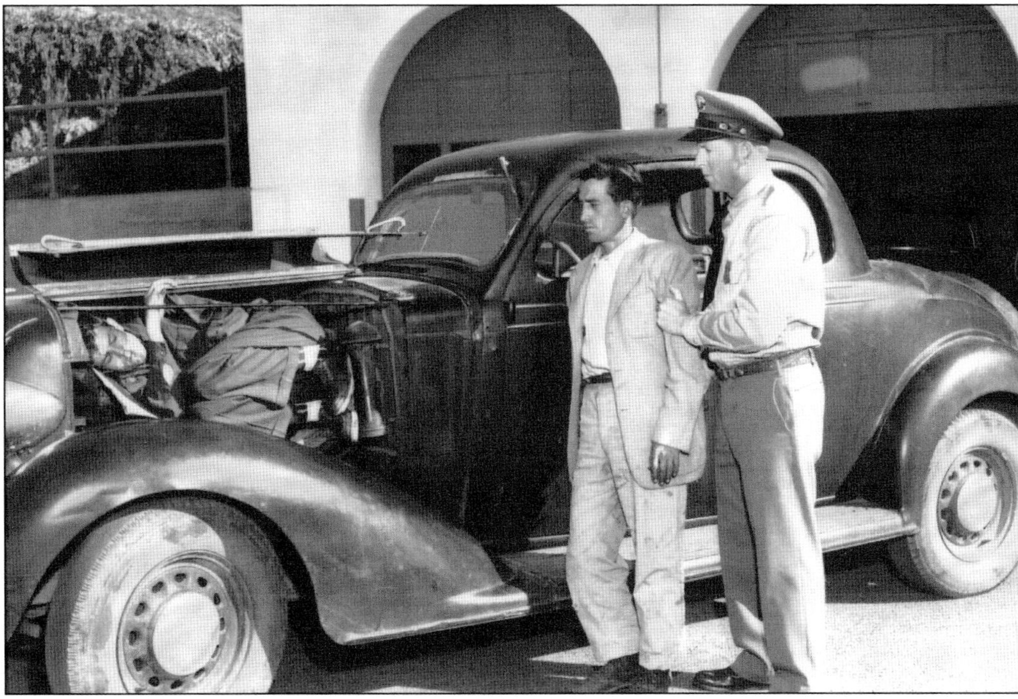

The end of the bracero program in 1964 had a large impact on the community. While the program was in effect, about 450,000 guest workers came into the United States legally each year—a total of about 4.5 million workers over the 22-year existence of the program. After the bracero program ended, migrants came across the border illegally. In this well-known photograph, a border patrol agent is arresting a man for human smuggling. (Evelyn Sevel.)

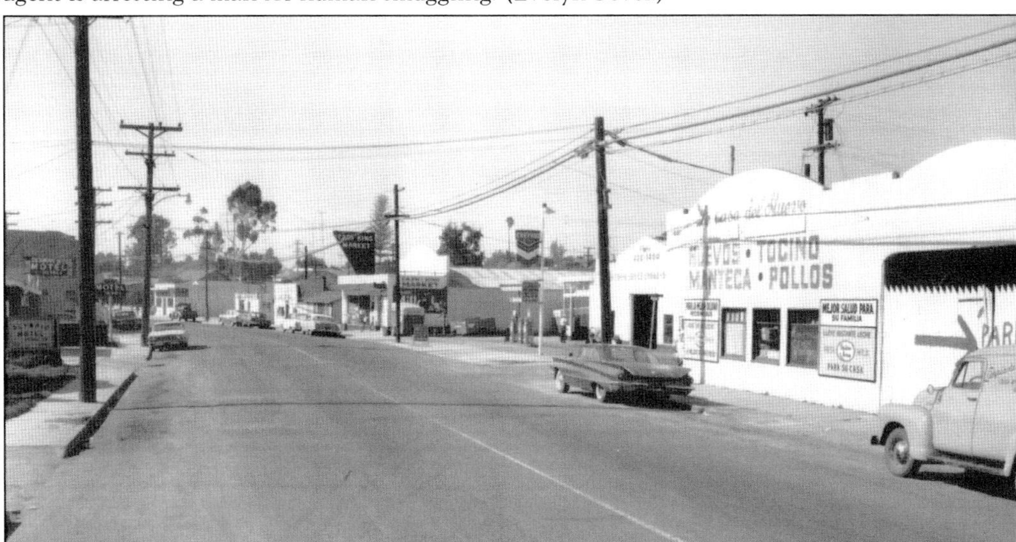

During the bracero program, which was in effect from 1942 to 1964, only about eight percent of immigrants remained as residents in San Diego (and San Ysidro); most returned to their homes at the end of their guest worker contracts. However, when the bracero program ended, immigrants tended to stay. During the 1960s, sixty percent of San Ysidro residents—in a community of 3,000—spoke Spanish. This picture shows Spanish/English signs along the road. (Evelyn Sevel.)

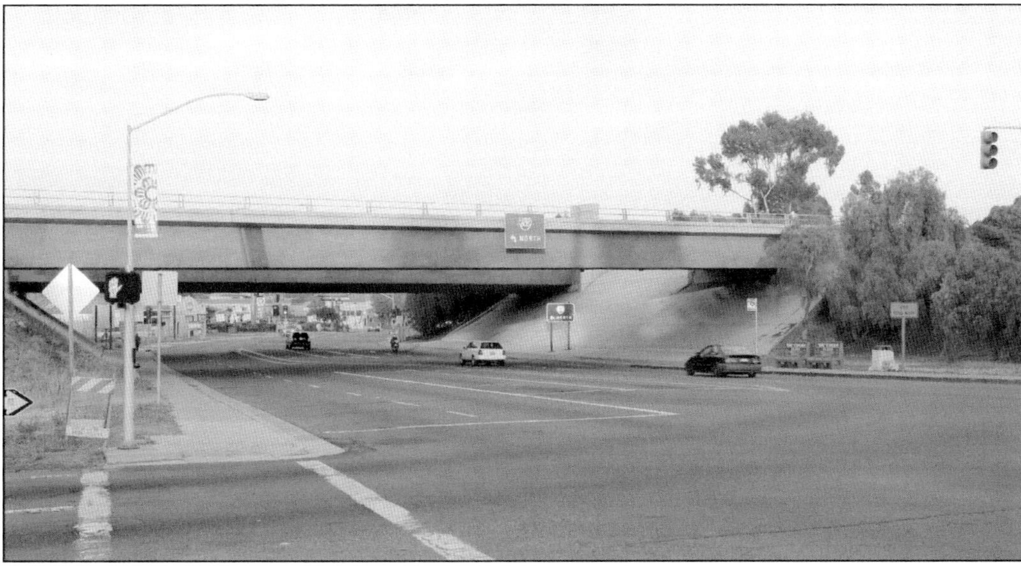

During the 1950s and 1960s, developers conceived grand plans, including a Skyride from San Ysidro to Tijuana, an upscale marina at the Pacific Ocean, and San Diego's application for a Model Cities Planning Program for San Ysidro. Although many plans never came to fruition, the construction of freeways running to the border heavily impacted the community. In 1951, the John J. Montgomery freeway (now Interstate 5) was built, which caused the razing of the Argüello family's historic La Punta home. In 1967, ground was broken for the Interstate 805 freeway. The City displaced hundreds of residents and businesses, including Cuen's Feed Store, which moved into this old US Customs garage (pictured below). Robert Egger's community center also moved. Interstate 805 was completed in 1975, with the freeway cutting through San Ysidro Boulevard and ending the area's small-town feel.

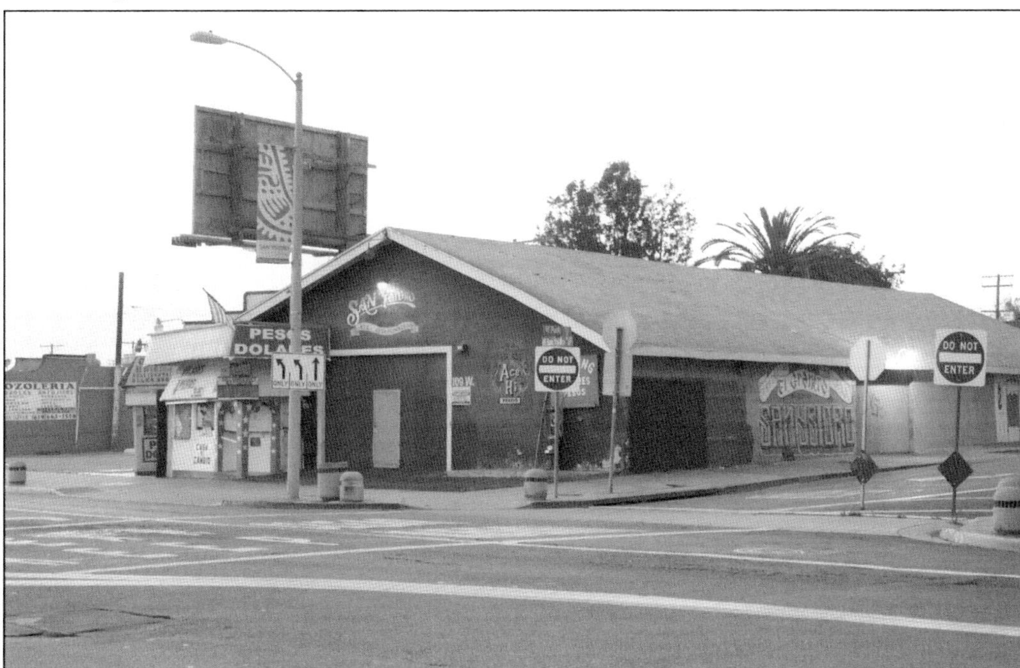

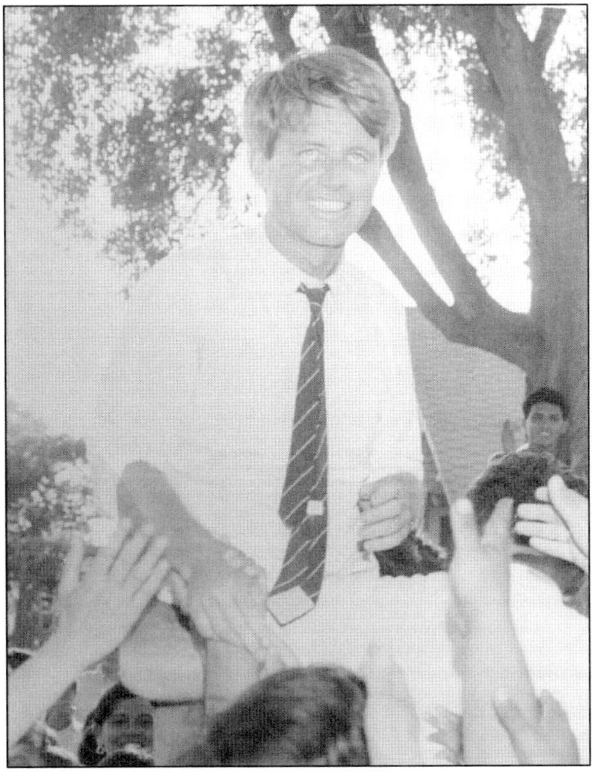

The San Ysidro community became an essential political focal point, as shown in these pictures, when Robert (Bobby) F. Kennedy visited the town on June 3, 1968. Campaigning for president on a platform of civil rights, Kennedy worked closely with activists such as Cesar Chavez. The Latino vote particularly important, these pictures show the large crowd of San Ysidro supporters who came out to shake hands with Kennedy. Two days later, he was assassinated in Los Angeles by Sirhan Sirhan. (Both, Jaime Mercado.)

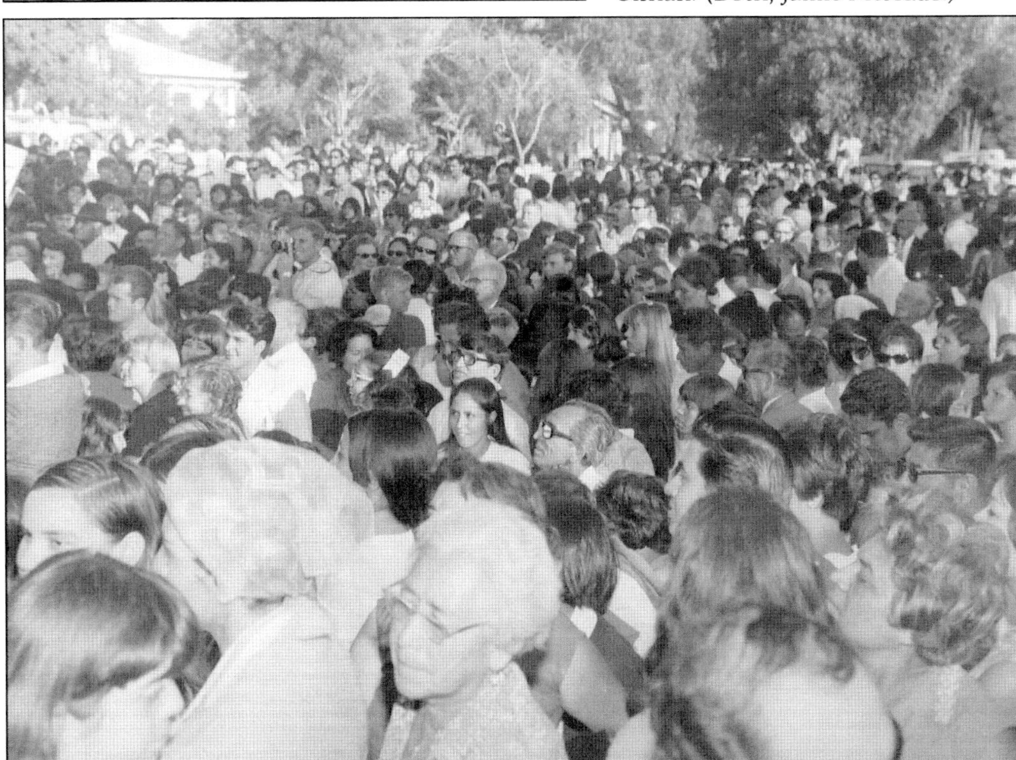

By 1969, the Hispanic population in San Ysidro had grown to encompass 80 percent of the town's residents. With the 1960s in full swing, recognition of immigration issues translated into grassroots movements. In San Ysidro, only one doctor was available for 7,000 residents. Many had to go to Tijuana to receive care until a concerned group of women created El Club de Madres and, through community support, opened "La Casita." Located in a small, wood frame house at 223 Mesa Road, the health clinic began with only three nurses and two physicians who volunteered twice a week in the afternoons. Thanks to ongoing promotion and generous donors, the clinic expanded and grew, eventually moving to a larger facility at 4004 Beyer Boulevard, where it remains today. (Both, San Ysidro Health Center.)

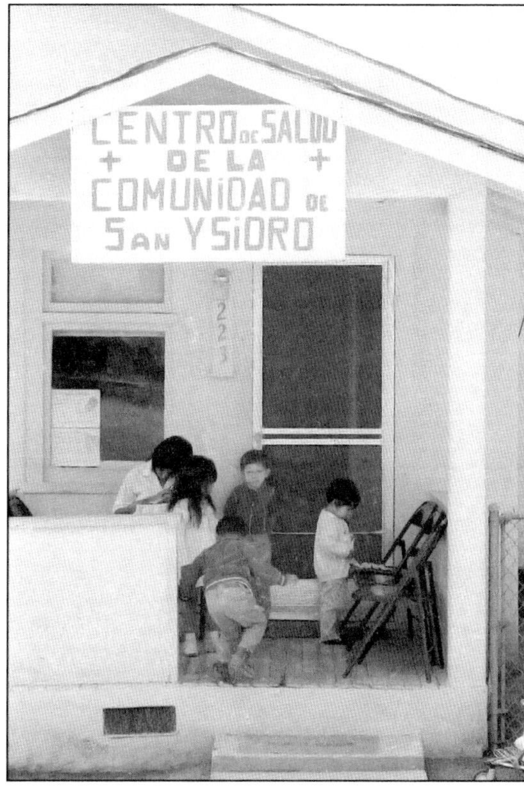

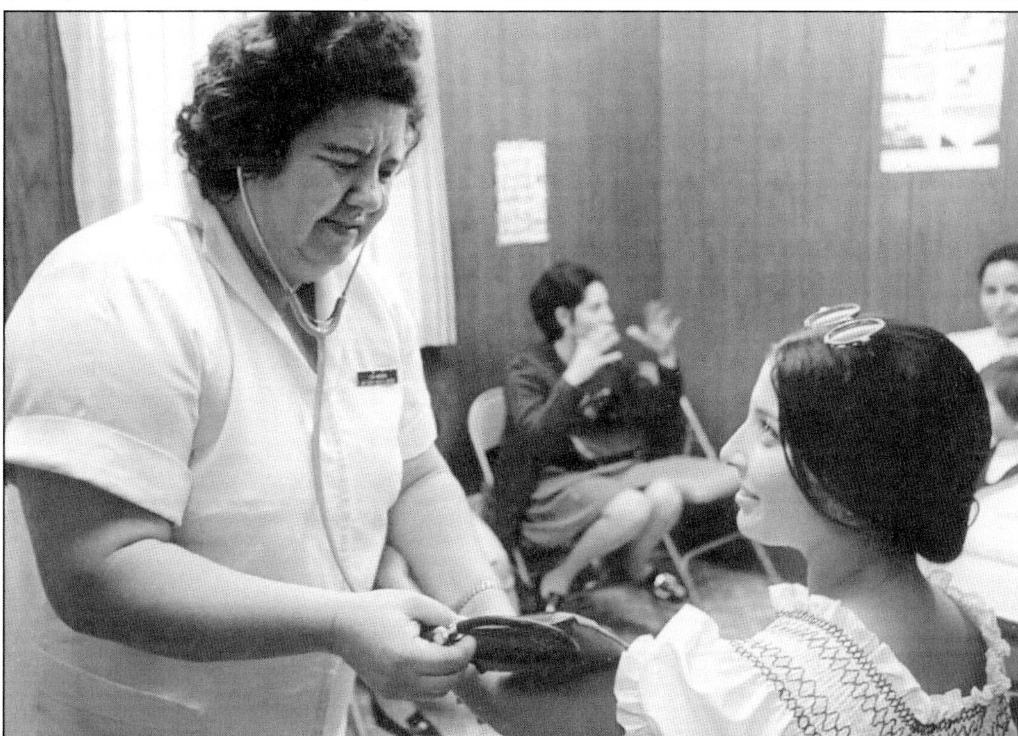

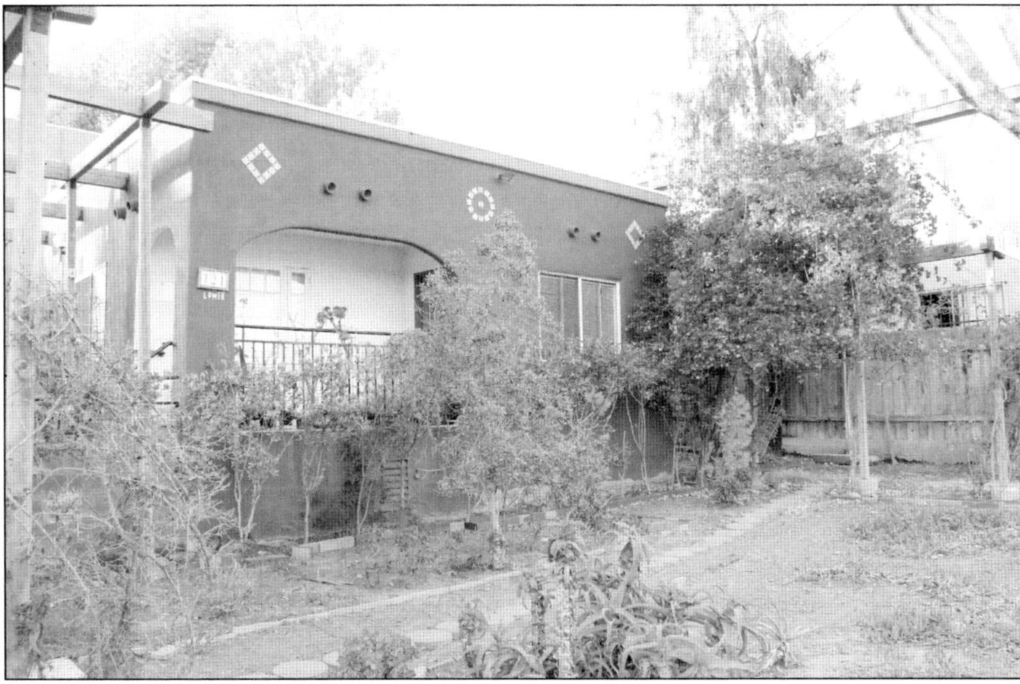

A statewide organization of Latino social workers called Trabajadores de la Raza began operations in 1968. They incorporated in 1972, changing the organization's name to Casa Familiar, and ran an alternative mental health facility for monolingual Spanish speakers. The group's original offices were in this building in the heart of Little Landers. The building is still owned by Casa Familiar but has been converted into low-income housing for the elderly. (Author.)

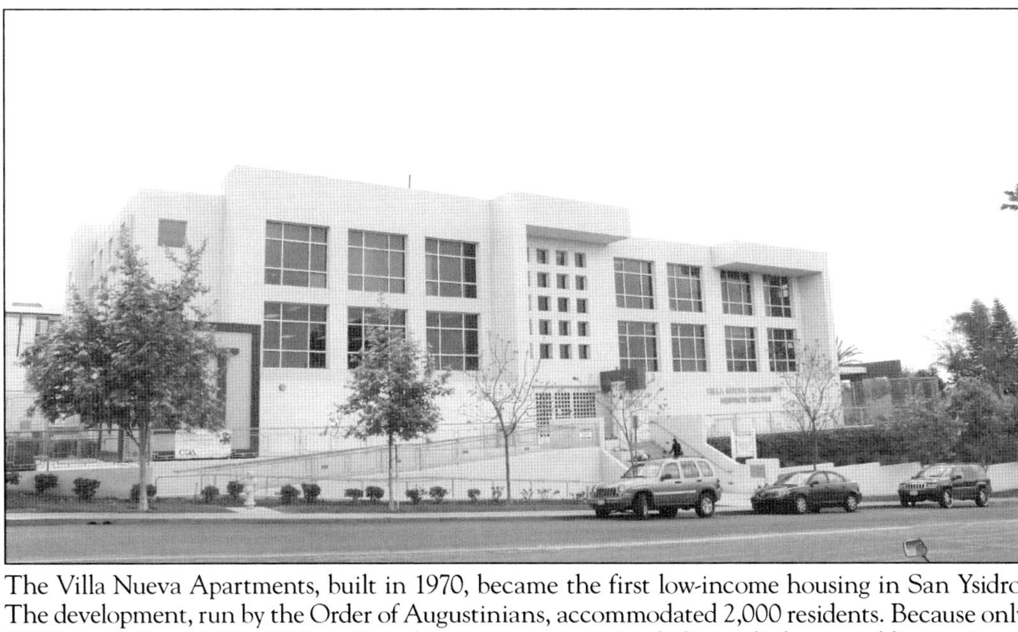

The Villa Nueva Apartments, built in 1970, became the first low-income housing in San Ysidro. The development, run by the Order of Augustinians, accommodated 2,000 residents. Because only 7,000 people lived in San Ysidro, when these newcomers arrived, the media began to blame a rise in drugs and gang-related activities to this complex. This picture shows the newly renovated building, which is now home to the main offices of the nonprofit organization Casa Familiar. (Author.)

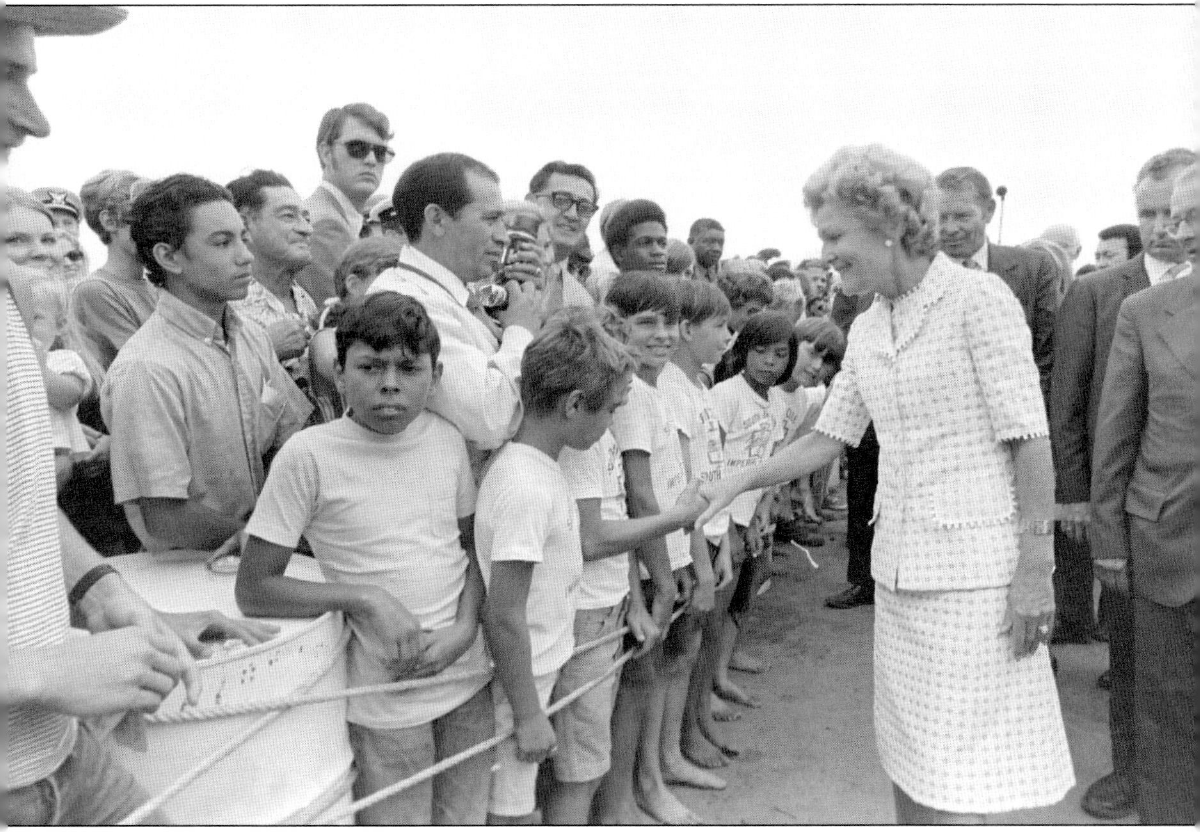

First Lady Pat Nixon came to Border Field State Park on August 18, 1971, and dedicated the land surrounding monument No. 258, calling it Friendship Park. She recognized the multinational use of the land and stated, "I hope there won't be a fence here too long." (National Archives and Records Administration.)

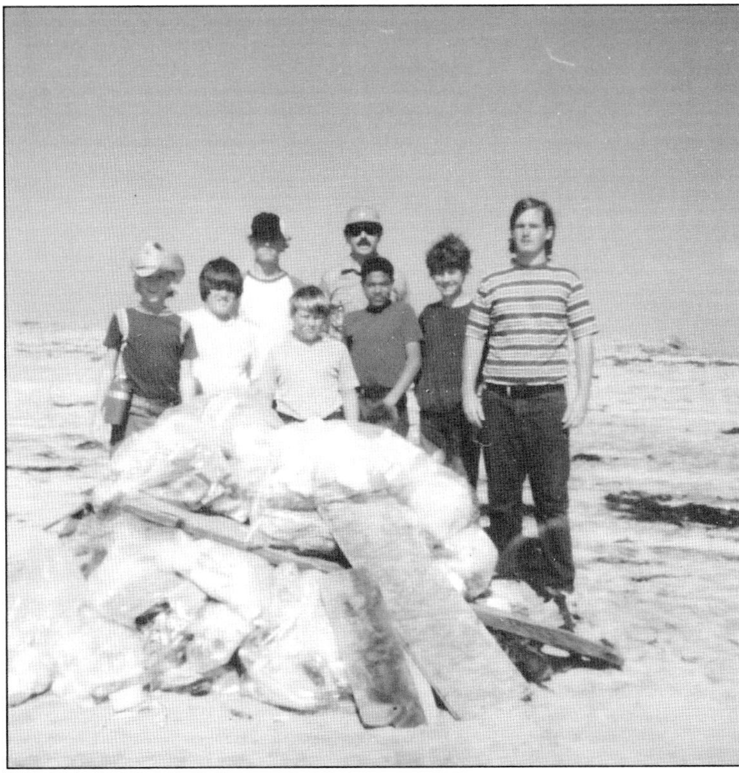

Although the Navy handed 372 acres of property over to the State of California for use as a park in 1971, five years later, newspapers reported that the area lay in waste. The Boy Scouts set up camp along the boundary line and began a cleanup of the area. Here, Boy Scouts stand next to the trash they collected. (California State Parks.)

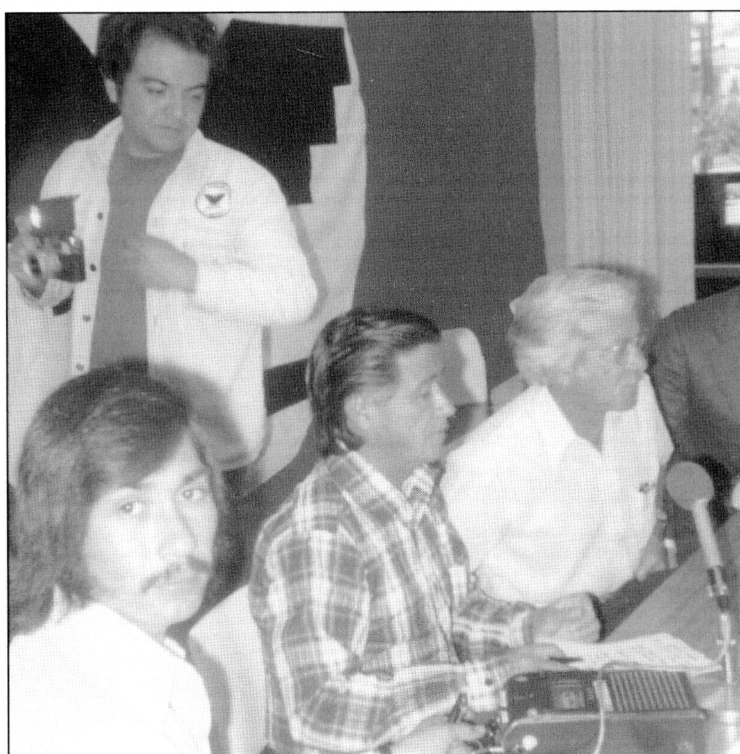

The 1970s also saw a rise in the Chicano movement in San Ysidro. American farm worker and civil rights activist Cesar Chavez came to the San Ysidro Community Park by the civic center to give talks. In this particular picture (from left to right) San Ysidro activist Carlos Perez, Cesar Chavez and tomato rancher Samuel Vener sign a farm-working contract in 1977. (Carlos and Juanita Perez via Guille Perez.)

Developers began to lobby the federal government to turn Border Field State Park into an upscale marina. Local biologists noted the importance of preserving the Tijuana Estuary, and a decade-long struggle began. Dr. Mike McCoy, a veterinarian, and his wife, Imperial Beach councilwoman Patricia McCoy (pictured at right with Mike), along with other biologists, spearheaded an environmental movement against urban sprawl to save marine wildlife. In 1980, the US Fish and Wildlife Service bought 500 acres of the estuary and established the Tijuana Slough National Wildlife Refuge along the Pacific Flyway. Today, the refuge is the largest coastal wetland in Southern California not crossed by a freeway and is home to a number of endangered species. The 1980 image below offers an aerial view of the preserved Tijuana estuary and the river valley. (Right, Mike and Patricia McCoy; below, California State Parks.)

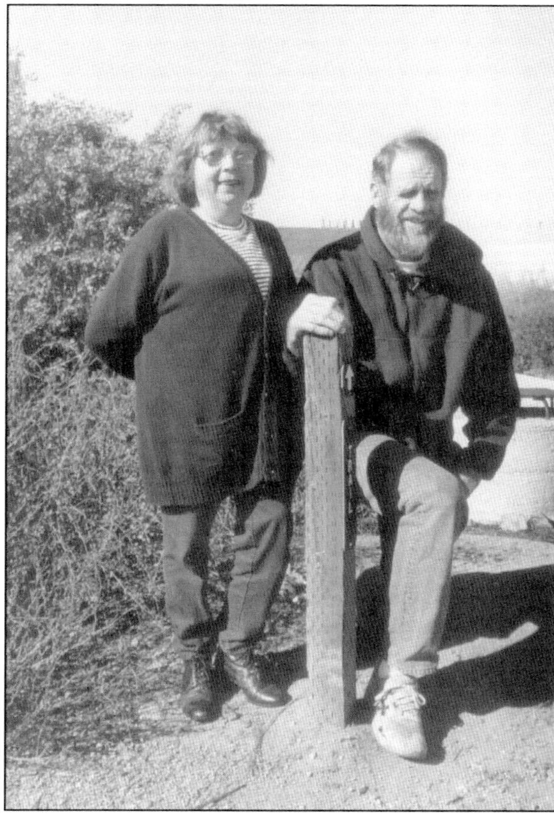

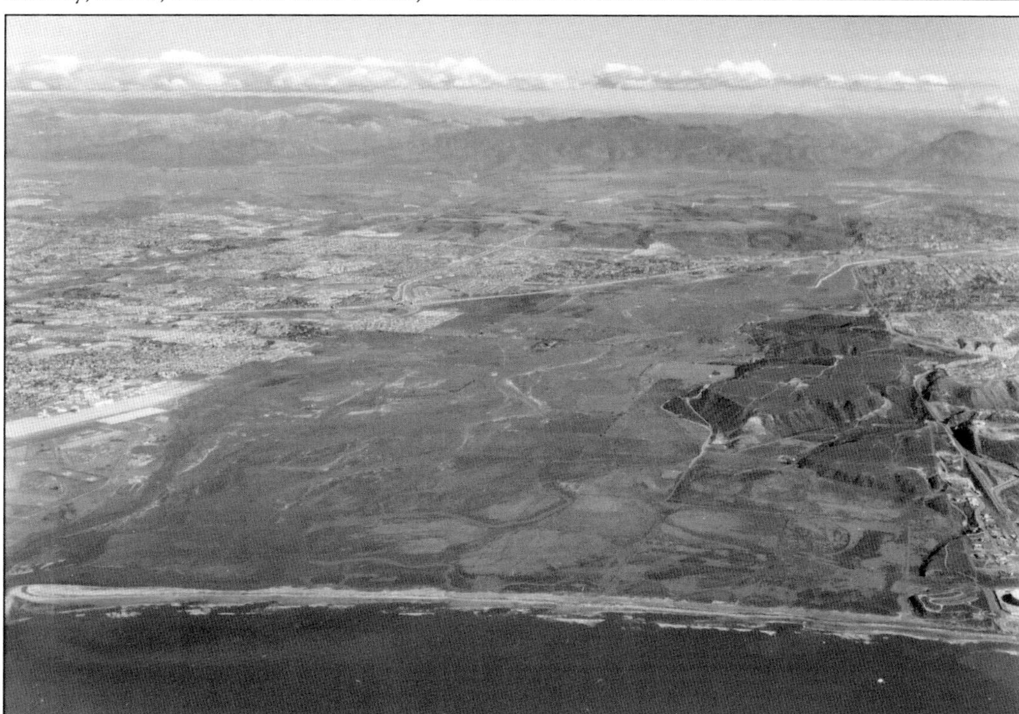

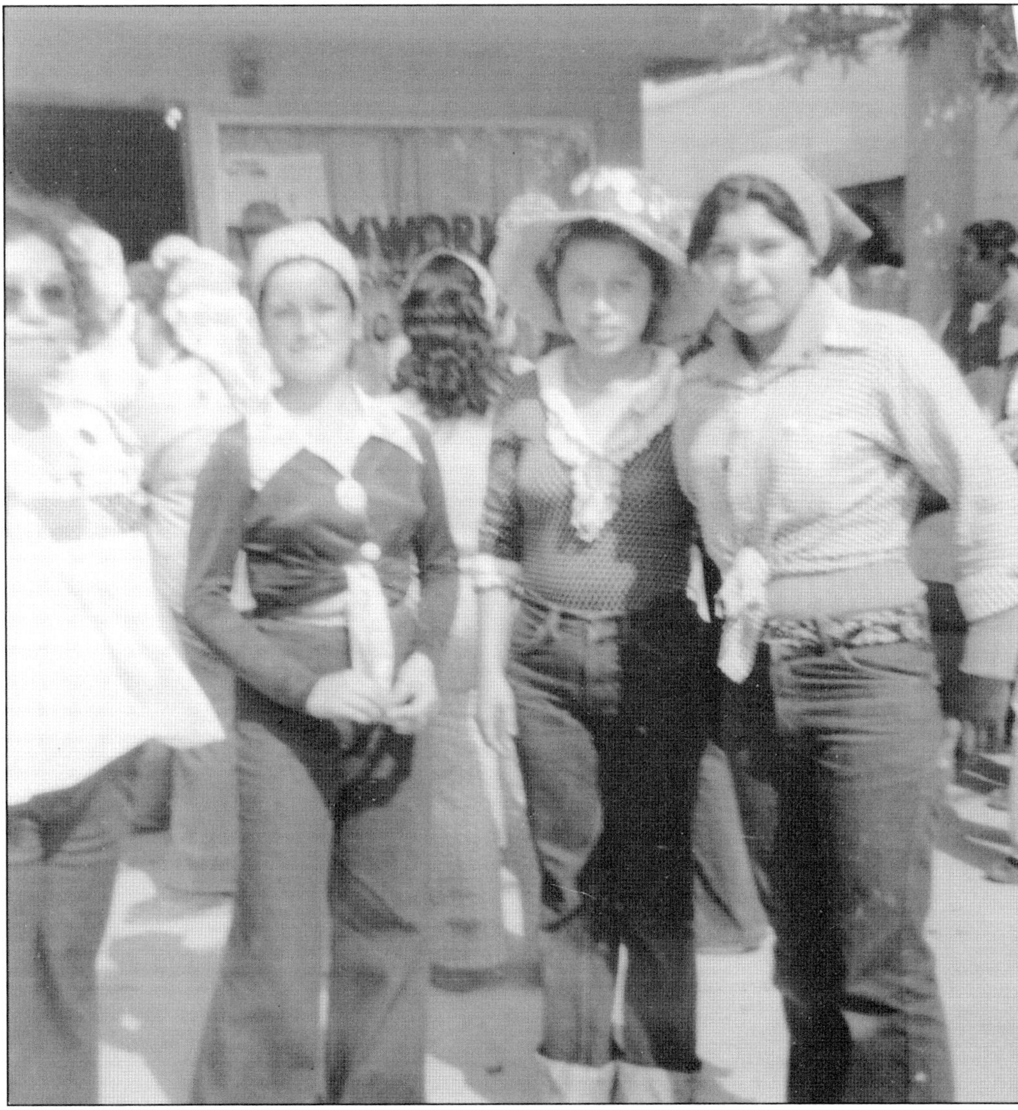

In this picture, Juanita Ruiz (second from the left) stands in front of the United Farm Workers (UFW) Service Center with her friends. She went on to marry Carlos Perez. This UFW office was located in the heart of downtown San Ysidro. By the 1970s, many farm workers of Mexican descent lived in San Ysidro. (Carlos and Juanita Perez via Guille Perez.)

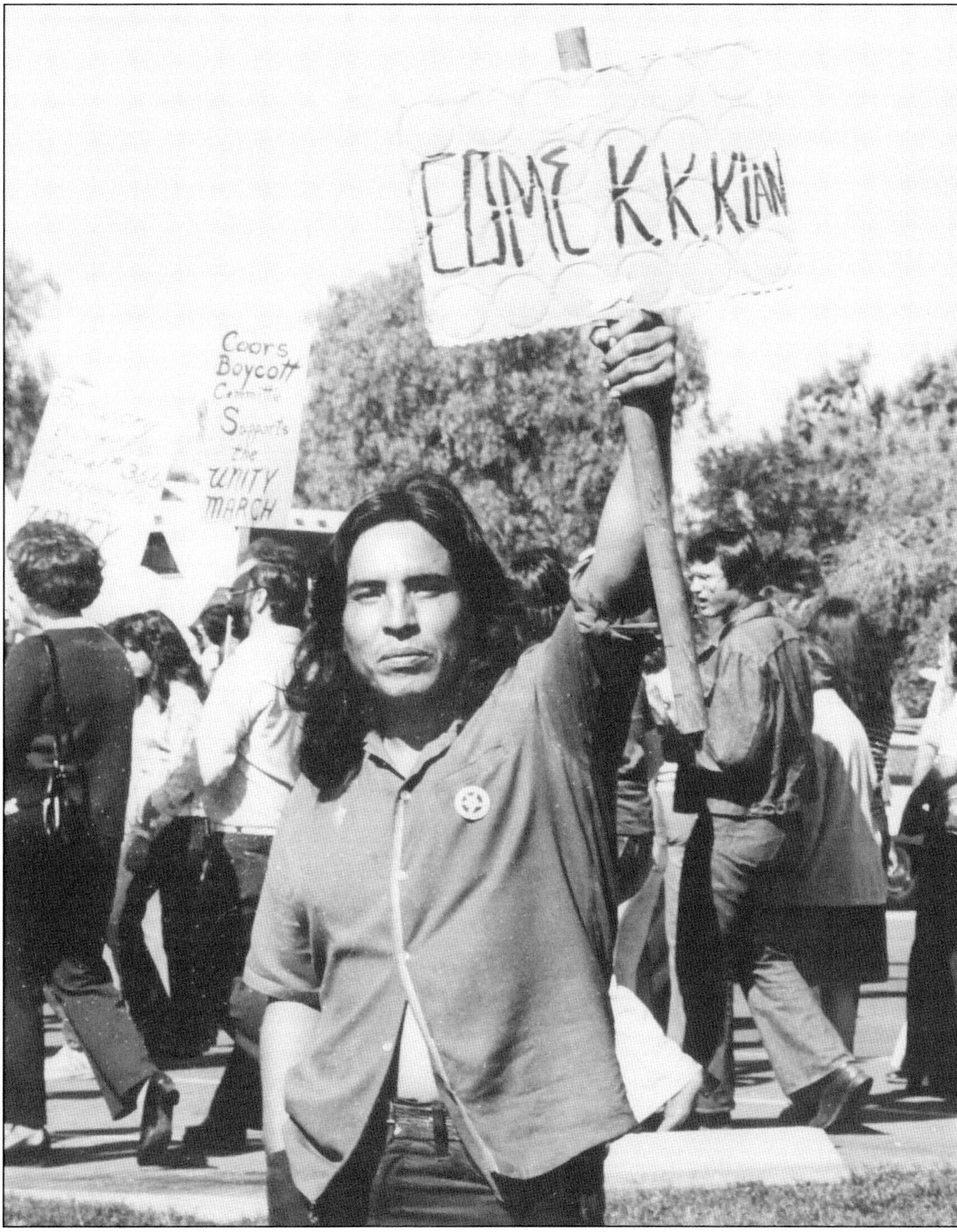

Another local South Bay Chicano activist, Herman Baca, launched demonstrations along the border. On October 29, 1977, demonstrators gathered near the San Ysidro Port of Entry to protest the presence of the Ku Klux Klan. (Herman Baca Papers, Mandeville Special Collections Library, University of California, San Diego.)

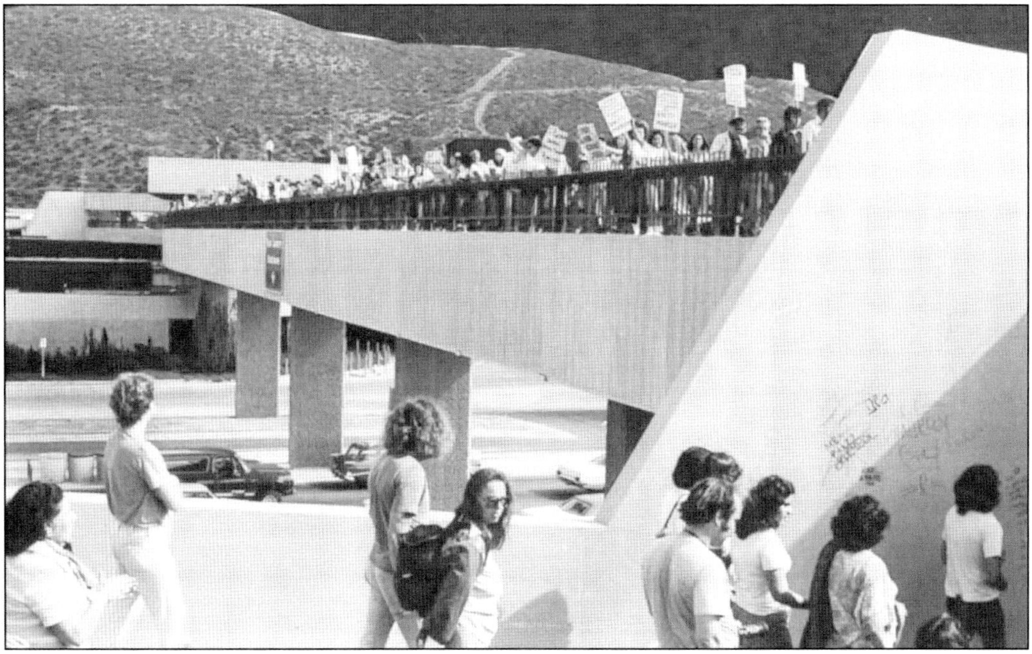

Herman Baca organized a gathering of more than 2,500 people at another rally at the border to protest the Carter Curtain on February 11, 1979. Baca, the owner of a print shop in National City and Chairman of the Committee of Chicano Rights (CCR), worked closely with Cesar Chavez and other Latino activists. (Herman Baca Papers, Mandeville Special Collections Library, University of California, San Diego.)

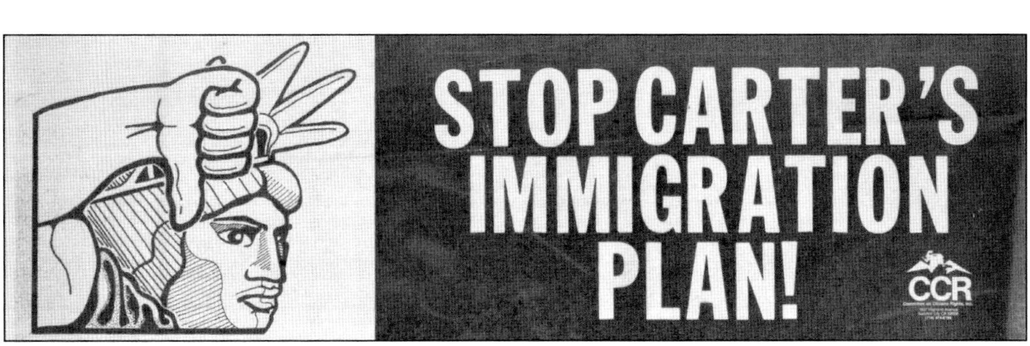

Protesters felt that if the United States kept an open border with Canada, the same treatment should be given to the border with Mexico. They also wanted to protect the human rights of undocumented aliens. (Herman Baca Papers, Mandeville Special Collections Library, University of California, San Diego.)

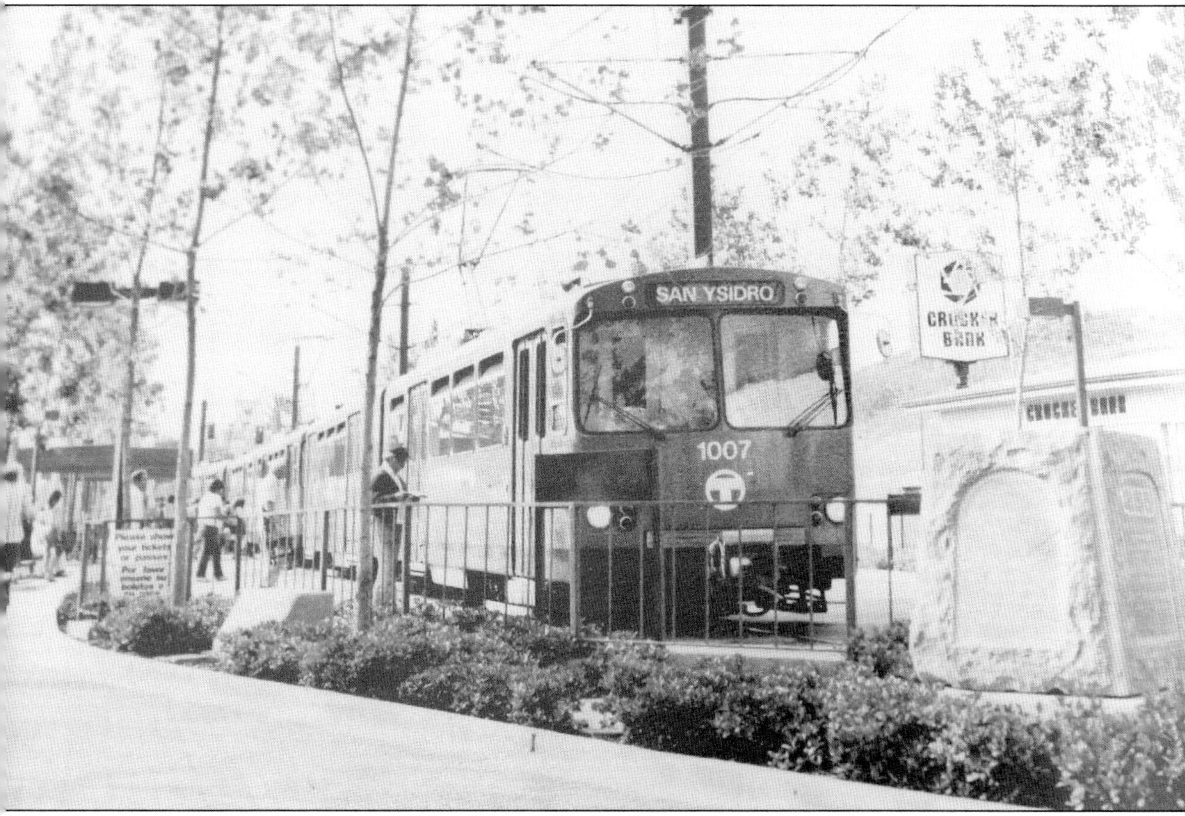

Many San Ysidro residents held out hopes that the border area would become a tourist destination. Developers constructed shopping centers such as Border Village, and construction began on the San Ysidro trolley station. During the trolley's inaugural week, which began on July 19, 1981, passengers could ride the trolley for free. (W.C. Whittaker photograph found in Robert M. Hanft's *San Diego & Arizona: The Impossible Railroad.)*

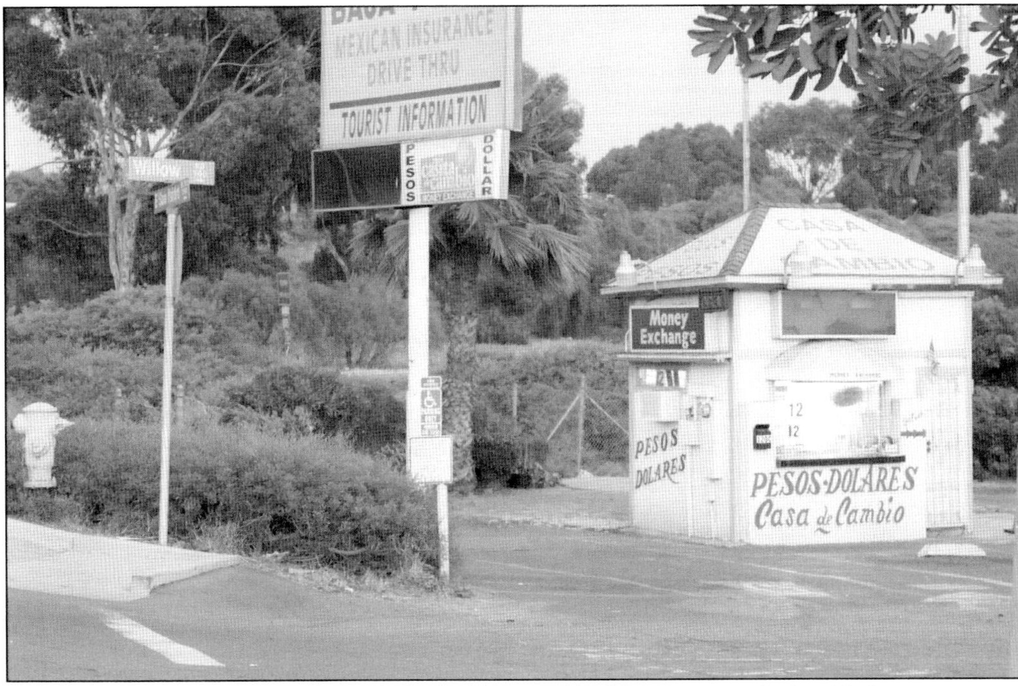

The devaluation of the Mexican peso dashed hopes of building an upscale San Ysidro community. In 1976, and again in 1982, the peso lost at least 50 percent of its value. Prior to that, 60 percent of all local sales were made to Mexican national customers, so the devaluations heavily impacted local businesses. With the devaluations, Mexican nationals could no longer afford to buy goods and services in San Ysidro, and the local economy became paralyzed. Unemployment rose to 50 percent. In an attempt to save failing businesses, many San Ysidro businesses converted their establishments partially or in whole to "Casas de Cambios," or money exchanges. During the 1980s, between 50–100 money exchanges existed in town, especially along San Ysidro Boulevard. Several still exist today. (Both, author.)

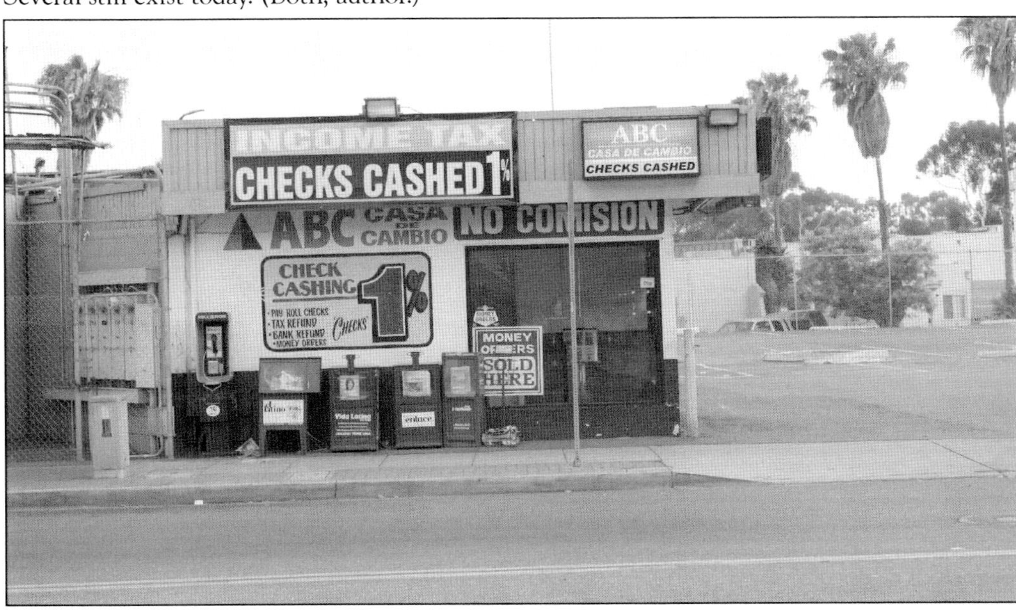

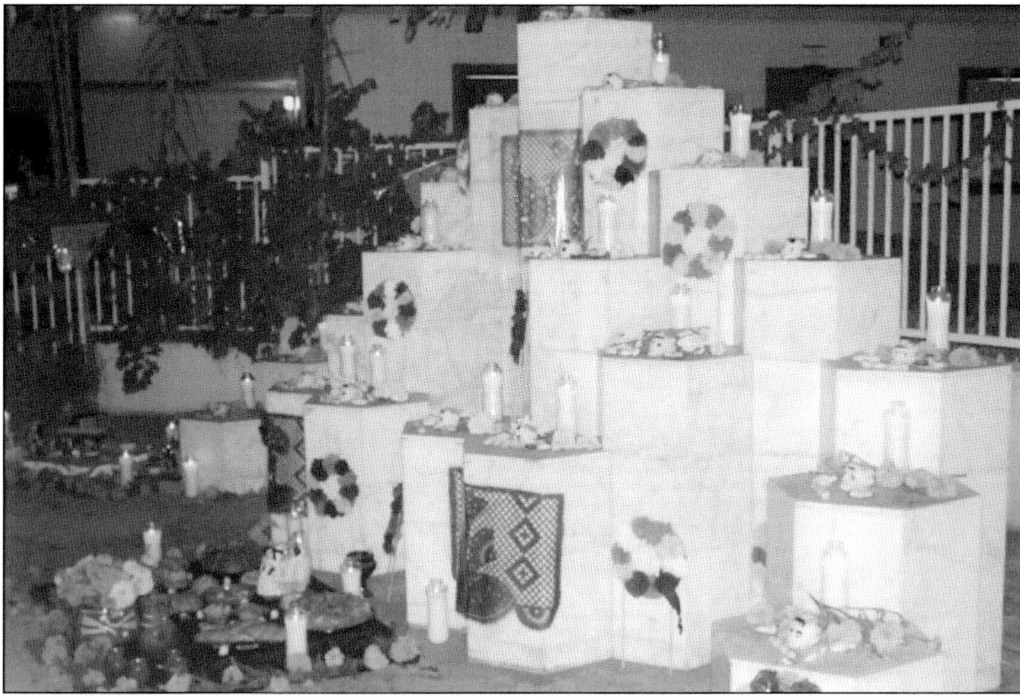

On July 18, 1984, James Oliver Huberty entered a McDonald's restaurant on San Ysidro Boulevard and began shooting to kill. He killed 21 people in the massacre and wounded 19 others; most of the victims were Mexican-Americans. At the time, this was the most deadly mass shooting in the history of the United States. A police sniper eventually killed Huberty. The San Ysidro Civic Center hosted the wakes of the victims, and Our Lady of Mount Carmel church held back-to-back funeral masses. The McDonald's moved to a new location and donated the former property to the city, which established an education center on the site as part of Southwestern Community College. The center began construction in 1988 (pictured below), and Roberto Valdes designed a memorial to the victims consisting of 21 hexagonal white marble pillars (pictured above). Every year on July 18, the monument is decorated with flowers. Candles are also lit on behalf of the victims each October on the Mexican Day of the Dead holiday. (Both, David Flores of Casa Familiar.)

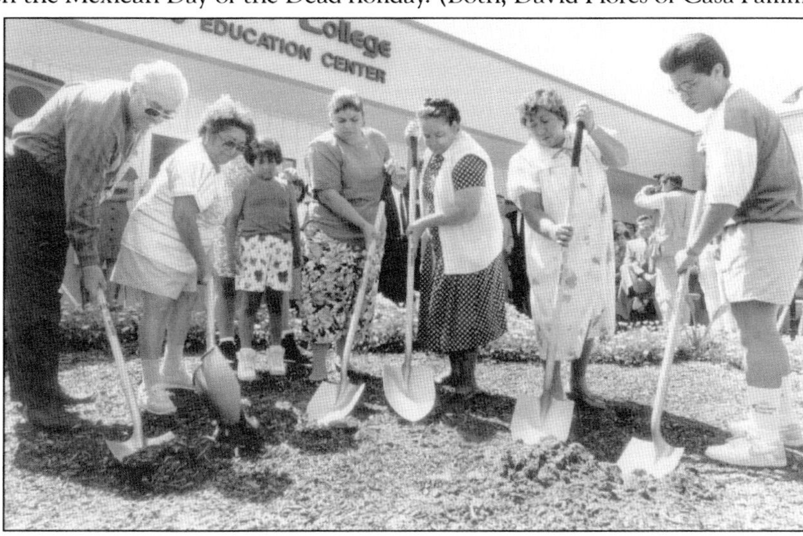

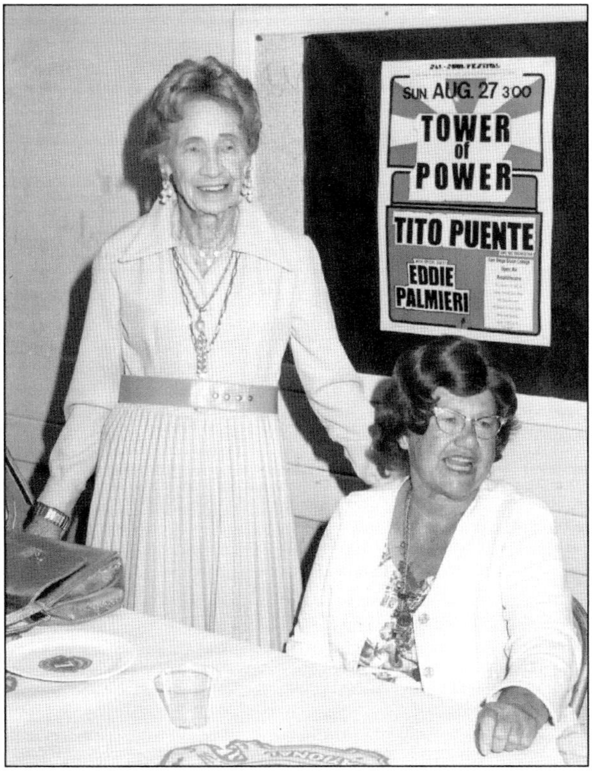

As San Ysidro shifted from a small town to a bustling border with a majority of Hispanic residents, "old-timers" actively participated alongside newcomers in the daily life of San Ysidro and the Tijuana River Valley. Mattie Larson (left) and Joyce Hettich, pictured in 1979 at a Lions Club dinner meeting, were two active members of the community. (Yolanda Gaudet.)

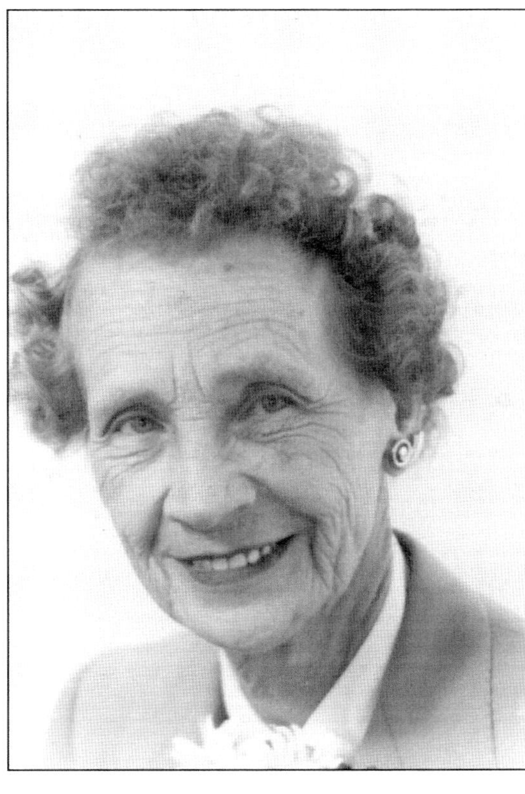

Mattie Larson taught at San Ysidro Elementary School in 1907, left for a time, and returned in 1927, when the town was thriving thanks to horseracing. She bought a house off Pepper Street in 1935. By 1942, she was the principal of San Ysidro Elementary School. She retired in 1952 and continued to participate in community events. (Yolanda Gaudet.)

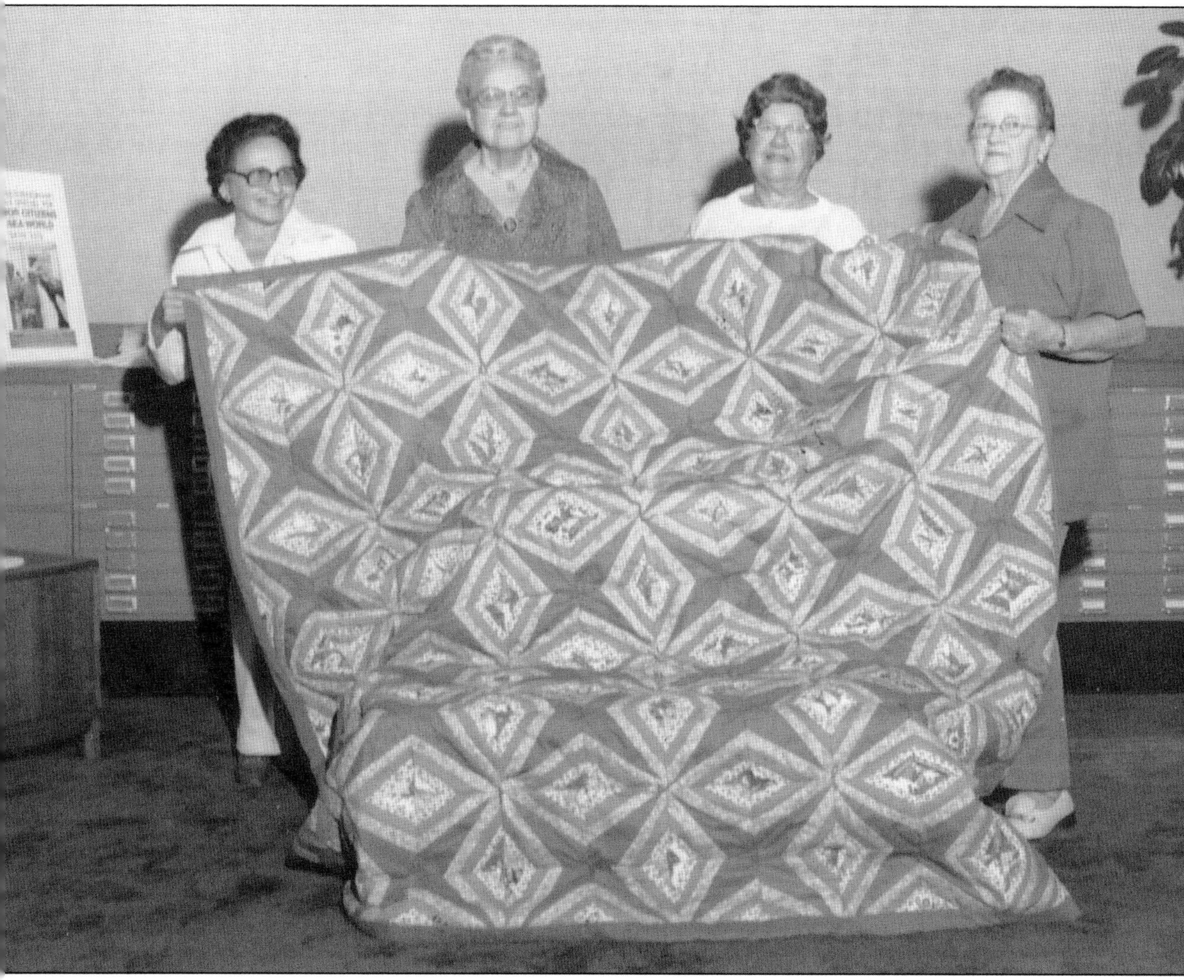

Joyce Hettich (second from right) is pictured here with the San Ysidro Women's Club. She became a member after she began teaching at San Ysidro Elementary School in 1945. She went on to teach at Sunset School and Willow School until her retirement in 1971. Many considered Hettich to be the unofficial historian of San Ysidro. (Miguel Guerrero, Joyce Hettich Collection.)

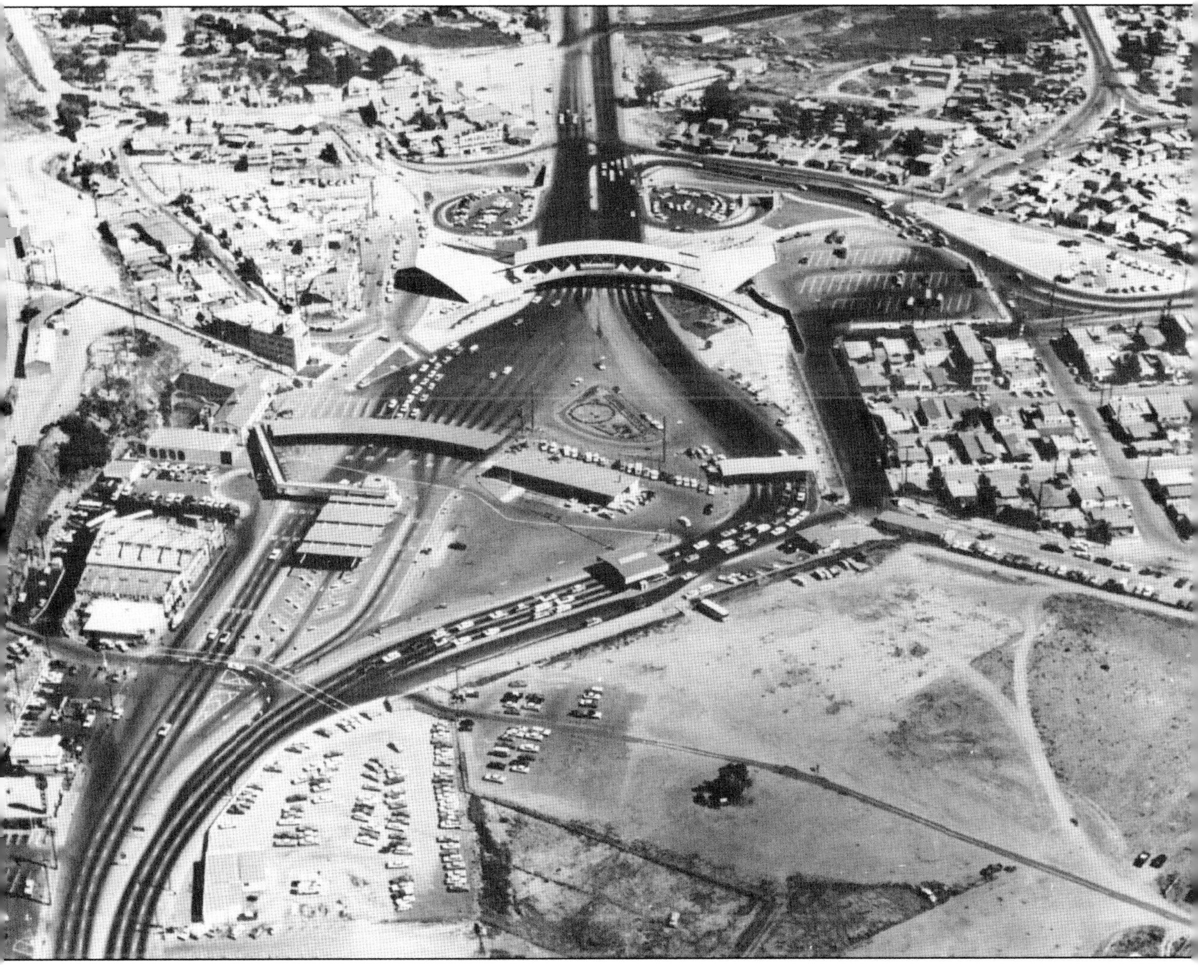

Once the city completed building Interstates 5 and 805, San Ysidro became the largest land port of entry in the world, with an estimated 47 million vehicles passing through each year. This 1980s picture shows the border crossing with the broad interstate roads cutting through the suburban community. (SDPHA.)

Nine

The Fence

San Ysidro is no longer a sleepy town catering to local farmers and passing tourists—it has become the largest port of entry in the world. A grand outlet mall, Las Americas, sprawls along the border wall, while San Ysidro Boulevard is still home to iconic buildings such as El Torredor and the public library.

Although most of the farmers have left the Tijuana River Valley, Suzie's Farms grows more than 100 varieties of fruits and vegetables throughout the year. Many ranches dot the valley up to Border Field State Park and the Tijuana River Valley Regional Park, both of which attempt to preserve the rich ecology of the region. The area also contains the largest protected coastal wetland in Southern California, which comes to an abrupt halt at the boundary fence.

After the terrorist attacks on September 11, 2001, Washington, DC, intensified its focus on securing America's borders. By 2008, the federal government had constructed a double fence along the Tijuana River Valley. Maria Teresa Fernandez, who spent more than a decade photographing the border in this region, noticed that it seemed to be alive, ever growing and reproducing. Fence construction damaged the environment, including Smuggler's Gulch, where the government filled the canyon with 1.3 million cubic yards of dirt with no consideration of the area's plant and animal life. Government-contracted workers were commissioned to have the marble obelisk exist exclusively on the Mexican side. Border patrol continued to increase, as did wait times at the border, causing more concern over high pollution levels, including for children at San Ysidro schools.

Although the border patrol and the fence make visiting the marble obelisk difficult, people on both sides remain undaunted, coming to Friendship Park during opening hours to wave at one another, hold religious services, and even take binational yoga classes. Still, the most daunting issue faced by San Ysidro's residents, farmers, ranchers, and environmentalists alike is the unilateral decision-making by the federal government that impacts their daily lives.

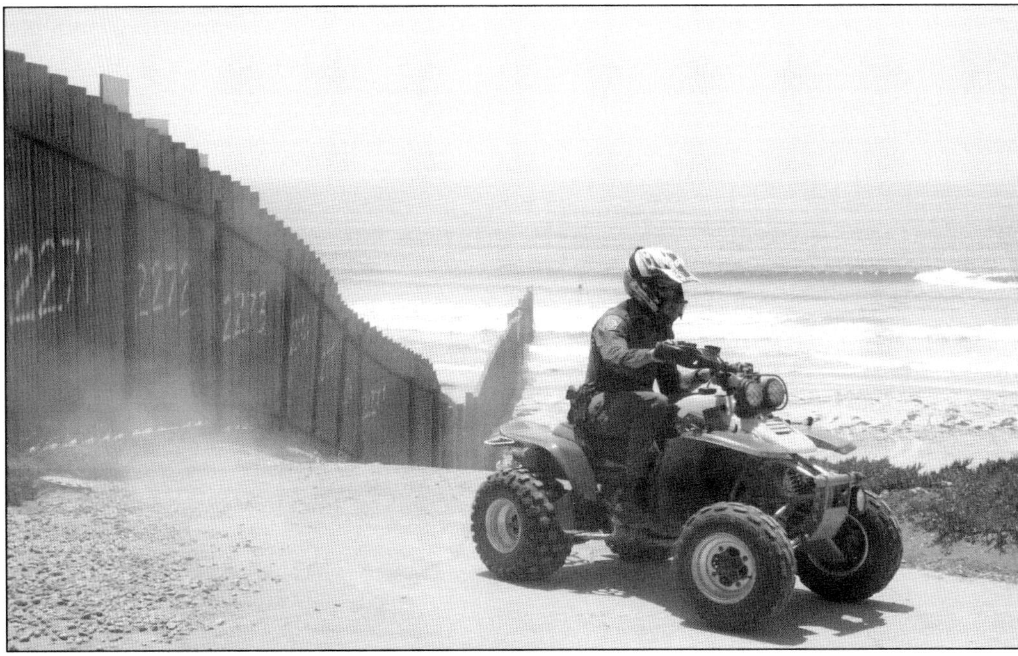

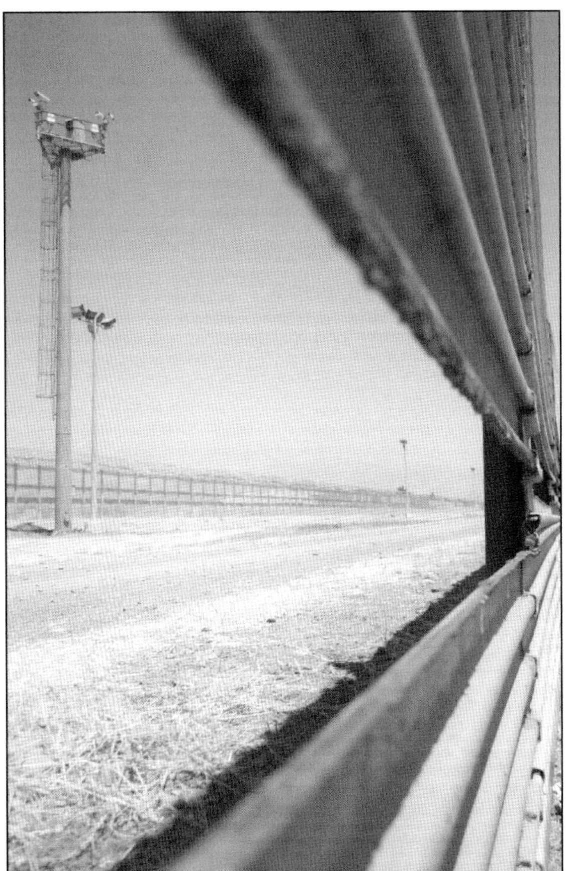

The focus on illegal immigration intensified during the 1990s. The Clinton Administration launched Operation Gatekeeper in 1994, which doubled the number of border patrol agents. In the photograph above, a border agent drives an all-terrain vehicle next to the fence. In 1993 and 1994, the government replaced the chain-link fence with surplus military landing mat material which then extended into the Pacific Ocean. Over the next 10 years, the fence corroded, and by 2005 it was reconstructed. Cameras, censors, and stadium lights were also added. The picture at left shows a camera tower; these were placed approximately one mile apart along the border. (Maria Teresa Fernandez.)

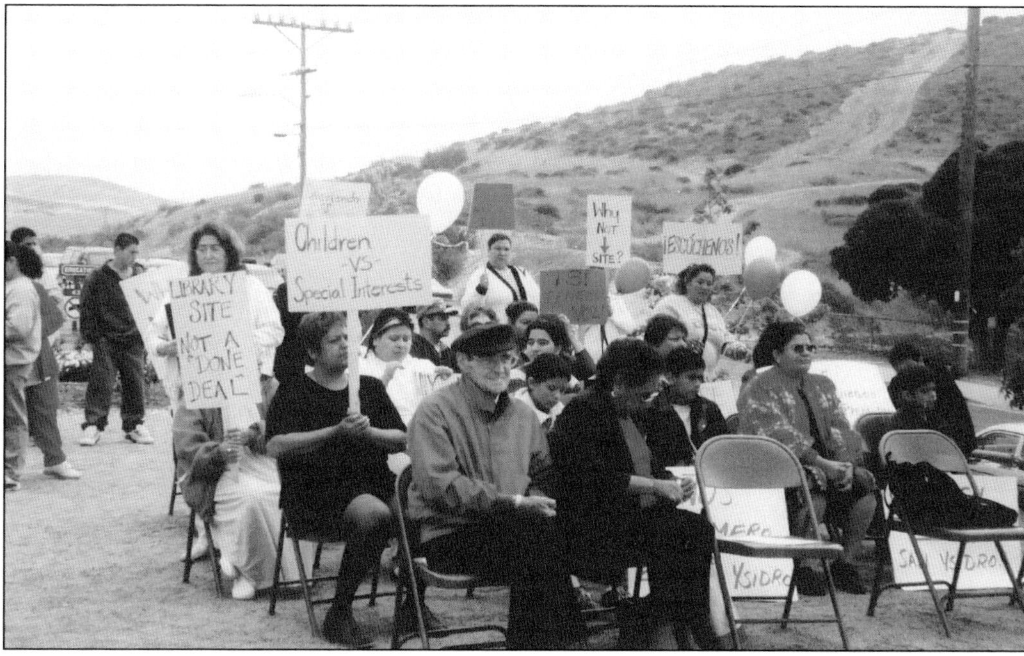

In the 1990s, while headlines focused on drugs and illegal immigration, the San Ysidro community shifted attention to the area school district and its need for new supplies and renovations. In 1997, largely due to grassroots efforts, area PTAs campaigned for a $200-million bond issue, Prop C, to support school renovation. The bond received support amounting to an overwhelming 87 percent majority vote, and the legislation made history as the largest bond of that size ever passed in California. (Alicia Jimenez.)

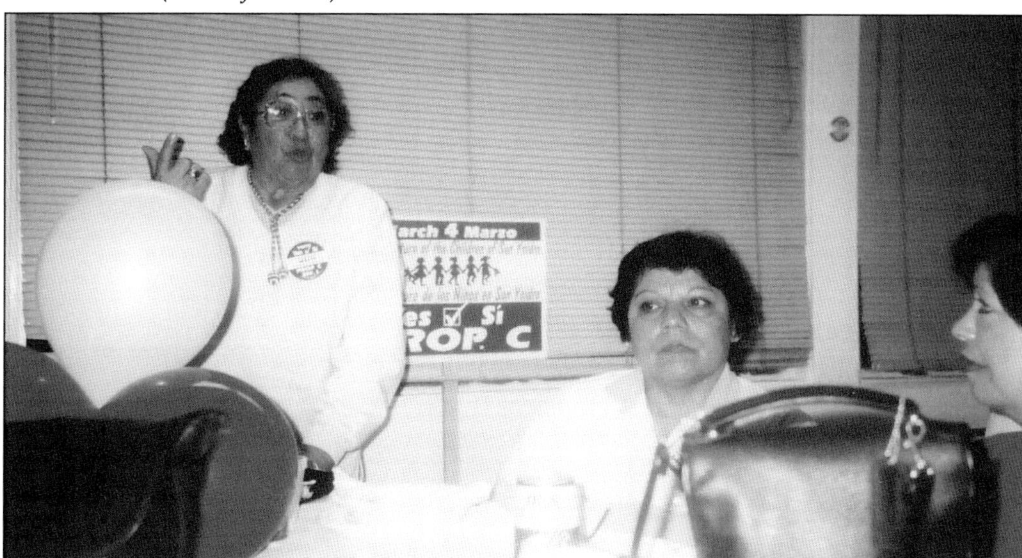

San Ysidro residents were instrumental in passing Prop C, including "Abuelita" Adelina Moreno Hernandez, born in 1931 and raised in Mexico City. Hernandez (left) moved first to Tijuana and then to San Ysidro in 1969. She spent 35 years as a volunteer at Sunset Elementary School, inspiring children with her stories and work. Her campaigning during Prop C was instrumental to the passage of the measure. (Alicia Jimenez.)

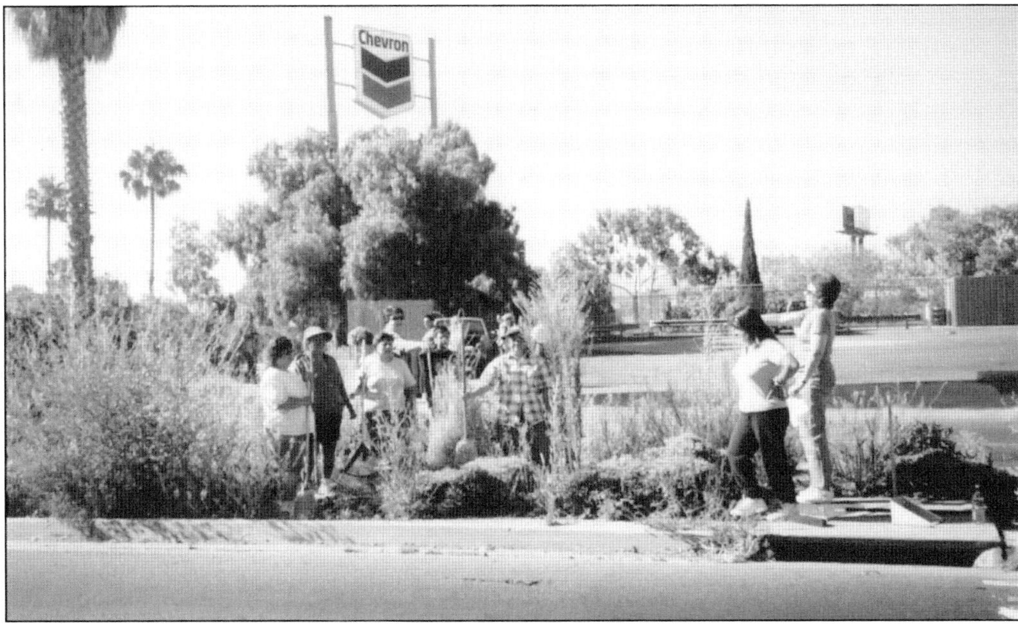

During the 1990s, San Diego often neglected San Ysidro's most basic needs for street cleanup. In 1998, Alicia Jimenez—along with 20 other members—created Hearts & Hands, a charitable organization. Each week, three workers driving golf carts set out from the community service center and cleaned the streets from San Ysidro's central area to the border. The San Ysidro Business Association paid them $400 per month each. (Alicia Jimenez.)

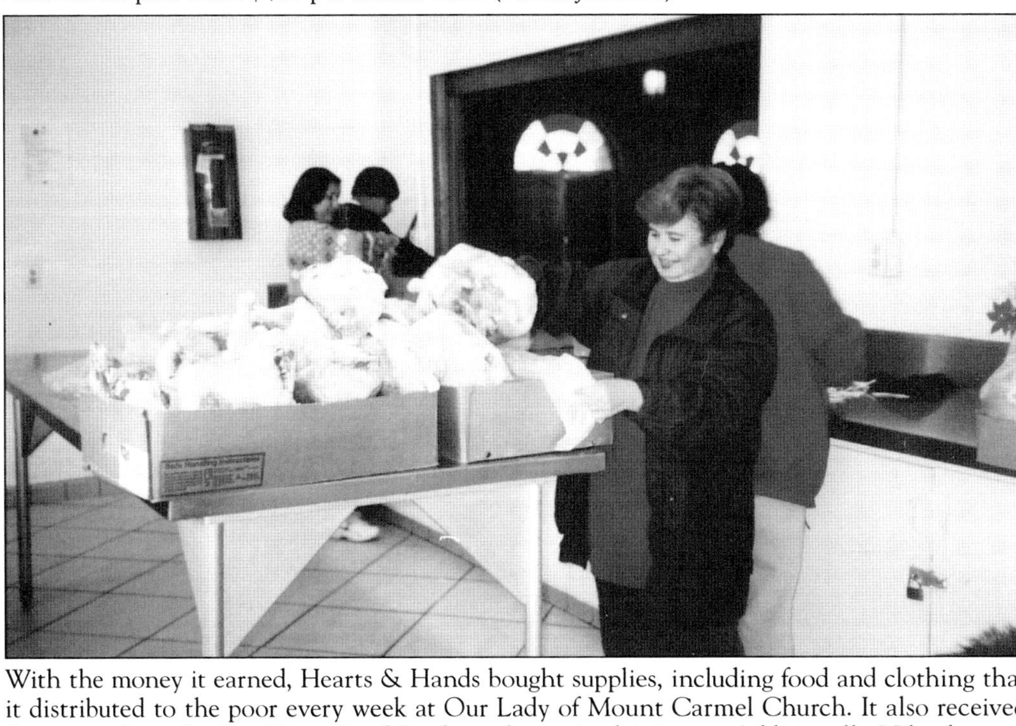

With the money it earned, Hearts & Hands bought supplies, including food and clothing that it distributed to the poor every week at Our Lady of Mount Carmel Church. It also received donations from the San Diego Food Bank, as shown in this image. Additionally, Nike donated shoes to the organization. (Alicia Jimenez.)

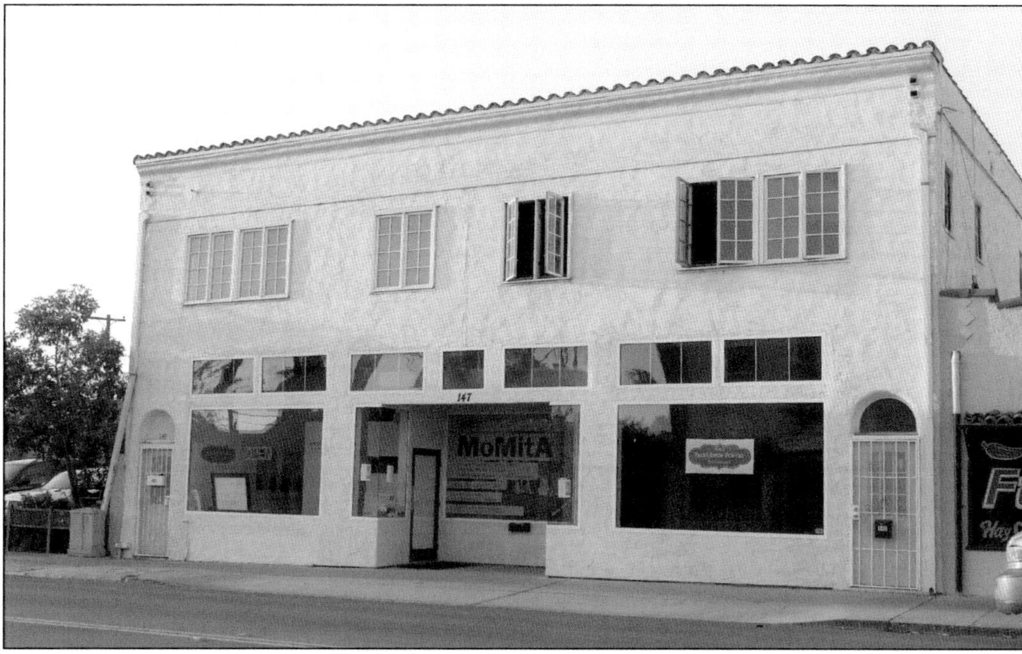

Casa Familiar offered more than 50 programs with subjects ranging from education and community development to arts and culture. Run by Andrea Skorepa since 1982, Casa Familiar also bought the historic San Ysidro Commercial Company designed by Louis Gill. Casa Familiar established an art gallery called the Front, which hosts exhibits often featuring community artists. (Author.)

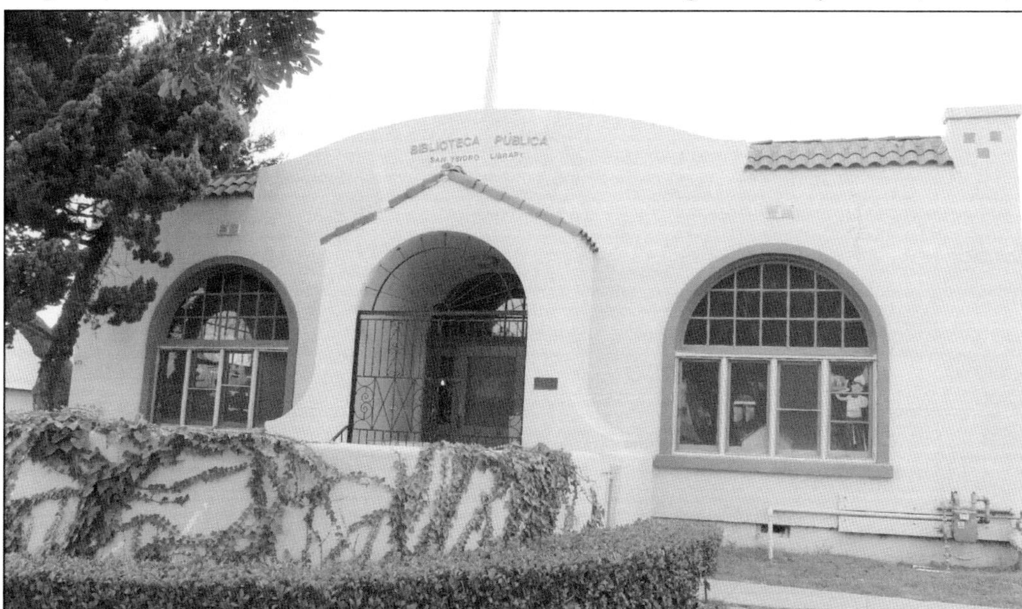

The San Ysidro Public Library, opened in 1924, still stands at its same location at 101 West San Ysidro Boulevard. To better represent the Spanish-speaking community, the front placard was changed in the 1970s to read "Biblioteca Publica." The pictures of Frank and Blanche Beyer are still on the wall in the front entrance of the library, but instead of a men's smoking room, the library now has a sunny atrium. (Author.)

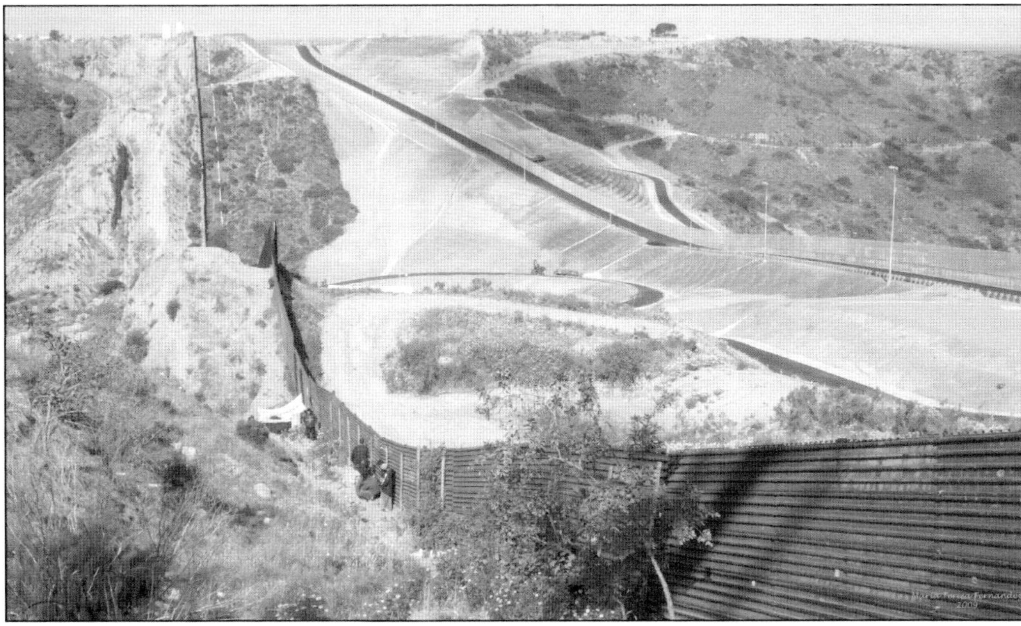

In 2005, Congress passed the REAL ID Act, which stipulated a double fence along the entire United States–Mexico border. In a few areas, they erected a triple fence. Section 102 of the act gave the secretary of the Department of Homeland Security the right to waive any law that would impede the rapid construction of the walls. (Maria Teresa Fernandez.)

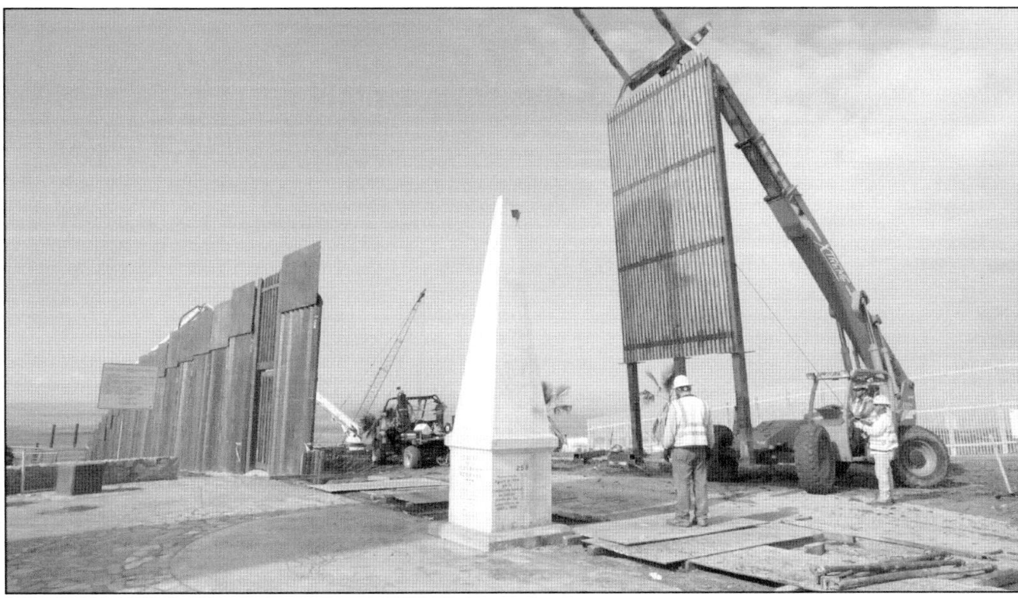

Despite the National Historic Preservation Act that protected the marble obelisk known as monument No. 258, federal construction workers redesigned the area around Friendship Park in 2011, making it so that the obelisk stood exclusively on the Mexican side surrounded by a mesh fence. This blocked access to the monument from the United States by three feet, with the intent to deter people from touching each other, passing drugs, or exchanging documents. The obelisk was eventually enclosed within several more fences, and the public could only visit the monument at certain times. (Maria Teresa Fernandez.)

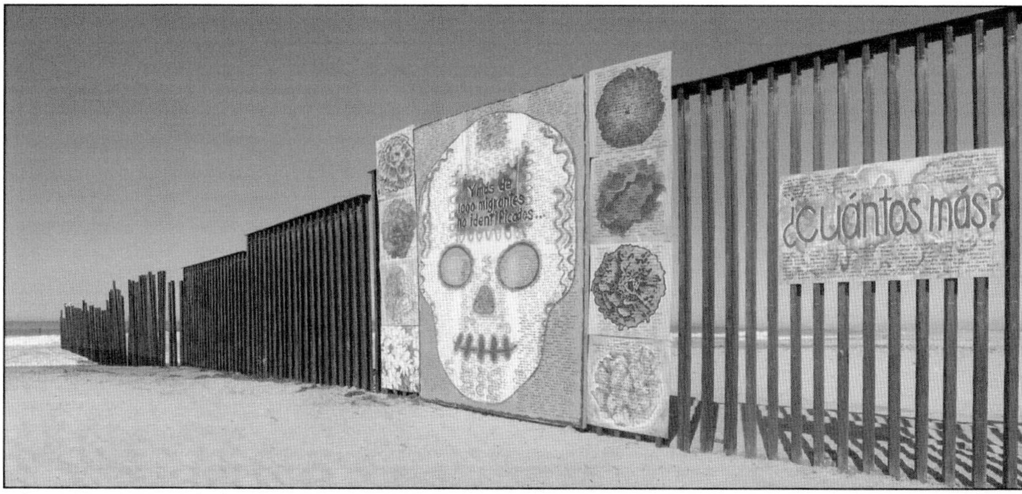

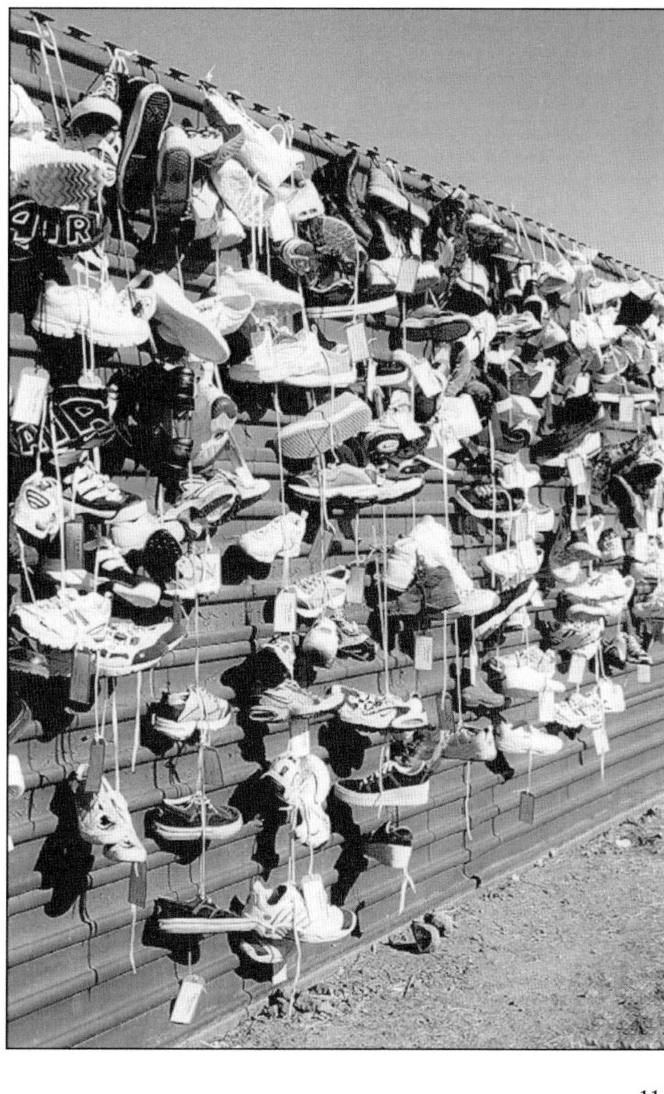

The rise of maquiladoras (multinational corporations located in Mexico, often in Tijuana) that started during the 1960s intensified in the 1990s. Many people from Latin America came to Tijuana in hopes of finding a better life. They took jobs working under harsh conditions—for companies like Sony, Mattel, and Nike—in hopes that the work would be a way station before going to the United States. Art installations on the Mexican side of the border fence commemorate the shoes that many immigrants wore while trying to come to the United States. Enrique Morones founded a grassroots organization, Border Angels, to stop the unnecessary deaths, due to extreme heat and cold weather conditions, of individuals traveling through the desert and mountain areas. Border Angels brings recognition to the approximately 5,000 corpses that have been recovered in the borderlands since 1995. (Both, Maria Teresa Fernandez.)

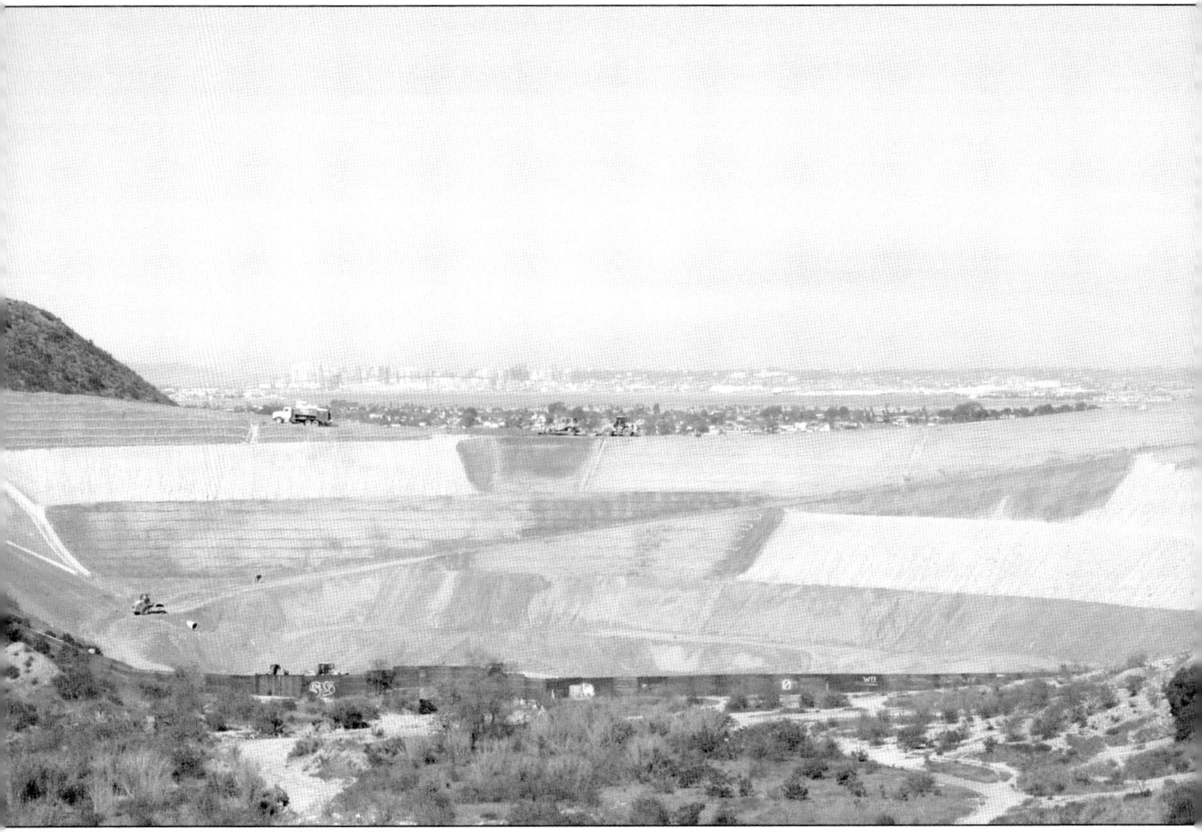

To create a more secure border, Secretary of Homeland Security Michael Chertoff filled in Smuggler's Gulch (an area where Mexicans often crossed into the United States) with 1.3 million cubic yards of dirt in 2008–2009, although it opposed the Clean Air Act, the Endangered Species Act, and the Coastal Zone Management Act. (Maria Teresa Fernandez.)

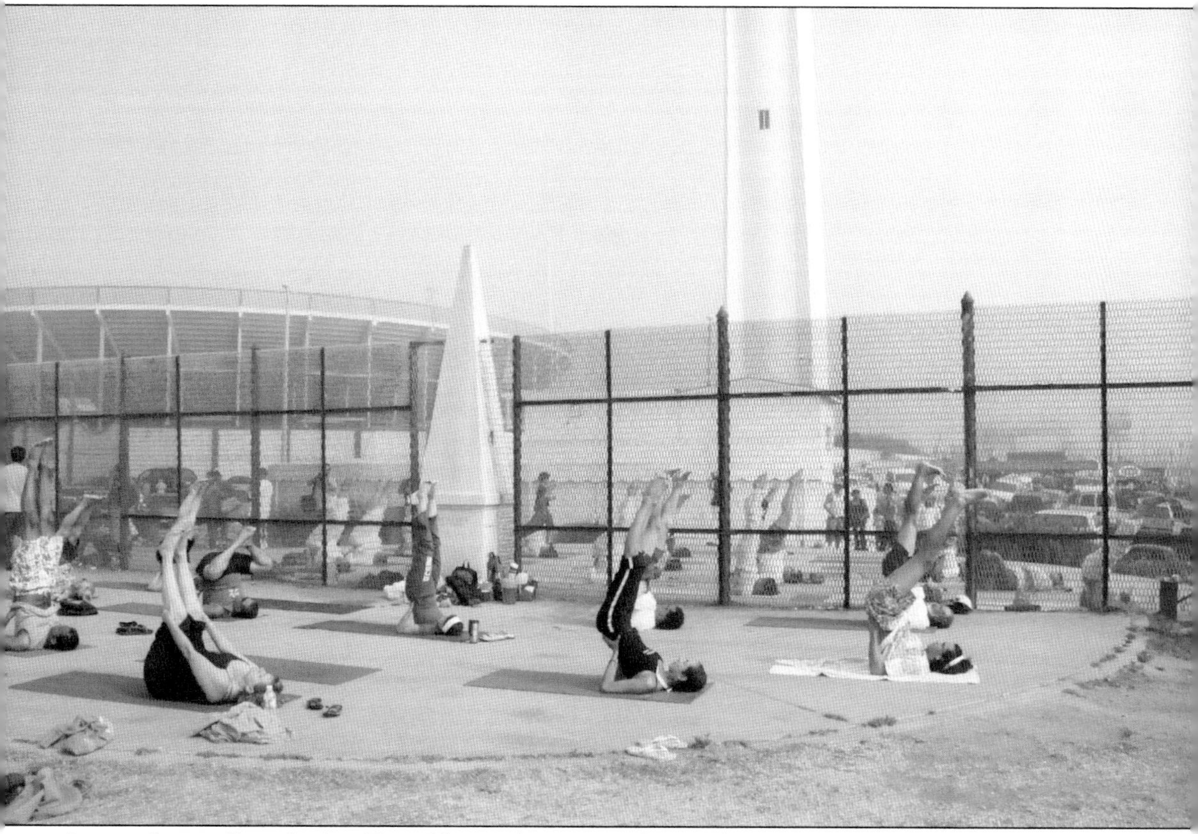

A secondary wall was built at Friendship Park in 2009. The area between the primary and secondary wall was considered a no-man's land. Grassroots groups protested, and eventually the area was opened at certain times. Dan Watman created an international garden on the American side, and Protestant minister John Fanestil held international religious services. Poetry readings and even yoga classes are still held at the marble obelisk. (Maria Teresa Fernandez.)

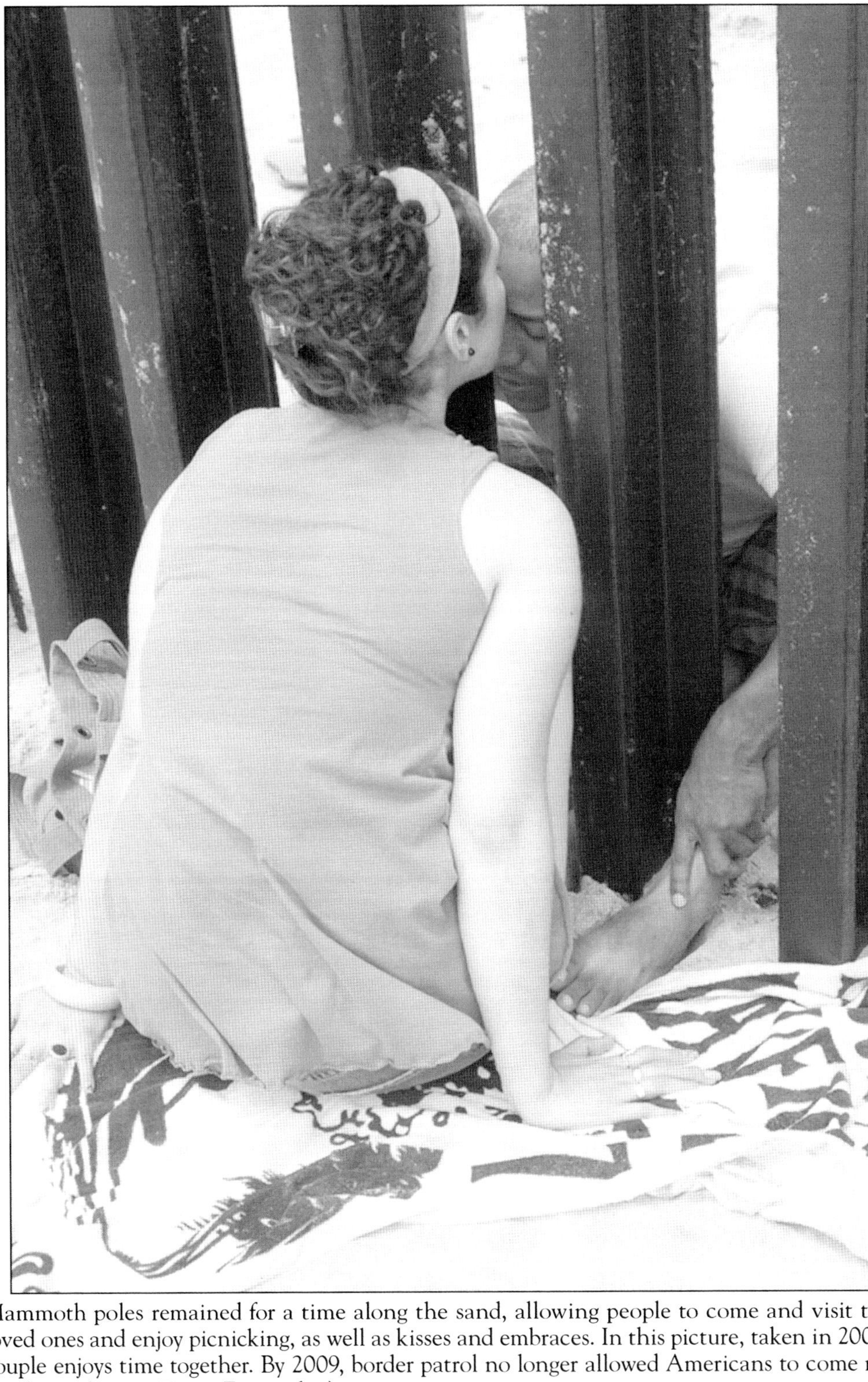

Mammoth poles remained for a time along the sand, allowing people to come and visit their loved ones and enjoy picnicking, as well as kisses and embraces. In this picture, taken in 2008, a couple enjoys time together. By 2009, border patrol no longer allowed Americans to come near the fence. (Maria Teresa Fernandez.)

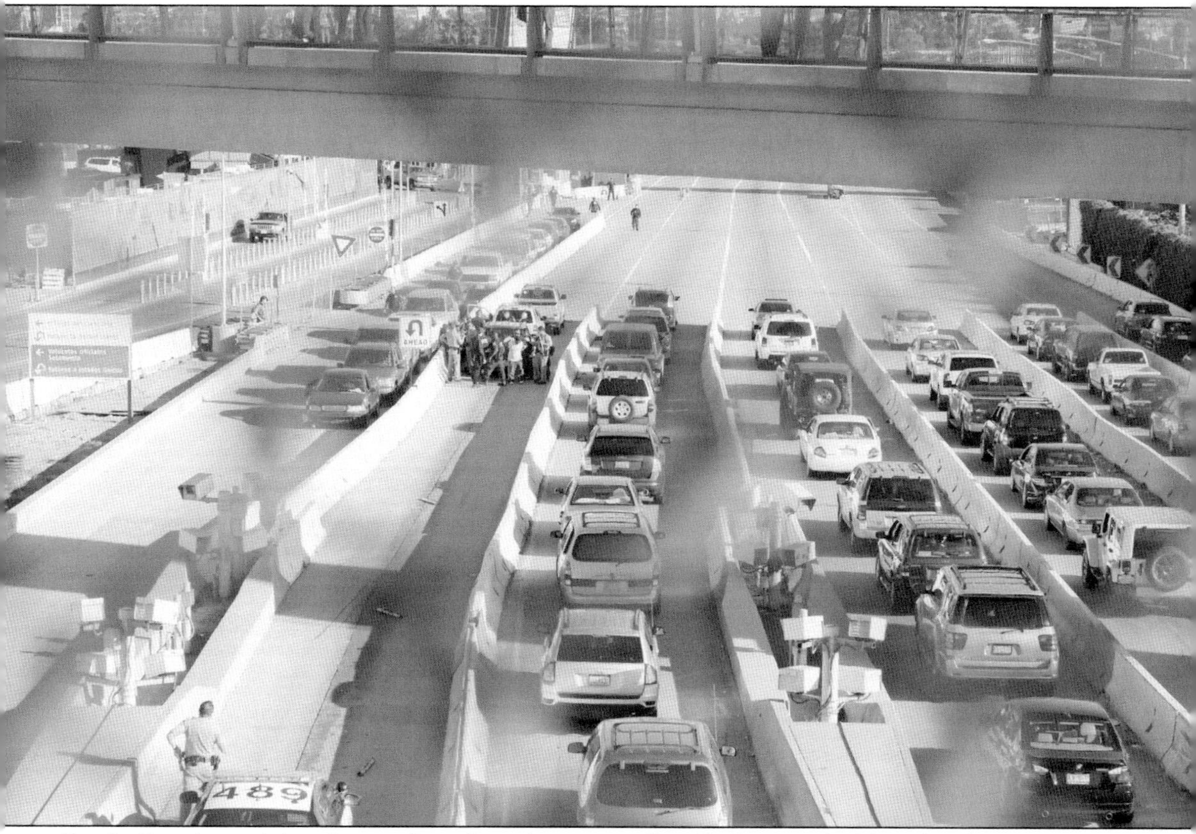

Border Patrol noted that the number of people crossing illegally decreased, although it did not stop. Arrests continued. Tightened security meant larger wait times for those coming into the United States. This translated into higher pollution levels for the San Ysidro community, from business owners along San Ysidro Boulevard to children attending schools in the area. (Author.)

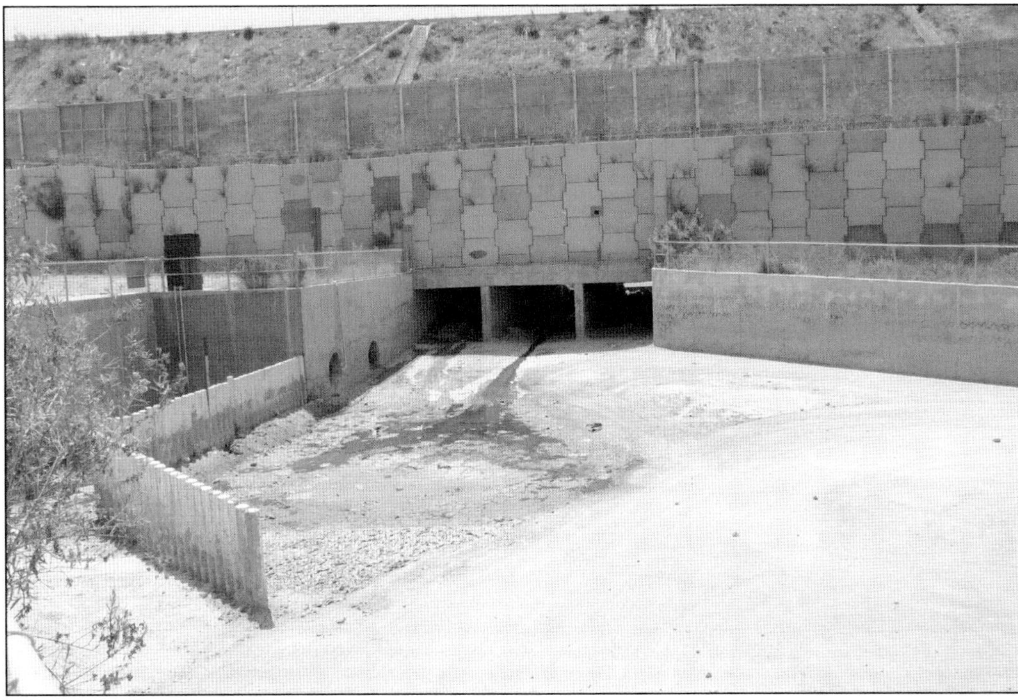

The International Water Commission maintained that sewage needed to flow from the city of Tijuana into the Tijuana River. The South Bay International Wastewater Treatment Plant established a sewage treatment plant (below), but during the rains, Tijuana's sewage flows through four holes along the border, including one in Goat Canyon (above), on its way to the Pacific Ocean. Local grassroots organizations such as WildCoast, cofounded by Serge Dedina, address these issues through international talks and cleanup projects. (Both, author.)

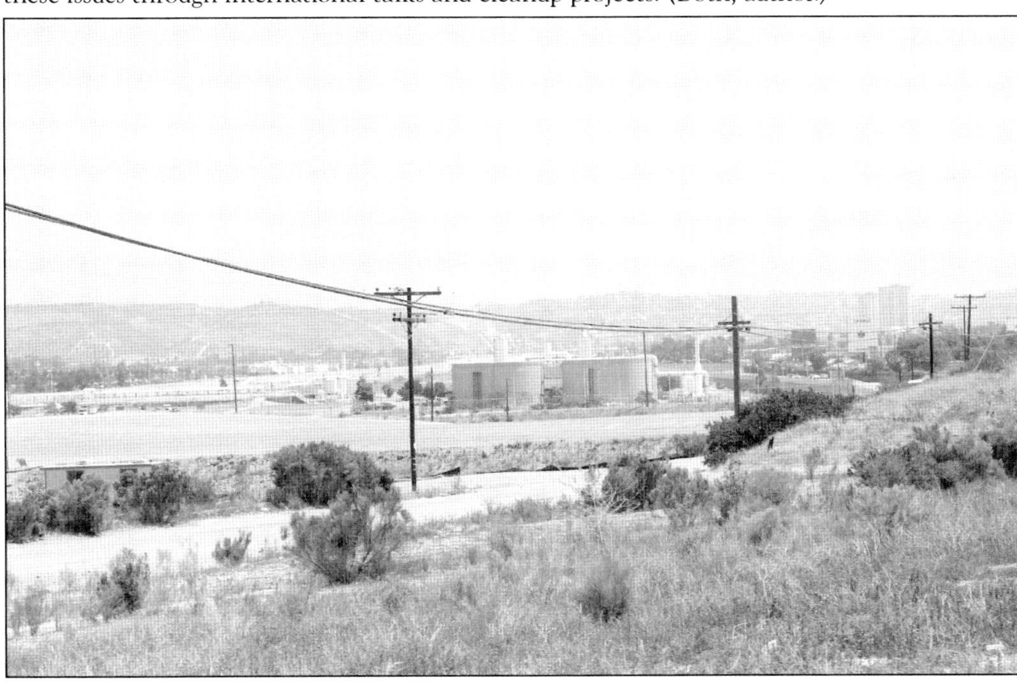

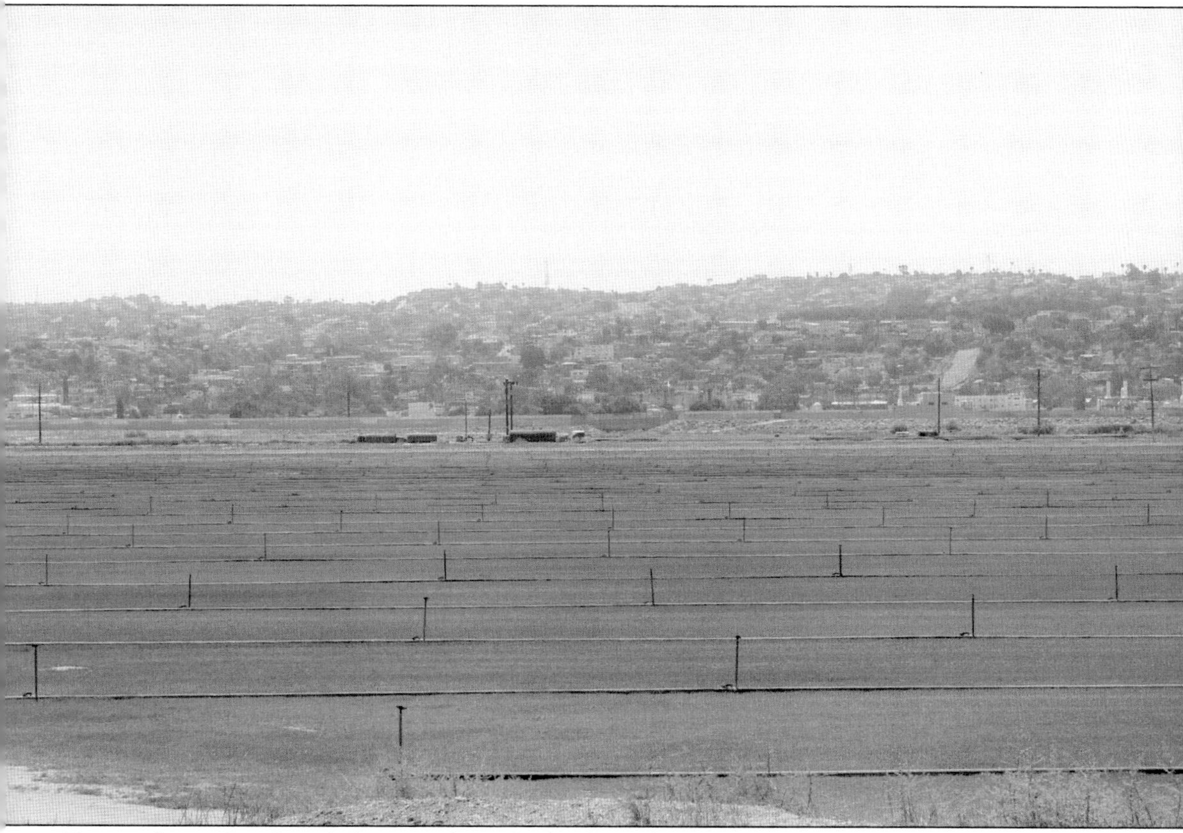

Farmers have abandoned the area along the border. The only viable crop cultivated is sod feed, shown here in an area where farmers once grew a variety of crops. In the background, the city of Tijuana, now exclusively in Mexican territory, burgeons with urban sprawl. (Author.)

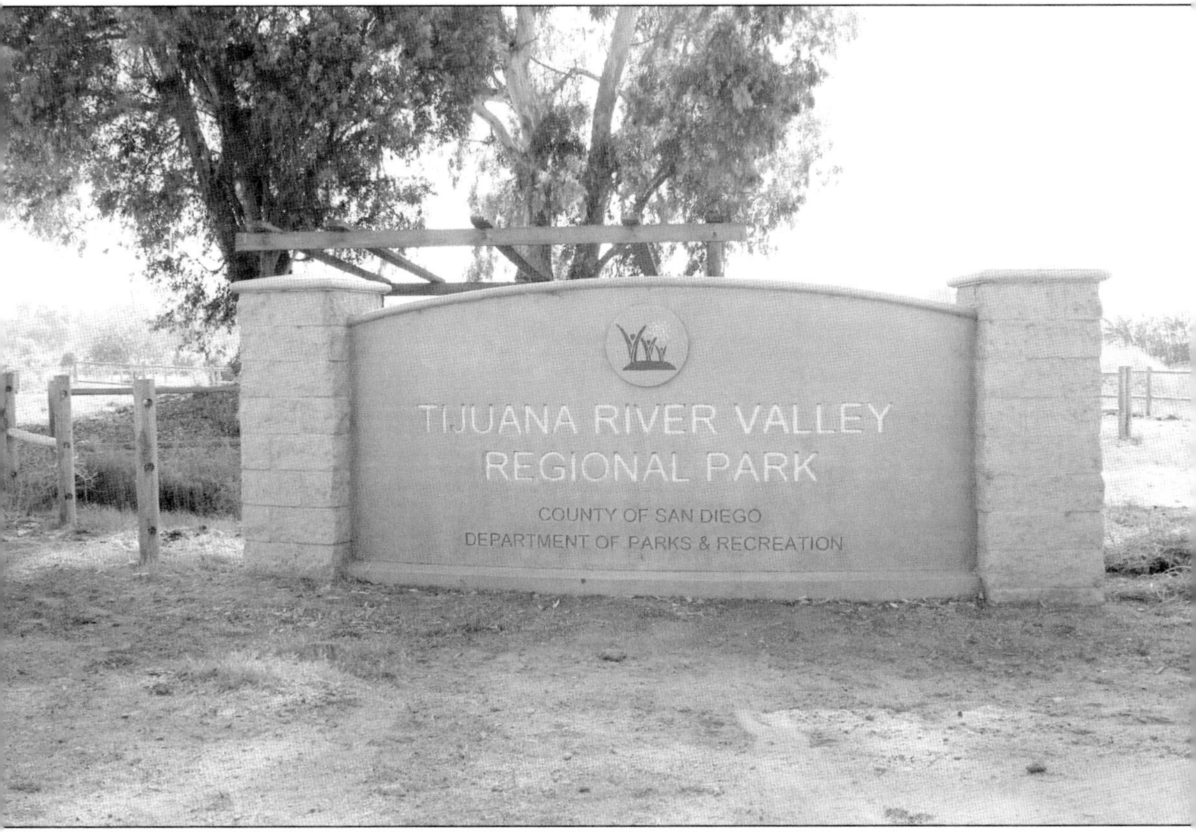

Federal, state, and county governments own different patches of land along the border. While Border Field State Park stretches to the Pacific Ocean, the adjacent Tijuana River Valley Regional Park encompasses 1,698 acres and 22.5 miles of riding and hiking trails. This park preserves the area's diverse ecosystem, including riparian forests along the Tijuana River and high mesas. (Author.)

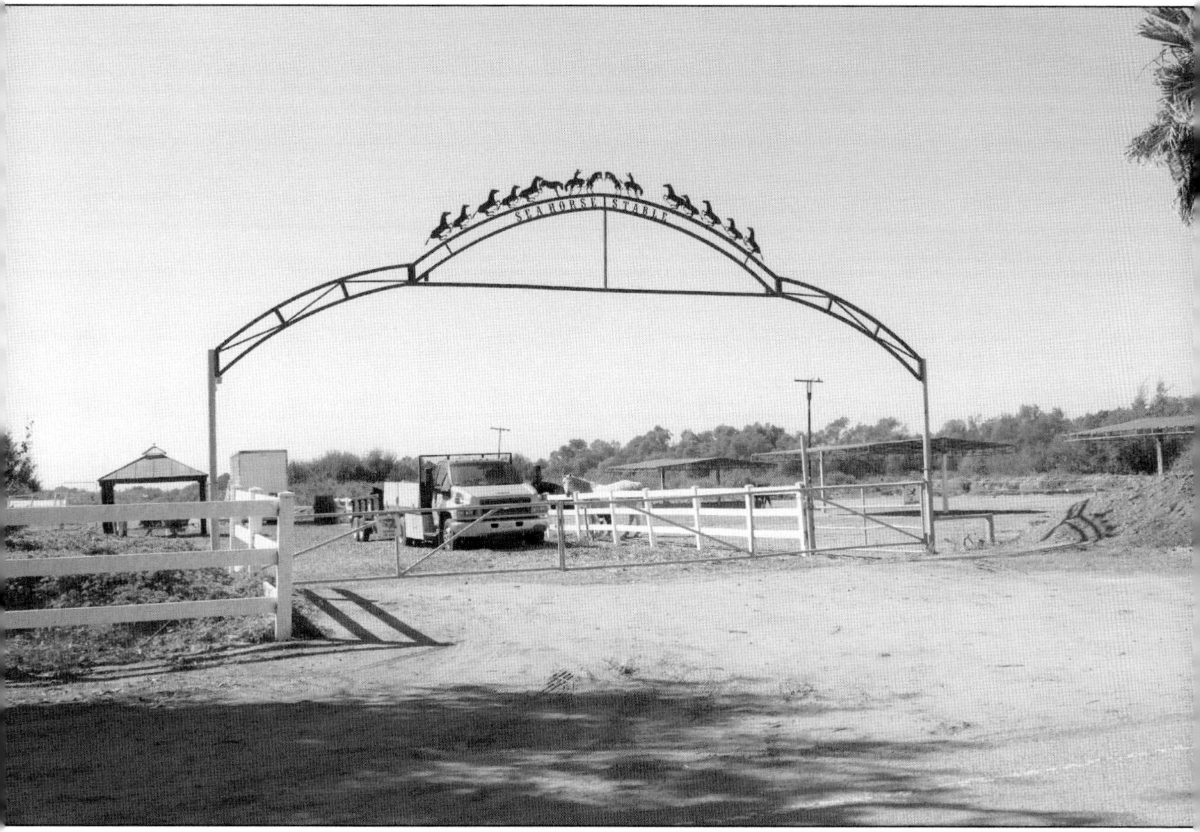

Further inland from the Tijuana River Valley Regional Park, many public and private ranches still breed horses for racetracks as well as for other equestrian pursuits. Some ranches dotting the landscape include Suncoast, Wigginton, Blanco Brothers, Kimzy, Rancho Machete, Border Patrol Stables, and Rancho Los Amigos. The entrance to Seahorse Stable is pictured here. (Author.)

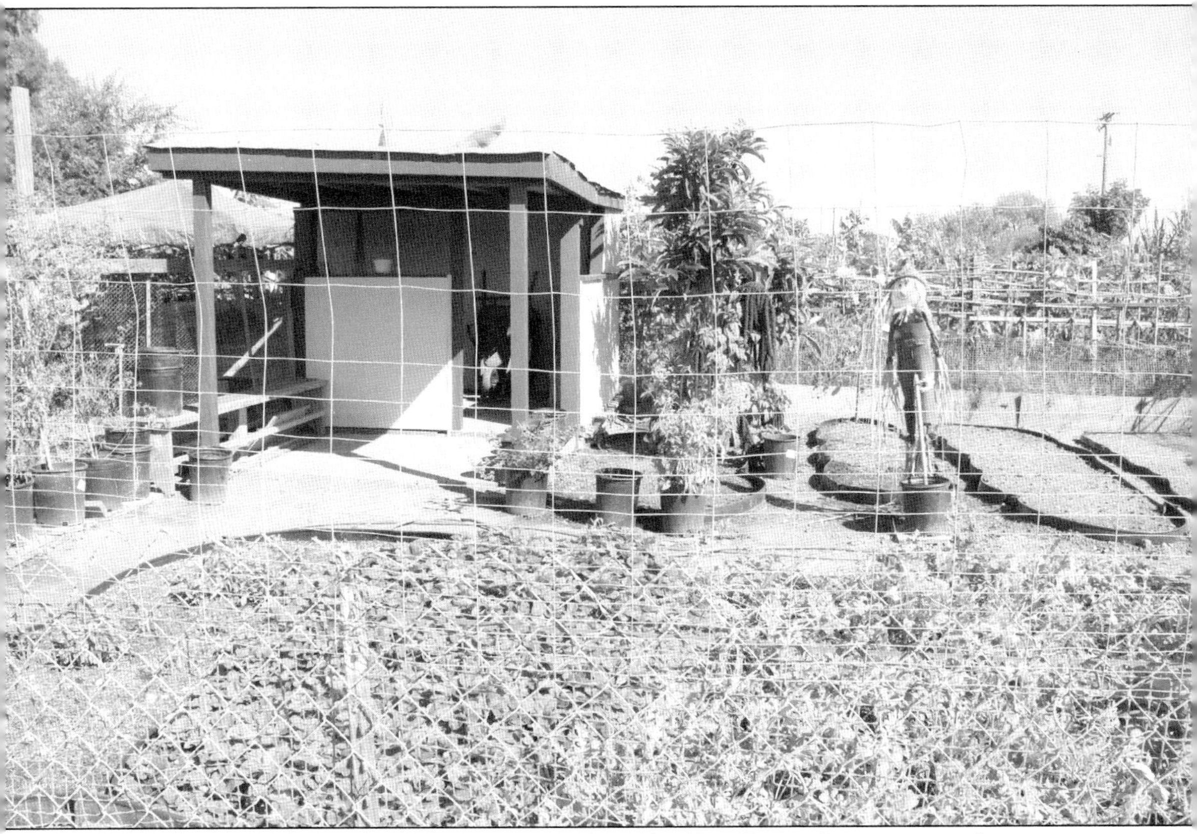

In 1999, the Resource Conservation District (RCD) of San Diego County created a community garden on a 25-acre plot of land in the Tijuana River Valley, an area that had historically been used for agricultural production. A $12,000 grant allowed for the installation of a water meter, irrigation pipes, and fencing, and in 2005, the garden expanded to contain 46 more plots. Residents now come here to plant their own organic produce. (Author.)

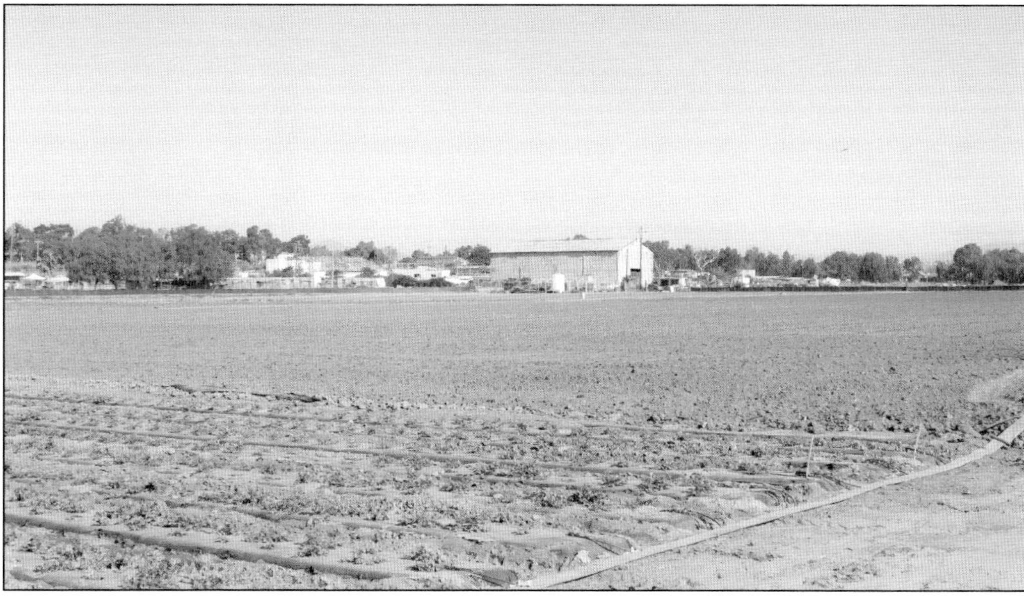

Inland from the border, the Egger family still owns farmland, much of which is leased from the US Navy. The Eggers, in turn, sublease 140 acres to Suzie's Farm, an organic farm in San Diego. Created in 2004 by Robin Taylor and Lucila De Alejandro, Suzie's Farm not only grows more than 100 varieties of fruits and vegetables year-round, but it is adjacent to the 25-year-old Sun Grown Organic Distributors, a sprout and wheatgrass company also operated by the same owners for the last 25 years. Committed to increasing awareness of food and farming within the community, Suzie's Farm hosts many events and programs such as a CSA (community-supported agriculture) program, a yearly autumnal equinox dinner, yoga classes, tours of the farm, and camps for children. (Author.)

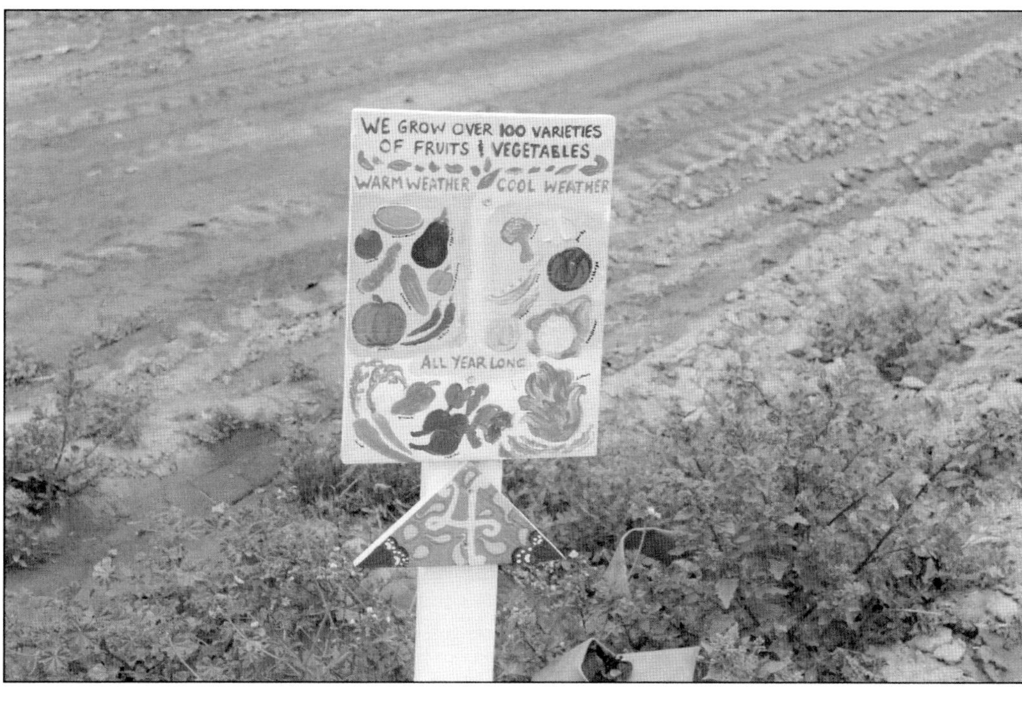

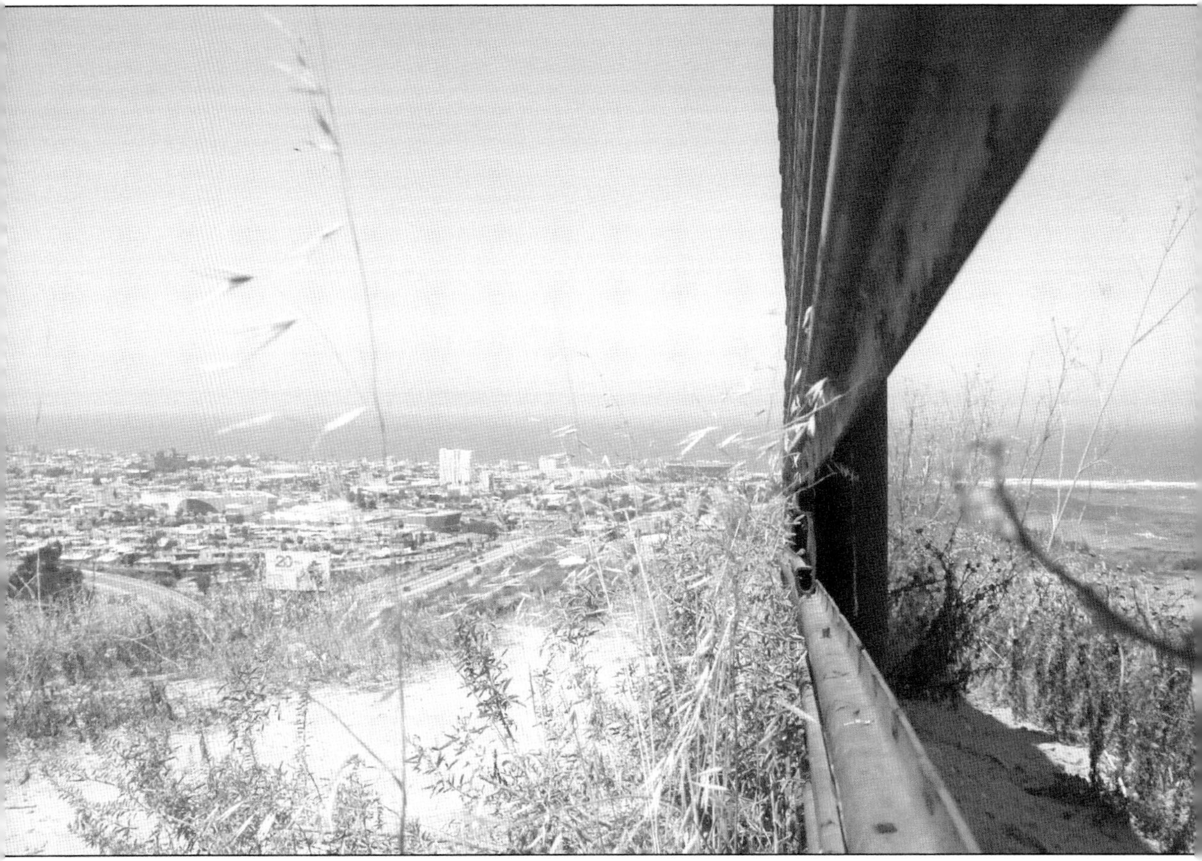

Border Field State Park preserves the coastal wetlands on the American side, while the urban sprawl of Tijuana juts up against the border fence. This picture, taken on the Mexican side, shows the stark differences between the environment on either side of the border. Additional construction of border fencing beginning in 2011 probably destroyed many buried Native American artifacts. Somewhere within the State Park, however, a Native American village still remains unexcavated. (Maria Teresa Fernandez.)

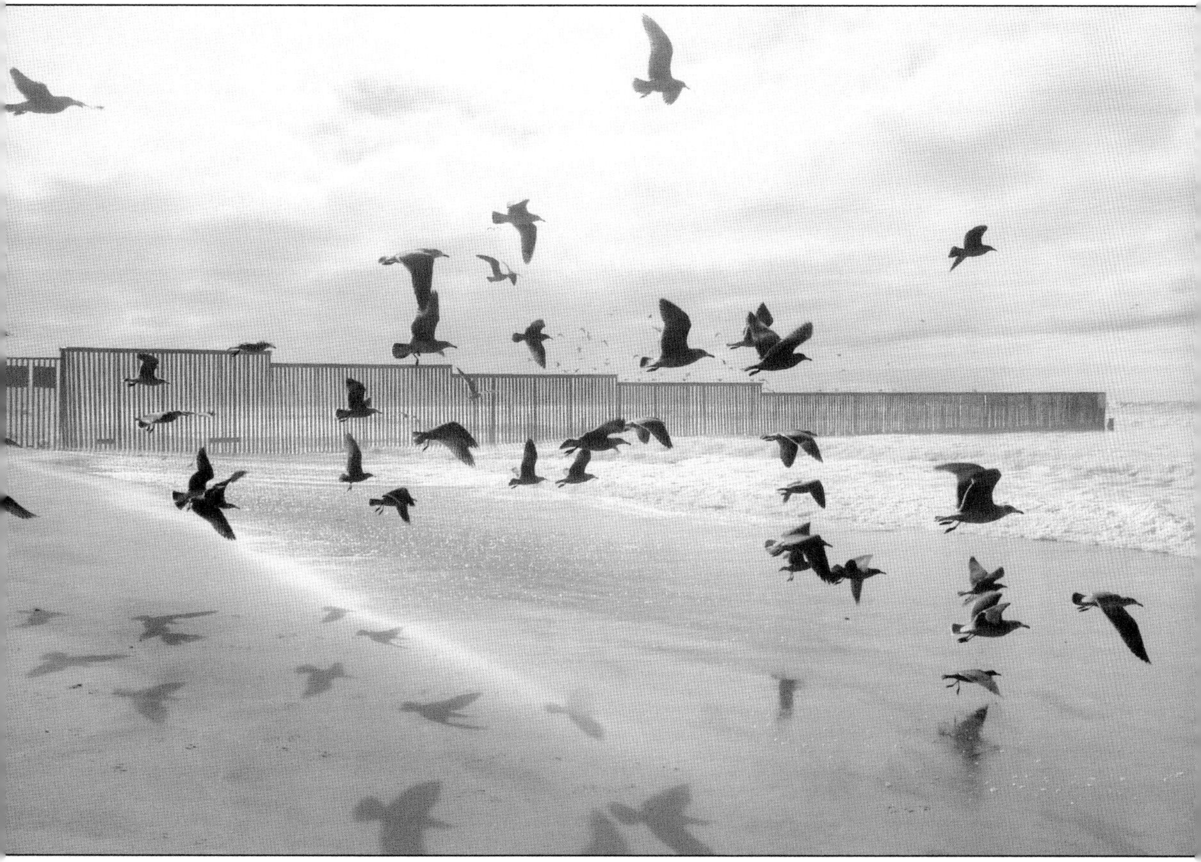

Like the Native Americans who came to the area thousands of years ago to fish beyond the surf line, and like the Argüellos, who spent much time with family and friends here, visitors still come to both sides of the border to enjoy the beach and mild weather. The San Ysidro and Tijuana River Valley region, however, remains separated by a man-made line that has, over the last 150 years, shaped and influenced the area's ecology and culture. (Maria Teresa Fernandez.)

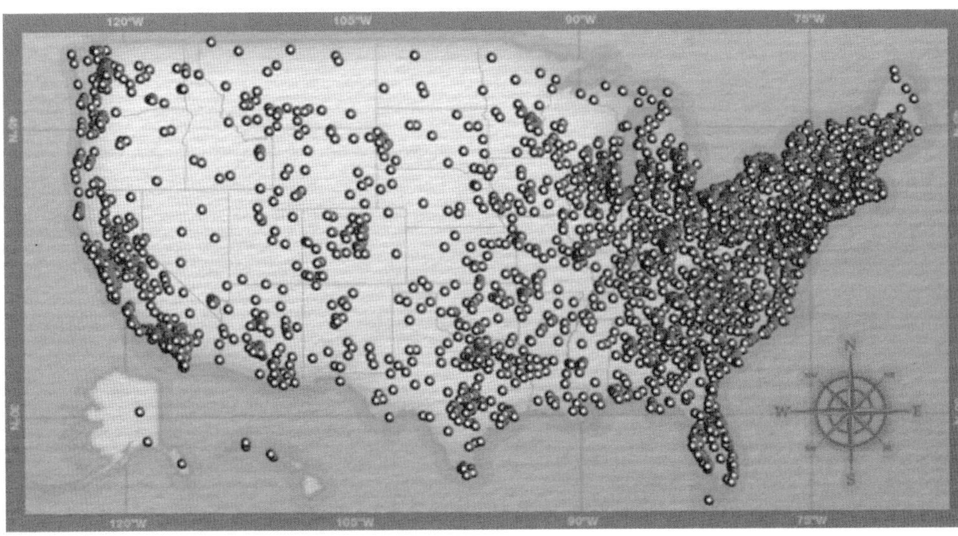